Love in a Time
of Politics

Katherine Zappone is the first open, married lesbian in Irish politics. Appointed to the Seanad in 2011, she went on to win a seat in the Dáil in 2016 as an Independent Progressive. She negotiated with Fine Gael to join its government and was subsequently appointed Minister for Children and Youth Affairs.

Katherine brought her convictions and experience as a human rights advocate and educator to her work as a politician, influencing Fine Gael's social agenda for marriage equality and reproductive justice, and prompting its economic agenda to include combating children's poverty and reducing income inequality. She was the first politician to establish a legal entitlement for parents to receive economic support for childcare.

Katherine's life-partnership and eventual marriage to her late spouse, Ann Louise Gilligan, shaped all her political work. Theirs was an extraordinary love story. Prior to politics, Katherine and Ann Louise were known for the case they took against the Irish state to have their marriage recognised in Ireland. This legal action kick-started the marriage equality movement, resulting ultimately in a constitutional win in 2015.

Love in a Time of Politics

A MEMOIR OF
FACING LOSS AND
FINDING HOPE

KATHERINE
ZAPPONE

HACHETTE
BOOKS
IRELAND

First published in Ireland in 2025 by
HACHETTE BOOKS IRELAND

1

Cataloguing in Publication Data is available from the British Library

ISBN 9781399747943

Designed and typeset in Adobe Garamond Pro by
Palimpsest Book Production Ltd, Falkirk, Stirlingshire

Printed and bound in Great Britain by Clays Ltd, Elcograf S.p.A

'A Vote for Love' poem by Michael Murphy, permission granted by Michael Murphy, reprinted
in *Ministry of Dreams: Collected Poems* (2019). 'Yes' poem by Brendan Kennelly, permission
granted by Suzanne Fairless-Aitken of Bloodaxe Books. 'Spinning Women' poem by Anne
O'Reilly, permission granted by Anne O'Reilly, who wishes to keep the copyright. 'Beloved'
lyrics by Zrazy, permission granted by songwriter Carole Nelson. Book extract from *The New
Heart of Wisdom* by Geshe Kelsang Gyatso, permission granted by Tharpa Publications, UK.

Hachette Books Ireland policy is to use papers that are natural, renewable
and recyclable products and made from wood grown in sustainable forests.
The logging and manufacturing processes are expected to conform
to the environmental regulations of the country of origin.

Hachette Books Ireland
8 Castlecourt Centre
Castleknock
Dublin 15, Ireland
(email: info@hbgi.ie)

Authorised representative in the EEA

A division of Hachette UK Ltd
Carmelite House, 50 Victoria Embankment, London EC4Y 0DZ

www.hachettebooksireland.ie

For Ann Louise

Contents

Prologue

May 2018

I glance out the study window of The Shanty, my home in the Dublin mountains. August, my golden retriever, lies on the floor close to my desk. She sleeps quietly in the emptiness of the house. It's just the two of us now, after Ann Louise's passing eleven months ago. I have been hunched over the desk for most of the morning, working on the text of my next Dáil speech as minister for children. The birdsong outside interrupts my concentration, which is why I look out to the small enclosure, filled with wooden tubs of late-spring flowers. The magnolia tree has begun to bloom magnificently again, a gift from our solicitors to celebrate the initiation of the case we took against the Irish state because it would not recognise our 2003 Canadian marriage. Fifteen years ago. My stare freezes. Grief enters, and slows me down, again.

Eventually I pull my attention back to the desk and notice an unopened envelope. It is likely another sympathy card – I am lucky enough to have received many from people across the nation, each one easing the pain, at least for the moment. I open it to find a beautiful letter from a colleague who worked with me to save Seanad Eireann from abolition, a referendum put before the Irish people in 2013. He had met Ann Louise a couple of times, witnessing the playfulness and fidelity of our love. His letter concludes by quoting F. Scott Fitzgerald, from a letter in which he spoke about his wife, Zelda: 'I love her, and that's the beginning and end of everything.'

I put down my pen. I cannot work anymore.

I see Ann Louise running to class in high heels, at Boston College, where we met in 1981. We were going to be late because our squash game had run over, she defeating me yet again, as one of Ireland's champions in the sport. Her spirit held exuberance so naturally. Her beauty blew my mind. How magnetised was her power. My life would never be the same. We would begin a life journey together, looking for social change based on love.

This study where I work used to be part of the learning space for women from Tallaght West who were determined to get a second chance at education. We had transformed our garages into a community education centre – right outside our kitchen door. I see Ann Louise standing in front of a flip chart, the paper covered with the words 'feminism', 'imagination' and the French feminist philosopher 'Luce Irigaray' in her vigorous script. Her face fills with an invitation to each woman to step on to the path of finding her own life dream. Much later it is these same women, and their families, who join us to line Dublin's streets as we march together for marriage equality. What solidarity we feel. They are not afraid of difference. They rejoice in our love and a referendum that represents the heart of a nation opening towards us, and people like us.

And that was only part of it. In 2011, she gave up a dream that the two of us would start some new work so that I could pursue politics. I tried to do politics differently. Time and again she showed me how to be collaborative: 'Be kind, Katherine. Trust your team.' Before a challenging cabinet meeting she'd ask, 'How can they be your companions in what you want to achieve? And how can you support them?' Her petite frame appears in my memory as she listens to how I find allies in the politics of modern Ireland. My drivers, political and constituency teams, civil servants, neighbours and family. We did change the world. But mistakes were made and the opposition and media wore me down at times, calling me to rethink who I am and how to keep going in the midst of a torrent of public criticism.

August still sleeps. I stare into the future, realising even more deeply that Ann Louise is no longer here. What does 'everything' mean now? I am heartbroken. A couple of minutes pass. Maybe writing will help me to live with grief and heartache, and to find meaning again. Remarkably, Ann Louise herself stretched towards new meaning in the last year of her life by writing. But her book remains an unfulfilled intention, because something happened to her and she was not able to complete it, despite her best fight. Maybe I can take up the mantle and do it for both of us.

To make a record of our last years together and reach for the new.

I pull out a drawer to find an empty journal. I crack the spine and write one line:

Somewhere between grief and joy . . .

And I am transported back to a time, before politics or illness or grief, when our home was filled with the happiness of our forever love.

CHAPTER I

The Phone Call

It is May 2011 and Ann Louise and I wake up to the sunshine coming through the back window of our upstairs bedroom in The Shanty. I love lying next to her. We have both slept well. The room feels cosy and safe. I think it is because our home is made of cedar. It was one of the features that so attracted me to the house when we first set eyes on it in April 1985. I am 'originally American', as I often say, and we make wooden houses there, not too many concrete ones. An English hotelier from Liverpool, Major Gamble, had built The Shanty in the late nineteenth century as his hunting lodge. He may have hunted in the Dublin and Wicklow countryside on visits from England, but 'lodge' is a bit too grand for this small wooden house with a sagging apex. A leaking conservatory fronts The Shanty, and shabby cedar shingles line its sides and cover its roof. But as soon as you enter the sitting room, the warmth of wood cladding from top to bottom envelops you, especially when the copper-hooded canopy over the fireplace casts its heat. Outside is always two degrees colder than down in Dublin, and the snowdrops, daffodils and tulips bloom late in the big garden. We have a small paddock attached to the home property, where we delight in raising various types of hens, tending an organic garden, harvesting berries and finding solitude and silence in a one-room log cabin for painting and writing.

Brittas, in the foothills of the Dublin mountains, showers well-being on everyone when the sun shines. The air is crystal clear. I slip out of bed to open the bedroom windows and gulp the breeze. I remember the day in 1991 when President Mary Robinson arrived at our front door to help us celebrate the fifth anniversary of The Shanty Educational Project. She announced, 'The air is so pure!' I felt both happy and awestruck in her regal presence.

In her inaugural speech, Mary appealed to Mná na hÉireann, the women of Ireland, and it was like the opening of a new era. Ann Louise and I were part of this flourishing, though we were often slowed down by barriers held solidly in place: what a family was supposed to look like; how women were told to behave. In the mid-1980s times were bleak, with little or no educational opportunities for those who left school early, especially women. They worked in factories or bakeries or whatever jobs could be found to bring money into a household. Inner-city communities, character-ised by an architecture of greyness, were monuments to poverty. Housing estates on the outskirts of Dublin, Tallaght being a primary one, were originally designed to remove unwanted sights from the urban middle classes, intended ghettos that became communities. At that time, only the privileged had places in third-level colleges, and 'second chance' education was almost non-existent. There were few women in public life, and childcare was only for the wealthy. Rural poverty was extensive, though hidden.

But we were young and full of energy for something better, imagining that Ireland could be a different place if only people had equal access to education. Our dream was to found an educational centre for those – especially women – who wanted a second chance at learning, and we finally located The Shanty as a place to do so. We wanted to form a small community of committed people and to share our home with them as a way to begin. We believed that we could help to dismantle sexism, classism and other forms of social inequality. Ours was a spiritual as well as an educational venture, and our table would be open to all – for food, drink, compassion, merriment, visioning, storytelling and decision-making. Idealism filled our bodies and spirits, and it seemed to become magnetic. More and more people wanted to join us, and there were few bad days in the beginning.

Over the next fifteen years, at least one hundred women, and a handful of men, entered our property each week to take another chance at their education. Their children were minded in the community centre in Jobstown. Women and men, inside and outside Tallaght, worked side by side with us to ensure that more and more people could access their right to education.

While often exhausted by the non-stop work (including our respective teaching positions in St Patrick's College and Trinity College Dublin), Ann Louise and I were following our dream together. People related to us as a couple, though we were only 'out' to close friends. It sometimes felt like a high-wire act. We did not want to deny our relationship in the workplace but we knew that we risked negative consequences if it became public knowledge, especially from those with the most power. We carried on, though, because we had each other and a growing community of friends and colleagues. And we believed, somewhat naïvely, that the good would always win the day.

We worked with adults and young people from the Tallaght regions to plan a 'community forum'. Maria Jordan-Kelly, from Brookfield, Tallaght West, and Ann Louise published a report entitled *The People Speak*. This led to a plan to build a community education learning centre – for adults and children – within Tallaght West. Friends lobbied politicians. Community leaders raised awareness, held fundraisers. We travelled to America to garner financial support. Together we managed to raise one-third of the money we needed, with no commitment yet coming from the state.

Early in June 1997 the people of the community took a vote. Their decision was final. It was communicated to all local politicians, two of whom were members of the Irish cabinet. Women, men and children would spend the evening celebrating their graduation from Shanty courses, and then leave the Jobstown community centre. They would bring tents and sleeping bags and march to the Dáil, hand in a letter of protest, march back and put up their tents. They

8

would camp out until the government gave us the balance of the money, £600,000.

Just as the graduation ceremonies were ending, the doors of the community centre burst open. The minister for local development and one of the TDs in our constituency, Chris Flood, strode in, virtually jumped onto the stage and said he had an announcement to make. That afternoon in a special meeting, the cabinet members had agreed to subvent our project by a once-off capital grant of £600,000. It went towards building what has now become the largest independent community-based education centre in Ireland. The roof came off the community centre that night. The people had spoken and the government had heard. The tents were put away for another day.

Over the course of the next year we built An Cosán, a centre for learning, leadership and enterprise, with a large number of dedicated and generous people from the Tallaght communities and beyond. Located in the heart of Jobstown, one of Tallaght West's four villages, An Cosán opened its doors in 1999.

So, it was calmer these days at The Shanty. Ann Louise had retired early from St Patrick's College in Drumcondra, where she had been a professor of education for thirty-five years. We had started a consultancy together to help respond to social and economic challenges. And with close colleagues and friends, we were building a campaign for marriage equality, to support our legal case to get the Irish state to recognise our 2003 Canadian marriage.

Ann Louise starts to run her morning bath, and I descend the spiral stairs. In the kitchen our beautiful Siena is stretched out on the wooden floor, waiting for her morning rub. We brushed the long-haired Lassie dog just yesterday, and what a job that always is. But it's worth it. She is gorgeous. Siena, named after St Catherine, is our fourth collie – succeeding Habermas, Julian of Norwich and Paulo Freire. They were all special and loved the activity of the women coming and going.

I begin to prepare breakfast, casting my eye over the empty egg-holder. *I'll get Ann Louise some fresh eggs*, I think. *It's the day for it*. This morning four eggs have been laid by our hens. I feel like a gleeful child as I scoop them up. While Ann Louise is the real genius as a natural chef, I at least can cook a good breakfast. We talk about the day over delicious scrambled eggs and the brown bread Ann Louise baked the day before.

She is preparing to give coaching sessions to a couple of her clients. I need to go into Dublin. We are preparing to go to the Supreme Court with our marriage equality case. We lost in the High Court, but we are appealing it. I want to meet with our solicitor, Kevin Brophy, to talk about strategy before a consultation with our barristers in a couple of weeks. At least things are moving again. I feel satisfied and hopeful. When we started preparing to take a case in early 2000, never did we anticipate that it would last so long! Just as well, or we may never have started.

Ann Louise is more philosophical about how time has lengthened our legal journey. She has been reading several Buddhist texts and has discreetly taken up a disciplined meditation practice each day. She lives in the present considerably easier than I do. Her meditation often fills The Shanty with a peaceful yet vibrant energy. While it seeps into me a little bit at times, I rarely find that kind of peace within myself. My restlessness comes from my father. As a businessman and charitable leader, he spent his life looking for ways to make a major impact, and it rarely happened for him the way he wanted it. He was a deep thinker, though, and that also influenced his efforts to improve the lives of others. Maybe I am taking up his mantle. I do feel driven to do something great. Followed by doing something else great. That's not to say that this is my sole motivation for the way I live my life and forge a professional path, but it is always there. Right alongside my deep desire to make things right and good for others. This I feel at my core too. But the pursuit of greatness is stuck in my gut, where a feeling of never being good enough lies. Because I am female? Because I am lesbian? Probably.

*

After breakfast I dress, leaving aside the country clothes for something a little more smart yet casual. I step into Ann Louise's red Renault van, the only transport we have – but useful for carrying animal feed and whatever is needed for the flowers in the long bed at the front of the house and the vegetables we grow in the paddock.

I drive the long distance to town and park in the city centre. I have the morning to do shopping before meeting the lawyers. The late-spring sun on Grafton Street warms my face and I welcome it. I have started to worry about the Fianna Fáil government's enactment of civil partnership legislation in 2010 and its potential negative impact on our future court proceedings. 'Why do the gays need marriage equality if they get all those rights in civil partnership? Why do these women need more?' ask many in Irish society. I am worried that this legislative change could influence the Supreme Court to rule that civil partnership is enough, and that it is allowed *within* the constraints of the Irish constitution.

My head starts to feel heavy, as it often does when such thoughts swirl in my mind. Where did the peace of the early morning go? I walk past the street corner where newspapers used to be sold and my mobile rings.

'Hello, Katherine. This is Mark Garrett' (Tánaiste Eamon Gilmore's political advisor). 'I wonder if you would be free within the next forty-five minutes to take a phone call from the tánaiste?'

'Of course,' I respond with, no doubt, a stunned voice.

While I had been a member of the Labour Party for a brief period when Pat Rabbitte was its leader, I let my membership expire when his leadership came to an end. Why did his successor want to speak with me?

I start to look for a quiet place to take the call and slip into the Carmelite church on Clarendon Street. Such serenity amidst the lighted candles, each one lit for a special cause, slowly energises my spirit as I wait. I decide that I'd better head into a stairwell, though, so that I won't disturb those at prayer. When the phone rings, I answer immediately.

'Hello, Katherine. This is Eamon Gilmore.'

I admired Eamon's courage to form a government at such a challenging time. We are still in the midst of the bank bailout by the International Monetary Fund and the European Union, and subject to all the conflicting austerity programmes initiated by the previous Fianna Fáil-led government.

'I would like to recommend you to Enda Kenny as one of his appointees to the Seanad,' says Eamon after the pleasantries. 'As partners in government with Fine Gael, we have agreed that I may recommend a certain number of people to take up the seats of "taoiseach nominees" mandated in the Irish constitution under Article 18.'

Eamon is asking me to become an Irish senator, without going through the convoluted process of getting elected to the upper house! I am astonished. I have spent the last decade of my professional and personal life knocking on the doors of those who held powerful political positions – those on the 'inside'. Now I'm being invited in! For a moment, I can't find my breath. And then unexpectedly my voice says, 'It would be a privilege, Tánaiste.'

Oh my God – what will this be like? Between my various work commitments and our legal case for marriage equality, I am kept more than busy. But this will be an opportunity to try to change things from the *inside*. Will it be easier? I hope so. Will I know how to do it? Not right away. But it still feels as if I've just won the lottery!

I start to phone Ann Louise and then this huge sadness descends. My father had passed away just two months before. I spent the month of January with him in Seattle, where I grew up and where all my family still live, to cook for him, mind him, take him to a basketball game or two. He was grieving, deeply, for my mother, his beloved wife. She died six months before he did. I spent a lot of time just with my arms around him in his favourite chair. I came home to Ireland in early February, only to return again to Seattle to lay him to rest on 17 March. We did not have any unfinished business.

But now, suddenly, I'm looking for him. Where is my father? *Do you know, Dad, what has just happened? Why can't you be here?* I go back into the church and sit quietly for a few minutes. The sadness ebbs as I light candles for my parents. A soft joy visits me; a sense of well-being I have never experienced before.

Ann Louise is so thrilled when I ring her. Love, as St Paul says, is not jealous. Though we traverse a similar professional and advocacy territory, Ann Louise is never jealous of me. Her strong sense of self, she says, comes from her father. How about that? Dads and daughters. 'Katie, that is remarkable news,' she exclaims. 'I am so happy for you.' And then she says something I will never forget: 'This job will allow you to bring together all you have learned, and all your experience, so that you will be able to make really important public contributions. You will soar.' The Seanad would provide me with an opportunity to comment on the happenings in Ireland and our world in ways that might make a genuine difference. I wanted to develop law that would advance human rights and argue for government policies that could make our people's lives better, especially those people whose opportunities had been restricted because of social circumstances and conditions, like those who worked with us and for themselves in An Cosán, and especially people like me whose gender or sexual identity was still considered to be second class. Critics of the Seanad say that 'all the senators do is talk'. Well, I love public speaking. I love to craft words in order to engage the listener, to inspire action or offer meaning. I couldn't wait to get started.

*

About a week later, the news was out about Taoiseach Enda Kenny's nominees. Going through the gates of Leinster House as a new senator was like walking on air. Leinster House was built in the mid-eighteenth century as an exquisite town house, reflecting the wealth and status of its owner, James Fitzgerald, earl of Kildare. The staff at the gates and inside the house knew my name, were exceptionally respectful and full of congratulations. It just kept raining sunshine. Over the years they became like family, always there to assist in whatever way possible, without judgement and with an earnest desire to serve. The aura of the house was filled with power, a power to be drawn on, to use as a basis on which to think and act. It felt, at times, like being clothed in sparkling status when everyone addressed me as 'senator'. Never could I have imagined that title on myself.

The first order of business was to meet other senators and to decide where my political allegiance lay. As a neophyte, I offered to act as a Labour senator because of Eamon Gilmore's role in my appointment, and I was looking forward to working closely with Senator Ivana Bacik. At the time, she was acting pro bono as junior counsel in our legal case – *Zappone and Gilligan v. Revenue Commissioners and Others* (2006) – and was awesome at that job. She was also leader of the Labour Party in the Seanad. I initiated discussions with her on the first day. Later that afternoon I was directed to the Seanad antechamber to take a phone call. With high ceilings, a chandelier, large windows, a fireplace and some fine art, it provides a luxurious setting for senators to work or meet in before entering the chamber itself. I picked up the phone and to my surprise, for a second time, it was the tánaiste.

Eamon said, 'Katherine, we want you to be an Independent senator. There are enough Fine Gael and Labour senators in the sixty seats in the Seanad for us to win most votes with the whips. So we want to demonstrate our commitment to a new approach to politics. With a good portion of Independent senators, we hope that this will allow the deliberations to be more robust and thoughtful. Be free!'

I will always hold admiration for both Eamon and Enda for that decision. At the time, Enda Kenny was known for his religious conservatism, carrying strong views against abortion and with little openness to marriage equality. Early on in my tenure, I remember giving him a copy of *Our Lives Out Loud*, the memoir Ann Louise and I wrote in 2008. Afterwards I met him in his taoiseach's office at the end of the corridor on the second floor of Government Buildings. We sat down in sitting-room chairs between his sizeable antique desk and a gorgeous marble fireplace, and he began by quoting, from memory, several paragraphs from our book. I was dumbfounded.

Entering the Seanad chamber for the very first time during that same week bedazzled me. Used as a ballroom when owned by the duke of Leinster, its historic Georgian ceiling plasterwork and elaborate crystal chandeliers embody an extraordinary grandeur. Because visitors are not allowed on the chamber floor proper, to cross its threshold lifted my sense of responsibility then and every time afterwards, requiring perfect posture and often solemn speaking. I found my voting seat on the left of the cathaoirleach (the chair of the Seanad) in one of the last rows because I was an Independent. While you are required to sit in the designated seat to vote, you may sit anywhere else at other times, as long as it is on the correct side of the chamber. I would soon learn that this would be the easiest procedural rule to understand and follow. Otherwise, Seanad protocol was extensive and complex, and it helped to have an experienced (and friendly) senator share the intricacies of the rules from time to time. There was no rule, however, against sitting back in my big Seanad chair and gazing at the exquisite blue and white ceiling to collect my thoughts before speaking. It was my prime meditative technique, and also helped me separate the wheat from the chaff of other senators' contributions.

While we were the chamber with less weight than the Dáil, there was always an undercurrent of an intoxicating feeling of power. How would I negotiate such a feeling? I had so much to learn. It was the opportunity of a lifetime, and I did not want to waste it. After the last Seanad vote I would return to my office, respond to emails or more likely read some research or policy documents that would help me to craft a speech for the next day. Often that meant I would get home late at night. By the time I drove through our gate, Ann Louise would have cooked and ate her dinner, watched the nine o'clock news and headed to bed with a good book. She always left me a plate of gorgeous food in the kitchen, though, putting my eggs-on-toast to shame. As much as she adored me, she was fiercely independent and self-contained. And, above all, generous. If I were really lucky, she might be still awake, and I would tell her minute details from stories of my day. It was like writing a diary entry – only better, because I had a lover's audience. Her eyes would close then, and she would say, 'See you in the morning, Katie.'

CHAPTER 2

Save the Seanad

Feargal Quinn had steely blue eyes, a suave cut of whitish-grey hair and gentlemanly manners. He had founded the national supermarket chain Superquinn in 1960, and built his successful business empire on the philosophy that 'the customer is king'. He possessed celebrity status from his television series *Retail Therapy*, and had been a senator for many years. I had seen him in the corridors of Leinster House a few times, and had listened to him often in the chamber. He was funny and serious, kind and considerate – with the commitment of a patriot. He was prodigious in his approach, and could comment on just about anything with practical as well as legal know-how. I was in awe of him.

One day at the beginning of Seanad business, when I was

six months into the job, Senator Quinn's voice sounded more unsettled than I had heard it before. He was talking about Enda Kenny's intention to abolish the Seanad. As 'father of the house', the longest-serving senator, Feargal was not happy. I was riveted by his words. While I had heard talk of the taoiseach's proposal, I hadn't paid too much attention, because it seemed unlikely that it would come to pass. But Feargal sounded pretty clear: this was a serious threat to the Seanad's existence. And he didn't like it. Neither did I.

Doing away with the Seanad, I thought, would extinguish a diversity of voices that might never otherwise be heard. At times, its chamber allowed for more considered views than the speed of the Dáil, and its debates could be a litmus test for the government on certain issues. I had diligently trained my own mind in graduate and postgraduate work over the course of eleven years. It required enormous discipline every day, but I learned how to analyse issues critically, taking account of how others before me had done so. I adopted a human rights lens and a belief in the moral agency of every individual to judge what is right and what is wrong. I always tried to take account of the social and economic circum-stances of individuals, alongside their diverse characteristics, in order to envisage the different ways in which law affects our citizens and residents. How can our laws and public policies support our citizen and residents, so they can live a life of well-being and flourish? What do we need in the laws of today, in light of how the social context has changed over time? How can we train our ears to listen to the experiences of others, so that we can incorporate their needs and dreams into the laws we make? These were the questions I started to ask myself, and tried to answer, as I became familiar with my new surroundings and the opportunities they presented. The Seanad allowed me space to do so. I observed how Dáil deputies lived in a different environment. They breathed the cut and thrust of the raw power of politics, of the competition to govern or to take down those who govern. There was less time for considered thinking, less time to discern the right thing to do.

Nevertheless, I had certainly experienced some of the Seanad's impotence. Days begin with a session entitled 'Order of Business' and most senators use it to try to get media coverage on something topical. It has little function other than that. And if we wanted to sponsor a bill, it could not have any financial implications for the exchequer. Senators cannot spend money – that's only for the TDs! But I had participated in enough sessions critiquing bills and proposing and passing amendments to know that we could influence decisions made in the Dáil. Take that away, and the government would have even more power to ram through legislation. The Seanad needed true parliamentary reform to strengthen our democracy. Abolishing the upper house, however, would only copper-fasten the interests of a tiny elite. The Seanad had room for people with dissenting voices or for those living a minority experience. As the first open lesbian in either house, it had room for people like me.

In early December 2011 word went around that Feargal Quinn had invited former minister for justice Michael McDowell to an early-morning 'private' meeting in Leinster House. Topic – 'Save the Seanad!' I certainly needed to be at that. While still learning the ropes, I wanted to be at the heart of everything significant. And to get closer to men like Michael and Feargal, to study how they operated and what they thought, seemed like the perfect way to become more familiar with the political system. Michael was a big man, in both persona and height. I was hungry for intellectual stimulation and, as one passionate about being Irish, I longed to learn more of the island's history in ways that brought it alive. The meeting was packed with Independents, those nominated and those elected, and several other party-political senators attended, including a few from Fine Gael. McDowell was on fire. He argued that abolishing the Seanad would mutilate our constitution, and he put forward strong arguments for a two-house Oireachtas. The adversarial nature of the Dáil needed the 'check and balance' that the Seanad provided. Little money would be saved by eliminating it. Everyone listened with rapt attention. Senator Quinn, the meeting's chair, concluded the gathering by putting out a call to prepare for a civic campaign to say 'No!' to the Seanad's demise.

My Independent group met soon after. Jillian van Turnhout (former chief executive of the Children's Rights Alliance) was our leader, and Fiach Mac Conghail (director of the Abbey Theatre), Martin McAleese (dentist and husband of President Mary McAleese), Mary Ann O'Brien (founder of Lily O'Brien's Chocolates), Marie-Louise O'Donnell (communications lecturer in Dublin City University) and Eamonn Coghlan (Irish Olympian) were the other members. Enda had appointed us all, so we had that in common. It provided a good base to support each other through learning about politics, and finding ways to make an impact. Our differences, and there were many, did not often get in the way.

We all felt fired up by the abolition debate and started talking about proposals that we could put forward, things we could do collectively to influence a campaign. As we had all been appointed by Enda, media commentary often covered how we could and would be deferential to the taoiseach because of that – not *real* Independents, in other words. Someone coined 'Endapendents' but I couldn't stand that. I felt exceedingly grateful for the opportunity to serve, and I would write a letter to Enda at the end of each Seanad year over the course of the five-year term to express my gratitude. But having been an outsider, and still feeling that I wore some of that cloth, I believed that Independent meant independence. While not ruling out compromise – as I had often done as an activist – being an Independent meant that I had to think things through for myself, engage in lots of conversation with my colleagues, study some of the theory behind the issues, get expert technical help when I felt I needed it and finally make a decision about how to proceed.

I relished this opportunity. A lot of it was thinking about how best to present my opinions but it was also about entering into real dialogue with others. Good conversations are quintessentially about acknowledging our relationships with one another. The best conversations happened as we built trust, even if we disagreed. When it came to action for saving the Seanad, though, for various reasons some of those conversations broke down with other senators. I felt there was competition for the limelight in what would become a defining moment for our time. Could we save the Seanad?

Would Ireland change its form of democratic governance or not? How could 'the people' be better represented? These were, and still are, weighty topics. Emotions were bound to run high. Ideas for a proposal began to develop in my Independent group. Feargal Quinn continued to drive a way forward, looking for people to join him. Other members of the house, such as the oncologist consultant and Independent senator John Crown, developed their own bills to reform rather than to abolish the Seanad.

As I listened to the various proposals for moving forward, and considered who was making them, I eventually discerned my way. I chose to support Feargal Quinn's efforts. I judged that his would be the most effective, and had the greatest sense of urgency and savvy, especially with Michael McDowell on board. His involvement would ensure that Seanad reform could be substantive even within the confines of the constitution. Others wanted me to go with them and were angry when I did not, but to me their proposals were less developed and they didn't contain the legal heft necessary to engage the electorate. However, I regret that I did not entertain longer discussions about those choices then. I am guilty of at least that.

I was eager to help Feargal Quinn's efforts and to push back against the abolition of the Seanad. We needed allies for such a momentous task. Eamonn Mac Aodha, my friend from the Irish Human Rights Commission, had insisted that as a new politician I must connect with one of his best buddies, Noel Whelan. Could Noel help us? I wonder. Eamonn introduces us by email and we agree to have lunch in One Pico, a fine restaurant on Molesworth Place in Dublin, close to Leinster House. I feel a bit nervous, wondering if I will get on with the big burly man I am about to meet. A barrister, journalist and tallyman/political nerd, Noel is keen to meet up; he's intrigued with the new senator on the block. I love him immediately. He is generous, kind and hugely intelligent. He calls things as he sees them, respectful, albeit straight-talking.

I mention that Senator Feargal Quinn wishes to meet him: as Noel is aware, Enda Kenny is preparing to keep his promise to the Irish people to abolish the Seanad and Feargal is gathering folks he thinks might be interested in saving it. Noel immediately says he is eager. Passionate about parliamentary reform, he insists that getting rid of the Seanad is not the way to do it. His great grasp of Irish history hovers behind his strong words. The Irish sought freedom for everyone, and it is up to the next generations to ensure that we find ways to protect it. That we look to extend democracy for the people, and not let any political party take control from the people. Three hours later Noel and I shake hands, and I leave with a feeling of excitement and a touch of mischievousness.

*

The number 65 bus serves seventy-eight stops, departing from Poolbeg Street in Dublin city centre and ending at Main Street, Ballymore, County Wicklow. It was the only form of public transport between The Shanty and Leinster House at the beginning of my Seanad term. From my home, it took me twenty minutes to walk to the closest bus stop on the N81, then a fifteen-minute interval because I did not want to miss the bus, at least an hour to get to the Liffey Quays and another twenty minutes to walk to Leinster House. Including waiting for the bus, and traffic, it amounted to an approximate two-hour commute on a good day. We had only one vehicle in the family at the time, and no excess cash to buy a second one. Starting a small training and consultancy business after the 2008 crash took any extra resources we had.

Most days I ended up using Ann Louise's Renault. She worked mostly from home at this stage. But it was far from an ideal arrangement. We started to talk about getting a car loan for another one but were concerned about meeting the repayments. And I loved cars so much that it would be hard for me not to be extravagant. We were stuck. I hated that feeling, especially at this point in our lives. Both of us wanted to change the world, together, but I couldn't even get around efficiently! Yet some days we were full of hope, especially after returning from a board meeting of the organisation that we had helped to found: Marriage Equality. Gráinne Healy and Denise Charlton – warrior women individually and together – co-chaired the board and were fortunate to find Moninne Griffith and Andrew Hyland as its executive leaders.

Marriage equality in Ireland was conceived in the late winter of 2007. Ann Louise and I had lost our High Court case in December 2006 to have our Canadian marriage recognised in Irish law. Justice Elizabeth Dunne had said, 'No!' We did not have the right to marry in Ireland under the constitution because that right was confined to the union of a man and a woman. It took 138 pages to say that our marriage was not valid in Ireland. What a terrible day that was for us. We were shattered. Not that we really expected to win, but we were crushed by the immeasurable weight of such a solemn rejection. We had prepared ourselves over the previous five years for this moment, always bringing our upbeat and hopeful vision of an equal world that would reach to us, and others like us.

Actually, maybe that was it. This day, of all the days, felt personal. As we left the courtroom, we looked at each other, and, without saying anything, we held our heads high, knowing our hearts were low. It showed on our faces. I know it did. Ann Louise rarely, if ever, looked beaten. But traces of defeat slowly crossed her face. I turned to her and whispered, 'Darling, we'll be okay. So many people are with us. Our day will come. Just not today.' She continued to look forward as the cameras appeared. A little startled by the first flash, her features softened and we both did our best to smile. Because we had agreed to comment on radio, we did not say anything to the reporters there, and just kept walking. As we reached the lobby of the Morrison Hotel to take a private break before heading out to RTÉ, she linked her arm in mine and brought me to the first couch to sit. It was only then that we let the tears come.

Later that day we were shown photographs of the hundreds of friends, colleagues, union organisers, LGBTQ+ groups and people we had never met who were protesting outside the entrance to Leinster House. They had cleverly decided to go to that location, rather than to the courts, to hear the judgment. I can still see Ailbhe Smyth with the blowhorn, and so many of Ann Louise's colleagues from St Pat's, along-side a big crowd of friends from Tallaght and An Cosán. It was such a sunny day, and most of the photos were taken before the judgment came out: 'our' people were beaming. They really believed in our right to joy.

Solidarity is something you can feel, a deep connection, a physical energy between and among those who gather for a purpose. And it travels. It is not bound by physical proximity. A couple of weeks later, Ann Louise and I sat one night in front of our wood-burning open fire with Siena and Paulo at our feet. It was the warmest place in the sitting room, and their favourite spot! I picked up a piece of wood, one I had split in our paddock on a carefree day earlier in the year. As I tossed it in the fire, I turned to Ann Louise and said, 'Let's plan a bigger campaign.'

Over a series of dinners for various friends, human rights activists and lawyers, we laid out a number of strategies. These included a legal strategy to appeal the High Court decision, communications to build public awareness about the rationale for equality through access to civil marriage, mobilisation to engage supporters from all sectors, a political strategy to work with public representatives, and a funding strategy to sustain the organisation. Great excitement and some dissonance filled the air as the conversations progressed. Some wanted to go softly, softly – an incremental approach – while others forcefully stated that we had waited long enough, and we should go straight for marriage, without the 'stepping stone' of civil partnership. We wanted the straight path, so we rolled up our sleeves together. In early 2008, the organisation Marriage Equality was formally launched in the

Mansion House on Dublin's Dawson Street to a packed audience.

When I took up my senatorial role, Ann Louise began to put more time into the Marriage Equality work than I did. She attended most, if not all, the board meetings, and often visited the office to assist the few staff there in whatever way she could. They all wanted her around for her wisdom, creativity and courage. They knew she would always speak her truth, graciously, even if it was hard to hear at times. So much was at stake for all of us. Yet her tone was never harsh, nor did her words sound critical. Above all, the staff loved her creativity. She always had a solution to the problem at hand, and she knew when not to interfere. We would discuss everything when she got home from meetings I was not able to attend. It took a lot out of her, though, and it would have been easier if I could have been by her side more frequently. At least I could take up a role in my senatorial capacity. The government had promised a constitutional convention – a forum of citizens and parliamentarians – to consider a possible referendum on the marriage of same-sex couples. I got one of the assigned places for the convention. I was hopeful, then, that we could still fight this together, albeit on different fronts.

Sometimes I felt selfish or self-cherishing by keeping my prime focus on my work in the Seanad. This rarely bothered Ann Louise when it came to the task of cooking, and I loved coming through the kitchen door to the smells of roasted chicken, vegetables sprinkled with cumin, tarragon or dill. It was the brown bread and the scones that were my favourites. Ann Louise was famous for those scones, served most days during Shanty courses. 'What is the recipe for your scones, Ann Louise?' she was often asked. 'I love swirling the bowl!' she would respond. But she was not happy about being left with all the cleaning. Rarely was I excused from those domestic duties no matter what was going on in Leinster House. I can see now that she was right and I was wrong. There were probably not enough 'sorry's on my part. I just felt my work was *so important*. But that did not wash at all with her. I eventually learned that teamwork outside of professional activities is at the heart of an equal relationship. (Thank you, Ann Louise.)

One day, out of the blue – and with a touch of magic – our car problems were sorted when a close friend kindly offered to lend us their blue Volkswagen Beetle, for as long as we needed it. Memories of a twenty-seven-year-old me driving from the Bronx to Manhattan in a vintage orange Beetle came to mind. Though I could feel every bump, the tyres responded with precision as my hands turned the wheel and I easily learned the rhythm of the unwritten rules of the road. But the heat didn't work and the Beetle showed its cracks. This one would come with all the mod cons – I couldn't believe my luck.

I put down the phone and sprinted out the door, through the paddock gate, and across the field to Ann Louise's log cabin. 'Annie, Jenny is loaning us . . . well, me . . . a car!' And that was that. I just delighted in driving that sharp-looking little bug through the big gates of Leinster House.

Ann Louise was all for anything that made my Seanad duties easier. She had expected that by taking early retirement in 2009 we could build again a way of working together. We had put a lot of time into the establishment of our consultancy, the Centre for Progressive Change, founded in 2009 as a response to the enormous economic and social upheaval Ireland was undergoing post-crash. We ran leadership programmes, offered executive coaching, governance advice for non-profits and seasonal 'retreats for change'. We started from scratch on all this, and my work included everything administrative (marketing, financial accounts, website) as well as teaching in the programmes with Ann Louise. It was a heavy burden. I really did not want to do this any longer, but she was so happy, freed from the drudgery of academic life. It had become more about raising funds for the next research project than about teaching undergraduates and advising postgraduates about philosophies of education and the imagination, which Ann Louise loved.

When I was appointed to the Seanad, she could see that things would change and that, eventually, she would have to let go of this dream we had started to build together. She kept at her executive coaching, and planned to offer retreats with Anne O'Reilly, a former academic colleague. She never complained, but she did ask me to continue to keep the accounts, and run the website and the emails. I really did not like that, albeit minor, work, but I did it. Of course I would do anything for her. I felt the heavy-heartedness of her loss, though it was not my loss. I still have my Centre email address and every year I pay a small fee to continue to host the server for the website. It is over a decade since we closed the business, but I haven't been able to let this go. Ann Louise's generosity in our life-partnership taught me, because I felt it at my deepest core, the true generative nature of a love commitment. She never failed to support me in anything I tried, even if it cost her something she wanted for herself. Because of this, I have thrived at times, and survived at others. Perhaps that is why I hang on to a website and an email that are essentially redundant. They represent the dream she was willing to let go of, for me.

*

January is a forbidding, damp and dark month in Ireland. Though the light starts to come back, it struggles to do so on most days. Both houses of the Oireachtas are still asleep, and the ushers begin to unlock the doors only during the second week. Senator Feargal Quinn is keen to get going on his crusade to save the Seanad, though, and so early one morning he invites Michael McDowell, Noel Whelan, Joe O'Toole and myself to attend the first meeting of what we eventually dub 'the Seanad Reform Group'.

Three men. Actually four, including Feargal. And one radical feminist lesbian. I know I do not look or sound like that. What is 'that', though? Often someone who is super creative and edgy with the clothes she wears. She does not fit the mainstream. I never wanted to experiment with clothes. I was aware that a woman's choice could be integral to her resistance to the norms of patriarchy, but I really like much of traditional female design. My favourite professional outfit at the time is a light grey fine woollen tailored jacket and skirt, with a white cotton shirt. I wear it for my Seanad photo. Although it makes me look like part of the establishment, I am clearly an outsider, and get in only through the intriguing actions of powerful insiders.

But it does matter what people wear. Some of the effort to don 'proper' clothing comes from what I thought my mother wanted. My father loved the way she dressed. He always talked about her 'New York style' and how it had first caught the eye of a boy from Montana. So, maybe what I heard is how her feminine style was integral to his attraction for and love of her. One day, she gave me an extraordinary gift. In her last decade, on one of my many trips back to Seattle, she said to me, 'I always knew you were different, Kay. We are so proud of you.' I wish I could have felt more of that in my earlier and even middle years. While I was eventually public about my lesbian identity, and my love for Ann Louise, I still struggled to love myself 'regardless', as Alice Walker once said. Most days I carried the contradiction well. Its resolution happened slowly, through the bestowal of a long life-partnership with Ann Louise.

I was about to enter Leinster House 2000 (the new wing erected in 2000) on a drizzly and dreary January night. The newer wing is to the left side of Leinster House, as one faces the majestic entrance, and it was built with an architectural design that combines modernity and a Georgian ambiance. Home to several offices for deputies and senators, and a suite of rooms for the main opposition party, it also houses the parliamentary committee rooms down a modern, sleek stone staircase. There's a comfortable coffee dock, opposite an enormous open-space, cathedral-ceilinged room with agreeable couches. Journalists hover there too. If you want to be seen with the person you are meeting – to pique interest in what you might be up to – the coffee dock is the place to go. It's also conveniently close to offices and committee rooms. But as I walk through the entrance that quiet night, there isn't a soul to be seen.

Feargal, already in Room B – behind a thin wall at the entrance – must have heard me enter and so he walks out to greet me with the gait of a happy man. We shake hands, and I spontaneously brush his right cheek with my right hand, as I do with those I am fond of. He thanks me for coming, and then we both turn as we hear Joe O'Toole and Noel Whelan arrive. They had met each other at the gate, no doubt joking with the ushers there who wanted to know what they were up to. 'Always tell a good secret!' I imagine is what Joe might have retorted. Former Independent Senator O'Toole, a great friend of Feargal's, having served for several years together in the Seanad, is very expressive, often erupting in laughter or employing a stern and billowing voice. A teacher by training, he became president of the Irish Congress of Trade Unions and then secretary general of the Irish National Teachers' Organisation. Ann Louise loved the INTO, admiring the canny way it dealt with various governments over the years. She really liked Joe too.

Noel is raring to go. He travels a lot for his work, often driving the Waterford–Dublin road before our meetings after a full day practising as a barrister at the Waterford circuit court. Tonight he is still on holiday. Noel was engaged in politics in his earlier life, working in the Fianna Fáil headquarters for a time, before taking up an advisory role for a minister of state for European Union affairs in the early

1990s. Noel is hooked on politics, bringing a detailed understanding of it to our campaign. He is familiar with every constituency and local electoral area across the country. He wears this immense knowledge lightly, but it provides a major storehouse for the work we are about to do. As I kiss his cheek, Michael McDowell barrels through the doors. He, too, has more energy than usual, both from the break from his work as a senior counsel and because he loves a good fight. And this is going to be a serious struggle. Early polls provide evidence that the majority of the Irish hardly care about the Seanad and do not know what takes place in that chamber. Why not abolish it? This will be our sizeable challenge – to answer that question and to get people to care enough to vote, and to vote 'No'.

Room B is very small. All four gentlemen are well used to talking and to having the floor. I muster my will to bring my voice to this table. I feel intimidated by their experienced and clever minds, so I fall back on a familiar tactic: stay quiet, take time to assess the mood, and then steadily express my own views. Feargal lays out his initial thoughts on the development of an offensive plan. Michael responds first, regaling us with a bit of history, then moving to a thorough analysis of how the Irish constitution could host a more democratic Seanad than current laws allow. Joe lays out his forceful feelings and views. He had used the Seanad well during his time to voice the concerns of the working man and woman. 'Union members can be persuaded to vote for the value of the Seanad,' he concludes.

Noel has not said anything yet, though he immediately begins to sketch words and arrows that depict logical movements on his notepad. The first cuts of a campaign. Following up some of Michael's remarks, he confirms that we should write a bill to demonstrate how the Seanad could be reformed *within* constitutional parameters. This would allow us to shift the argument from an *abolished* Seanad to a *reformed* one. We all know that laws relating to Seanad elections exclude many citizens from voting. What if we write a law that gives the vote to everyone? Michael informs us that he is getting research done to confirm that this change is allowed by the constitution. Noel agrees, saying, 'This will be the cornerstone of our appeal to the electorate, so we have to get this analysis right.' He continues by proposing another idea – that we should write a consultation document that outlines some of our ideas for reform. This could initiate a national conversation, and ensure that the electorate approves of the direction of our bill.

At this point I finally feel prepared to speak. I have little experience at bill-making but I do know about the power of consultation and communication with the public. Perhaps we could take the consultation document to the people, hold a couple of public or town-hall-type meetings in Dublin, and perhaps in Cork and Galway. Between us we have many networks. We just might need a little cash, though. I am sweating at this stage, but think I have managed to sound clear and succinct. Feargal immediately responds with, 'I'll put in some seed money to get this thing going. Then we can write a letter outlining our intentions, and ask for a contribution to a reformed Seanad. We can start by sending it to all Oireachtas members, and then spread it to our national contacts.'

Something very distinctive is unfolding. Feargal assigns responsibilities to each of us, and we adjourn for two weeks. At the next meeting we are joined by two other men, both of whom bring complementary strengths to the group. Brian Murphy, a former advisor and speech writer for Taoiseach Bertie Ahern and one of Noel's closest allies in various political and writing ventures, comes on board to help compose the consultation document and guide the strategy. Brian Hunt, a solicitor and former advisor on EU affairs to the Department of the Taoiseach during Ireland's presidency of the European Union, brings his great skill in drafting legislation.

Over the course of the next eight months we met usually twice a month. On 26 September 2012, our work went public. We launched 'Open It, Don't Close It', our thirty-page consultation paper on the future of a reformed Seanad: how its election processes could be transformed; who is elected; what powers it holds; how it does its business. At the core of our proposals was a call for universal suffrage, a direct public vote for Seanad seats so that it could claim a greater democratic mandate. While we managed to build some momentum in this early period, the hill to climb was arduous and high. Initially we garnered strong media attention, but it was challenging to sustain. For months, we continued to work on a Seanad reform bill, but it had to be attractive to the public and constitutionally airtight. Feargal was unflappable, Michael impatient, Joe committed, Noel steady as she goes, with his eye on the prize. The two Brians were consistently generous. And I was getting used to all of them, able to speak more freely more often. Happy to take media and public meeting slots. Proud to be with this group of men. Though I was aware I had ideological differences with a couple of them, my affection and trust grew.

*

Working so diligently to save the Seanad propelled me to think more deeply about the work I wanted to do as a senator. I believed that the upper house was a place to test new ideas in law-making. This might demonstrate its potential to be more than a 'talking shop'. One of the best ways to display its promise, I thought, could come through developing private member's bills as vehicles for social change. What else needed changing, then, that aligned with my commitment to human rights? This question made me feel as if I had some genuine power to effect change. I just had to use it right. I looked around. I found something that caused me some fear at first. That was, however, to change as my heart opened.

Ireland was the only country in the European Union that did not legally recognise transgender individuals in their preferred gender. We were the laggard. In 1992 the courageous and kind Dr Lydia Foy had sex reassignment surgery and initiated a twenty-two-year legal battle to have her birth certificate reflect her gender identity. She is a tall trans woman with a big voice, a quick broad smile and glistening eyes. Lydia waged her campaign alone for a very long time. Her spirit is indomitable, and she was still conducting her crusade when I entered the Seanad. Though the Irish High Court had ruled in 2007 that Ireland's gender laws were not compliant with the European Convention on Human Rights, by 2011 the law still had not changed and Lydia was preparing to go to court again. As a human rights commissioner of the first Irish commission, I had worked really hard with my colleagues to influence the way in which Ireland should incorporate the human rights convention into the country's own laws. We wanted the convention to have as much impact as possible. My idealism in those earlier times tempered eventually. At first I could not understand why, if the courts had ruled that Irish laws were not compliant with the convention, the lawmakers wouldn't rectify this injustice as soon as possible. But now I was learning that there is nothing automatic in the pace of significant social change. Lawmakers hold the rudimentary power and sometimes they do not exercise it.

I first met Lydia in Blackhall Place, the headquarters of the Law Society of Ireland. Another eighteenth-century Georgian building, its ambiance celebrates the traditional norms of humanity and society with its exquisite architecture, beautiful ornate high ceilings and stained-glass windows. By her presence, Lydia broke down barriers and disputed norms contained within the setting. I felt the discordance alongside the hospitality being shown to her by those gathered for a human rights law seminar. I can actually feel social change at times. This was one of those moments. Lydia paused in her conversation with a colleague as she saw me. 'Senator Zappone!' she cried out. 'Over here.' From that moment our friendship began. She spoke a little about her legal campaign, but she also shared her love of foxgloves and her initial efforts to sketch and paint them. I told her how Ann Louise was the gardener in our family, but that I loved to plant her choices in our long beds and then to weed and weed, especially as the seasons turned.

The next week I decided to contact Belong To, the organisation for young LGBTQ+ people founded by Michael Barron, to ask if I could meet some of its members. I had never met young trans people before, so I did not understand how they felt about themselves, experienced their world or how different one trans person can be from another. I wanted to know this. I knew as a lesbian that the only way straight people might begin to understand my reality was to listen to lesbian experiences of being in the world. Six young people were brave enough to come to meet me in Leinster House 2000 one morning. They filed into Room B and sat around the table, the same table where my Seanad Reform Group regularly met. It felt apt. If we could retain the Seanad, it might become more of a place where lawmakers could take on political issues that the mainstream regarded as marginal.

I felt nervous, aware of my own cultural prejudices about transgender individuals. I had touched on some of that in my earlier exchanges with Lydia. After I welcomed them, a thirteen-year-old trans boy said, 'My name is Jimmy. Please call me "he".' Jimmy continued to talk quietly about the struggles he had in school, though there was one teacher who talked to him often and offered him a refuge from his schoolmates' taunting and shaming. Somewhere in him, however, Jimmy generated emotional strength and resilience during his schooldays, and also found companionship and care in his time at Belong To. Some of the others spoke too.

They simply wanted to be recognised for who they felt themselves to be. They were well aware that current legislation was not on their side. 'Why can't you just change the law?' one of them asked, looking directly at me. 'I will try,' I replied. As with Lydia, my heart and mind were converted by these young people and I left the room determined to do something. Their bravery is still with me.

My Seanad assistant, Magdalene Hayden, helped me in everything, but she was especially good at organising meetings that would be difficult or delicate. Originally from Finland, she carried that internal Finnish zeal for equality. We discussed what to do next and decided that it was time to meet the adults. Magdalene heard from TENI (Transgender Equality Network Ireland) about a couple who had begun some quiet advocacy for legislation that would recognise transgender individuals. Philippa and Helen Ryder married as husband and wife. Philippa, with the support of Helen, transitioned to being a woman during their marriage. Remarkably – and unremarkably – they wanted to stay married to each other. So, they needed two legal changes – a law that would recognise Philippa as female, and a law that would allow women to be married to each other. Jenny, their teenage daughter, wanted these changes too.

At the meeting, in walked Helen without Philippa. As a civil servant, Philippa did not engage in public lobbying for legal change. Helen was calm and respectful, but the power of her experience and commitment to what is right and good evoked a spell-binding, authoritative voice: 'I love Philippa. I loved her as the man I married. I love her as the trans woman she has become.' Helen then insisted that the law must recognise her partner for who she is, and it *must allow them to remain married*. 'We want to live in a land', Helen said, 'that supports us as we raise our daughter together. We are committed to whatever it takes, so that Jenny feels the love, safety and security she needs to withstand the eyes and tongues of those who do not understand or accept.'

Her conviction and eloquence blew me away. Helen knew a lot about the law, too. I was in unknown territory and she was educating me. She finished her story by sharing an exchange between their daughter and her wife, subsequent to Philippa's transition. 'Can I still call you daddy?' asks Jenny. 'Of course, baby,' responds Philippa. A parent's love, a daughter's love, never appeared more beautiful.

I left the room feeling ignited to set about my task as a lawmaker. Irish law and lawmakers were failing these citizens. The previous government had established a Gender Recognition Advisory Group in 2011, composed of members of various departments of state. They reported in 2012 to a new government. Joan Burton, as minister for social protection, was in charge of this issue. Advocates and human rights lawyers heavily criticised the group's review and recommendations as highly restrictive. In their words, they 'clearly infringed on an individual's right to privacy, personal dignity and family life'. The government was getting nowhere, no sight of even a draft head of bill on gender recognition – the outline of a bill, the first step in legislative development.

I telephoned my good friend and close colleague Michael Farrell. Michael and I had soldiered together for a decade as members of the Irish Human Rights Commission. While a soft-spoken Derry man, he was front and centre of the civil rights movement in Northern Ireland. In his early years, he was a hunger-striker during the Troubles, eventually qualifying to take on human rights cases in the Republic. He was a man of great heart as he tackled the hardness and complexity of the law. He was working at Free Legal Advice Centres (FLAC) at the time, and was Lydia Foy's lawyer. What a pair they were – indefatigable and brilliant. When Michael and I met, we started to sketch a plan to write a gender recognition bill. It was a big emotional lift for me. Progress felt possible.

*

I harness that feeling of possibility and apply it to my work to save the Seanad. We are doing everything we can. We hold debates in Trinity College Dublin and the University of Limerick. We write op eds and I do local radio. We stay in touch with a growing number of colleagues of like mind throughout the country. However, in February 2013 an *Irish Times*/Ipsos MRBI poll taken in the month indicates that a substantial majority of voters, 58 per cent, say they will vote 'Yes' to Seanad abolition. And the civil servants are speedily drafting the government's bill to do just this. For the first time, a strong foreboding starts to hang over the Seanad Reform Group. We might fail.

CHAPTER 3

Everything Changes

Several well-known women from business, the arts and public life – ten tables, each with six settings – have gathered for dinner in Dublin Castle. I guess I am becoming one of these women, but I still feel daunted in their presence. This sentiment starts to run through my body as I drive up to the Ship Street gate of Dublin Castle.

We have been invited to hear about an international club for professional women and to consider membership. One of the speakers is Sabina Higgins, wife of President Michael D. Higgins. Her presence calms me. While she is a remarkable woman, with many artistic talents and unbounded cleverness, her simplicity always relaxes me. I got to know her to a certain degree throughout Michael D.'s first presidential campaign. She rarely left his side. During the period in which he was still the underdog, his campaign manager, Joe Costello, phoned to ask if I could fire up the troops at a party meeting in the Westbury Hotel. I was both delighted and terrified by the request. Ann Louise came to my rescue, however, as she often did, and dictated to me some of the things I should say. By the time I stood in front of the crowd that afternoon, having witnessed Michael D. and Eamon Gilmore arrive a bit downhearted, I was determined to inspire the audience as best I could with my partner's words. I began: 'Michael D. is the only candidate who can build a "presidency of the people". Because he is *of* the people . . .' They liked what I had to say. Very pleased with the crowd's response, and how cheered her husband seemed, Sabina never forgot that moment.

Coincidentally, Ann Louise had been at Dublin Castle earlier on the day of my meeting with the professional women's club. She spoke at a conference on education, hosted by Quality and Qualifications Ireland, of which she was a board member. I did not hear how it went, so I text her just after the main course. No response. But now I remember that she was planning to attend her French conversation course at the Alliance Française on Kildare Street in the early evening. I am concerned that it might be too much for her. She has been quite tired in the past few days. Never one to miss an opportunity to converse in her beloved second language, though, she said we would meet back at The Shanty after my dinner. I relish our conversations together at the end of a day. I always start first because she is the introvert. I recount everything that has happened to me, whom I have met and what we spoke about, what I have worked on and my latest thoughts on our legal case or Seanad meetings. Ann Louise is a fantastic listener, never without insightful comments or an encouraging word. Then I stop and wait. Rarely does she have much to say at first. 'Come on, Annie,' I say, 'I can't read your mind.' And then she begins, in that beautiful refined Irish voice.

I text her again after dessert. She should be home by now. No answer. I try to keep down a modest unease and am one of the first to leave Dublin Castle. On my way out I meet Sabina.

'Where is Ann Louise?' she asks.

I tell her.

'Will you let her know that I was asking for her?'

'I will,' I say. 'And please tell the president that we are very much looking forward to lunch with him soon.'

Michael D. had invited me and Ann Louise to discuss his plans for one of his upcoming presidential seminars. Neither of us could believe our good fortune, and had used any spare time to read up on the writers and themes we wanted to talk to him about. It helped take my mind off the ominous tone of the latest news on the Seanad referendum.

I head to The Shanty, thinking Ann Louise's phone must have died but we will catch up at home with one of our usual evening chats. Then my mind drifts to Michael D.'s campaign theme of wanting to initiate a 'presidency of ideas'. I think that is very cool. I wonder, though, how it will appeal to the great numbers who had voted for him. Nevertheless, his first initiative is focused on ethics, something I taught in Trinity College Dublin in one of my past lives. When I arrived on Irish shores in 1983 I was a practising theologian, completing my doctoral dissertation for a degree from Boston College. I loved teaching ethics to both young and mature students. I insisted that the professor did not know it all, that the classroom was a place for us to learn from one other. The Trinity students were used to the traditional style of lecture given by the instructor and note-taking by the student. No fun, as well as no active learning; just a passive reception. Paulo Freire called it the 'banking method' of education. One of the courses that worked best with my approach I entitled 'Religion, Ethics and Literature'. I chose Alice Walker's *The Color Purple* (1982), Margaret Atwood's *The Handmaid's Tale* (1985) and *Beloved* (1987) by Toni Morrison. It was not hard to draw ethical dilemmas out of these novels, ones my students may not be used to in their day-to-day lives. The authors were women writing about women's experiences, women's ways of knowing and how women can make ethical decisions in ways different from men.

Traffic is so slow. I bring myself back to the present to try a new shortcut home. When I finally arrive, August – our newish golden retriever – is sitting just inside the gate, though it is wide open. She is shaking. *Why is the gate open? Why is August out?* Slightly alarmed, I get out and stroke August to calm her down. I get back into the car, drive up to the house and August shoots up after me. I could shut and lock the gate later. I drive around the house and park. There is Annie's car, its doors wide open, the lights flashing. The side door to our home is also open.

'August, where's Annie?' I call out.

She whisks through the door at a run. I follow into the kitchen and notice Ann Louise's mobile on the kitchen island.

47

There is a half-finished text on the screen, but she is nowhere to be seen. I run to our bedroom and there she is, in bed.

She looks up as I enter and says, 'Katie, I think I have the flu. My head was hurting all day. I thought it was maybe anxiety about giving a paper at the conference. When I got to my French class, I had to take three Disprin but my headache wouldn't go away. So I left early to come home. I pulled over at the Jobstown Inn and got sick. Thank goodness I rallied and managed to drive the rest of the way from there.' Then she closes her eyes.

I bend over and feel her forehead. No fever; breathing without trouble. I try to calm myself. Ann Louise sounds in control. But the car, the lights, the side door. None of this adds up to the way Ann Louise would normally behave. The Shanty is on a rural road, and there have been several burglaries in the area. We are two women together, without a man. Perfect prey, some might think.

'I just want to sleep, and I should feel better in the morning,' Ann Louise whispers.

Is she just imagining the positive, even in her depleted state? I wonder. It is so hard to tell with Ann Louise. She rarely gives in to any negative thoughts. I feel her forehead again.

'Okay, darling. Let me get you your nightclothes. You can't sleep in what you have on.'

She lets me help her, sleeping while sitting up. I lay her back down, still worried. I change my own clothes, slip in beside her and eventually fall asleep.

*

48

The next morning I woke early. We were scheduled to travel later in the day to London to spend the weekend with a friend. I did not think that Ann Louise would be able to go, but I checked her forehead again. She opened her eyes, was very drowsy and said she still did not feel well. I decided to ring our doctor, Máire Slevin. We had every confidence in her, especially since she had expertly helped Ann Louise through breast cancer. I got through to Máire and asked if there was anything else I should be doing.

'No, Katherine, but do continue to check her temperature. It does sound like it could be the flu. But please call me later in the day to check in.'

As the afternoon drew to a close, I still felt that something was not quite right. I phoned Máire again, then went back to Ann Louise, still resting in the bed, and told her that we'd be going to see the doctor. She sat up and insisted on dressing herself. As she went into the bathroom, I noticed that her left arm was hanging in an unusual way. But she came out with her clothes on and hair brushed, a smile on her face and perfume in her right hand. 'I need a little of this to keep me going,' she said.

'Right, Ann Louise. Let's go.'

How I loved her.

I got her into my car and we drove the half hour to Rathfarnham Shopping Centre where Máire had her office. It was the first time in twenty hours that I started to believe that things were going to be alright. Máire would check Ann Louise, prescribe something and send us back home.

Instead, after what seemed to be no more than a couple of minutes, Máire looked at me and said in front of Ann

Louise, 'Two plus two are not making four, here, Katherine. You need to bring Ann Louise straight to an emergency department and have them examine her. Tallaght Hospital.' For half a beat I felt immobilised. Then Máire took my arm, as I took Ann Louise's, and she walked us down to the car. I can still feel her healing touch from that gesture.

First Ann Louise had to sit in the waiting room. After thirty minutes, as I noticed her slumping, I went up to the reception and pleaded with them to allow her to skip the queue. 'This is a genuine emergency,' I said. 'And our doctor wants you to ring her as soon as you examine her.' I was not moving from that desk until they said yes. I had looked around, and no one seemed to be as ill as Ann Louise. Soon afterwards, someone came to us and took her in to a cordoned space behind reception, asking me to wait outside.

Thirty minutes later a nurse came out to tell me that Ann Louise had a bleed on her brain. Stunned, I asked, 'What does that mean? A stroke?'

'Yes, she's lost some blood from a damaged blood vessel in her brain. That's a type of stroke, but more commonly known as a brain haemorrhage. We don't know how bad it is yet, or how it will affect her. We'll keep her here until we can find a bed upstairs.'

I tried to slow down the feeling of trauma rising within me. Ann Louise was sleeping calmly. I sat in the space behind reception with her for a long, exhausting hour, with the loneliest feeling I had ever experienced, and then the nurse encouraged me to go home and get some sleep. What else was I to do? I had to be ready for the next day. I walked out of the emergency department alone, dreading the drive to a thoroughly empty Shanty. And then I remembered August; she could sleep on the floor of our bedroom next to me.

By the time I arrived at the hospital early the next morning, they had found a bed for Ann Louise. When I got to the room, she was chatting away with the doctors, even laughing a little. Everything seemed calm and normal. The doctors indicated that we needed to get Ann Louise to the brain ward of Beaumont Hospital, on the northside of Dublin. They would be much better equipped to care for her there and support her recovery.

I went out into the hall and dialled a Dublin number. 'Hello, June,' I said to Ann Louise's older sister, 'I have some bad news about Ann Louise, but we think she's going to be okay.' June came straight away to be with us.

Towards the end of the afternoon, a bed in Beaumont became available. As she was being lifted into the ambulance, Ann Louise looked out and asked, 'Where are my glasses? I don't have my glasses.' I ran back up to the room, looked everywhere, but could not find them. By the time I got back to the ambulance they had her strapped up and she was ready to go.

I was simply perplexed. Why, of all things, would Ann Louise ask for her glasses? She often did not wear them. I was just so relieved that our conversations had been going well, that her short- and long-term memories were intact, and that she knew her name, her age and her address. These were signs of wellness, I thought, yet uncertainty lingered. And I was right: the blindness had begun, though none of us knew it at that moment.

I settled Ann Louise in to her room at Beaumont. We would be waiting a while for her next exam, and I was due back at Leinster House to speak in a debate. I didn't want to leave her side, but I knew a short visit to the Seanad now would buy me time over the next few weeks. I needed to keep the ball rolling with the bill being considered, so I dragged my heavy body out of Beaumont Hospital and into Leinster House. I ascended the stairs, casting my eyes up to the exquisite painting of Countess Markievicz in a ballgown, hung on the wall halfway up. Her bravery and character amidst so much suffering always fortified me, no matter what the day or what work was in front of me. I was pulled out of my trance-like state when I met Orla Murray, secretary to Maurice Cummins, the leader of the Seanad, coming down the stairs. I told her what had happened.

She looked me straight in the eye and said, 'What are you doing here, Katherine? Go to Ann Louise!'

'Yes. Yes. I will do that shortly. I came back now to sort out my Seanad commitments for the next couple of weeks at least.'

There was so much going on. Our work to save the Seanad was increasing daily, as the polls continued to tell us what we didn't want to hear. The constitutional convention on marriage equality was coming soon. As a senator, I would hold one of the seats reserved for Oireachtas members. The development of my trans bill was taking longer than I thought it would.

I entered the Seanad chamber to find my seat, with a speech on the finance bill that Magdalene and I had prepared together. Magdalene was great at economics and we usually came up with some good critiques of the government's stand. Brian Hayes was in the chair reserved for a minister who attends the Seanad. At the time he was minister of state for public expenditure and reform. He also represented Dublin South-West, the constituency where Ann Louise and I lived, and the location for An Cosán. I knew Brian well from his work there, and respected him a great deal. He always found ways to support the educational mission of An Cosán. I sat in my chair and looked at him. He was listening to another senator's address to the house. I felt so overwhelmed with my circumstance, and I knew Brian was very fond of Ann Louise. So I texted him to let him know what had happened. His phone was on the table in front of him and he saw the text come in. Distress registered on his face. He looked up immediately, saw me there and texted back a word of support. At that moment all else in the chamber receded. His gesture of kindness helped me through the rest of the day. On my way out in the early evening I met Noel Whelan. I told him that I would miss a couple of Seanad reform meetings because Ann Louise was sick. Noel embraced me. No words were spoken, and I left.

The days passed slowly in Beaumont – so many tests, so many questions. Our conversations with the neurologists – led by Professor Norman Delanty – were inconclusive. Norman's healing manner was exceptional, and his ability to communicate complicated medical conditions in simple language gave me such solace. I did not have to struggle to understand. He and his team were trying to find the cause of the bleed, but they simply could not, no matter how many tests were carried out. Ann Louise's condition was difficult enough to process, but the uncertainty made it unbearable. While she appeared to be regaining her energy – and her positive spirit surfaced quickly – this contrasted with her doctors' deep concern.

June and her daughter Hilda – then in her mid-forties – accompanied me during many of those meetings. Their presence was a consolation. Hilda, who was devoted to Ann Louise, always came with her notes from previous meetings and her questions for the upcoming one. I still have her records. They helped me to feel a semblance of control when my hope began to ebb. Like it did that day I found myself alone in a corridor and one of the junior doctors sat down beside me. He said, 'We can see evidence of another small bleed in her brain. We don't know why it is there, or how it has happened.'

I was terrified. Though the tests had been inconclusive, this sounded as if something was really wrong. Nobody mentioned it again. I just decided to ignore it. The idea got in the way of mustering a positive approach. It surfaced in my memory only years later. The Beaumont staff provided exceptional care as the days passed. From the neurologists to the cleaners, an environment of safety and love grew around Ann Louise. She made friends with the people in the beds beside her. Eventually, the doctors said that, while the origins of her haemorrhage could not be determined, she appeared to be healing. Further tests confirmed this to be the case.

About a week later, I came in early one morning to find Ann Louise eating breakfast. I noticed that she could not find the food easily. Her table manners were impeccably gracious, and every lift of a fork would be executed with appreciation and delicacy, but now the cutlery missed the food again and again.

'Ann Louise', I asked, 'can you see the porridge bowl?'

She looked up at me, and with a pensive face said, 'Sometimes I do, and sometimes I don't. Sometimes it disappears, Katherine. But then it reappears.'

'I wonder, my love, if you are having problems with your sight. You often ask for your glasses, even when they are on your face.'

Ann Louise replied softly, 'I am not sure. So much of the day my mind is tired, and I think my exhaustion may be affecting my eyes. I'm going to sleep for a little while now.'

I sat in the chair by her bed, and quietly closed my eyes until I had to go back to work, and later to the dogs at The Shanty.

The next day I returned to her for lunchtime. She was very keen to talk.

'Katherine, since you asked me about my eyes yesterday, I just had to find out, so I went on a mission of discovery.'

She told me she had got out of bed and made her way along the corridors downstairs to the newspaper shop where she knelt on the floor and looked at the front page of each newspaper.

'I couldn't read any of the print before me,' she said. 'I had to feel my way back upstairs, and I eventually found my ward and bed. No one asked where I had been, which was fine with me. I just wanted to be left alone.'

She had her answer. She was blind.

*

To my regret, I did not take Ann Louise to the doctor right away that evening she got sick. I did not imagine there was something really wrong. I did not protect her. They tell you that with the first signs of a stroke you should get the person straight to emergency. Ann Louise spent the next four years of her life with no sight because I had failed to do this. She said, 'No, no, Katie. You did everything you could.' I felt blessed by her forgiveness, but the weight of her blindness will remain with me always. It is like a big stone on a beach. Though the ocean wears it away slowly, one tide after another, it does not disappear.

Ann Louise's meditation on the meaning of her blindness was to take many forms. What kind of 'unseeing' was it, though? From a physiological perspective, the occipital lobe on the left side of her brain was scarred. Everything was hazy and obscure. She could no longer read her books. The words would shake on the page or settle into a blur. She discerned the physicality of objects, of space and people around her, and she used every bit of that impression to learn how to move again, as if she could see. I think she called on the powers of every other sense in her body and relearned how to navigate her world. Activated together, they enabled her to appear as if she were a 'seeing' person.

Ann Louise attended Baggot Street Hospital regularly for physical therapy. I can still see her walking across Upper Baggot Street for the very first time after this haemorrhage – with her favourite occupational therapist, Aisling, by her side. No white stick. I felt terrified for her, and for myself. Her posture was as perfect, though, as it always was. She moved a little more slowly, but every step was determined, and she knew that she was being accompanied. My fear started to ease a little. I had learned a long time ago never to stand in the way of Ann Louise's will. I drove off, leaving her, with sadness and admiration in my heart.

Being the philosopher that she was, she mined the experience of blindness to come to terms with what she called 'the virtue of vulnerability'. What an extraordinary response. Vulnerability can be such a frightening experience, and so much of our cultural conditioning is to mask the fear of it. Instead, my Ann Louise found a way to discover something new, as she recounted in her journal:

Having a brain haemorrhage — especially one that left me with severely impaired sight — has brought me to very new expressions of my buried self. I am gaining confidence in talking about my disability and asking for help. The extraordinary thing is that I am finding new, deeper dimensions in myself, and new revelations in the potential depths of relationality and connection with others. There is almost a relief in not always having to be in control, and in charge!

While my grief began with Ann Louise's blindness, she began to look for new meaning and new ways of being human. She was so resolute in carving out this path. I was in love with Ann Louise every moment of every day for thirty-two years, but it was so hard now to witness her vulnerability. It shocked my heart. That's what it felt like – an electric shock to the heart.

I experienced my most agonising moment when I visited

her early one morning. They were the quiet times in hospital, with little nursing activity. She was awake. I looked straight into her eyes. She returned my gaze. I asked, 'Ann Louise, can you see me?'

She replied, 'I can see my memory of your image.'

I was devastated. Even as she reached for something positive to say, I felt her loss of me as well as my loss of her. I was grief-stricken with that double loss. I still find it so hard to believe that she could not see the precise contours of my face, the colour of my eyes, my look of love for her. And so my life narrowed towards her.

I looked out our bedroom window later that evening and thought, *I will never travel very far again with Ann Louise. It's a good thing we did so much travelling together earlier on in our lives. I will go to work each day, phone her often, make sure the neighbours call in on her when they can, and return as early as possible each evening. I will put my own needs to one side.* I didn't always succeed, but this was my promise. And I loved her with all my heart.

Another week passed and Ann Louise continued to recover. Tests began to focus on the little sight she had left and whether it were possible to recover any of it through a myriad of exercises. Always the answer was 'no'. But she refused to lose hope. She started to gain weight and the pain in her head subsided more and more.

Seanad work continued to pile up for me. Ann Louise agreed that the work must go on. My first phone call was to the president's assistant, Kevin McCarthy. Ann Louise and I were to have lunch with the president the following week. I explained to Kevin that she was still in hospital and would not be able to attend. His compassionate response assuaged my spirit: 'Katherine, please tell Ann Louise that the president sends her his warmest greetings, and that she should take as long as she needs to rest and recover. And if you both wish, the president would still be happy to have you attend the lunch.' I thanked him, and said I would come. Ann Louise and I had spent so much time preparing already, I trusted that she would not want me to miss this opportunity. We expected others to be there too, given the nature of the conversation. So the onus would not fall entirely on me.

*

On my way to Áras an Uachtaráin, I pass a herd of the wild fallow deer in Phoenix Park. My thoughts turn to the expanses of the park, of cycling there with Ann Louise. 'Not anymore,' I think with a laden sigh. But then my spirit lifts a bit as I see the United States ambassador's residence just off the same roundabout as the president's. It's an automatic response. I feel it every time, even during the Trump presidency. I grew up in an era when every day at school we placed a hand on our heart and spoke to the American flag: 'I pledge allegiance to the flag of the United States of America, and to the republic for which it stands, one nation under God, indivisible, with liberty and justice for all.' That went straight into my core, and still resides there somewhere.

The guards at the Áras gate let me in. As I drive up the long entrance to the parking lot, I don't see any other cars and am somewhat alarmed. Is it the right day? Am I too early? I walk towards the house and the very big doors open. One of the president's aides in full uniform comes out to greet me, and walking confidently behind her is Bród (Irish for 'pride'), the president's gorgeous Bernese mountain dog.

'May I pet her?'

'Yes of course,' says the aide.

I kneel down – we are at the same height now – and we have a natter.

I rise and enter, sign the visitors' book on the huge table and am brought into a room on the right. I've never been in this part of the Áras before. I walk past a small dining room on the right. I glance in to see two lunch places set. Two! Is it just myself and the president? My heart misses a beat.

The door in front of me opens and there is Kevin with his beautiful warm smile. He embraces me. 'Katherine, you are so welcome. Please sit in front of the fire. I'll go get the president.'

It is amazing to be here, in this room. I think it must be the president's private quarters. Then in walks Michael D. with another smile and an embrace. 'Katherine, I am so sorry to hear about Ann Louise. How is she?'

'As you can imagine, President, she is bringing every ounce of her positive spirit to the healing process. She sends you her love.'

At that, he gives me a kiss on the cheek. I can't believe she is missing this. But it will give me a good story to share with her in the hospital tonight. She will be happy that I am happy.

Kevin leaves. The president and I have an informal conversation. We are then brought to the dining room, sit down and begin the meal. A man known for his powerful intellect and imagination, he starts the conversation on ethics and speaks at length through the first course and then keeps going as the main course is placed on the table. I had come prepared to make, and elaborate on, three points related to the importance of Jürgen Habermas' notion of communicative action, Sharon Welch's theory of a feminist ethic of risk, and Martha Nussbaum's capabilities approach. When the dessert arrives, the president pauses, and I begin. He knows Habermas and Nussbaum, but not Welch. That is good enough for me. I tell this to Ann Louise in the hospital that evening. She is thrilled the meeting went so well, but I know it would have been better if she had been there. While I managed to enlighten the president about Welch, I know she would have run rings around both of us.

*

Our lives developed a new rhythm as I returned to work. A sense of fullness sometimes brimmed over – when Ann Louise's sense of normality appeared or I experienced a small win – but this was often followed by the deepest descent into numbed nothingness when progress eluded us everywhere. Towards the end of her Beaumont Hospital stay, one hundred citizens spent the weekend together in a Malahide hotel for a 'constitutional convention'. The Labour Party had stitched this requirement into the coalition programme for government with Fine Gael. The constitutional convention was Ireland's first experiment with a new type of deliberative democracy, whereby citizens would be selected randomly and then brought together to consider a current public policy issue. They would be supported by expert views, and small group discussions would take place. Ultimately the convention would vote on policy proposals that would be recommended to government. This convention, as a model, evolved into Ireland's internationally lauded citizens' assemblies.

In mid-April the weekend's topic was 'same-sex marriage'. Chaired by Tom Arnold (former chief executive of Concern Worldwide) and administrated by Art O'Leary (senior civil servant and chief executive of Ireland's Electoral Commission), the convention comprised sixty-six randomly selected Irish citizens, twenty-nine members of the houses of the Oireachtas, four representatives of Northern Ireland's political parties and an independent chair. We received carefully informed presentations from lawyers, academic experts, leaders of non-governmental organisations (including Marriage Equality, the Gay and Lesbian Equality Network and the Irish Council for Civil Liberties) and religious representatives. The press covered all the open sessions.

The stars of the show were Claire O'Connell and Conor Prendergast. They had been members of Marriage Equality's 'Believe in Equality', a group of adult children of LGBTQ+ parents, and were brought in to present some of their experiences and views. They stepped onto the podium together in the conference room and Claire began by saying, 'I am twenty-two years old. I study medicine in Trinity College and I teach piano on the weekends. We are a family like any other. We love and support each other. What's different about us from other families, though, is the way we are treated by the Irish state. In many ways my family is probably very similar to yours except for one big difference. My parents are not allowed to be married . . . for the simple reason that my parents are two women.' Conor followed with a similar tale: 'What this means in reality is that I only have a legal relationship to my mum who gave birth to me. My other mum, Bernadette, is a stranger to me in the eyes of the law . . . When I was little, she couldn't give legal consent to anything on my behalf, and although we were blissfully unaware of it, that left my brother and me in a legal vacuum, with less rights than other children.'

The silence was overpowering. Every member of the convention was transfixed. None of us had ever heard a 'bearing witness' like this before – and in such a calm and normal manner. Claire, tall and elegant, continued: 'People often ask what it's like to be raised by two mammies. And I fear my answer often disappoints them because the truth is that my childhood was fairly ordinary. I was never afraid to tell my friends that my mum was gay. And I was never bullied because of it. Was I worried about what my friends would think? Actually, most people would think that it was *cool* that I had two mums.'

Conor's voice was gentle yet authoritative: 'I'm lucky enough now to be engaged myself, which for us is wonderful, but it's still a little bittersweet. I have been with my fiancée, Elaina, for almost six years, but my parents have been together for thirty-two years, yet they can't have their love recognised by marriage, but we can. And that is what marriage is for. It is about recognising love.' At this point, one of the clergy at the top table, who had presented one of the opposing views just before Claire and Conor, bowed his head ever so slightly, and his face softened. He had looked quizzical, now he seemed pensive. Claire looked gently into the crowd, a sense of urgency in her plea: 'Marriage equality would mean that my parents, who are in a loving, committed relationship, can get married like anyone else. But, most importantly for me, no one could ever tell us that we aren't a family. So, for my family, and for all others like mine, I would ask you to recommend to government to provide for same-sex couples in the constitution. *Go raibh maith agat.*'

Joe Little, RTÉ social affairs correspondent who covered the proceedings and results of the constiutional convention, looked into the camera and said, 'Following another set of round-table discussions, they [the convention members] will vote around noon tomorrow on the question, "Should the government make provision for marriage equality in the Irish constitution?"'

The next day crowds gathered on Capel Street and in the plaza of Dublin City Council's Wood Quay offices – waiting patiently to hear the result that would sound from Malahide.

The answer was 'Yes'! In total, 79 per cent voted in favour of holding a referendum for the people to decide. Extraordinary cheers erupted and tears fell. A mighty rush of hope filled me up and spilled over. I could finally let it go – it had been gurgling for years. It was an astounding feeling of deep satisfaction to be part of something so magnificent. To see the joy on others' faces, especially those whose lives could now be changed for ever if the Irish people were to vote with empathy and generosity in the upcoming referendum. Ross Golden-Bannon, a board member of Marriage Equality, said in an interview, 'It was the most extraordinary expression of democracy that I have ever seen.' Before I left the hotel, I spoke to Joe Little on camera and declared, 'I am overwhelmed. We are almost there.'

I then raced out of the hotel, not stopping to speak to anyone of the hundreds gathered. I was desperate to get to Ann Louise in the hospital. I arrived in jig time, found a parking space quickly because it was Sunday, and ran to the entrance and up the familiar stairs. I entered the brain ward, trying not to run, and found Ann Louise resting, an extraordinarily contented look on her face. She had been listening to the radio. I went to the bed, bent over and said, 'We won!' She put her arms around my neck and said, 'Go to the celebrations, Katie. And give them my love.'

When I arrived in Capel Street, the adrenaline had left my body. As had my joy. I entered the front room of Panti Bar without her. And yet, it was so much about us. The entire movement and our own journey originated in love, and the people were now celebrating the opportunity to express their love relationships publicly in a way that is fair and equal. I did feel Ann Louise with me, but that day carried an extraordinary sadness for me, amidst the fantastic celebrations. Life, and the struggle to search for change, always moves between great joy and happiness and suffering.

I bore all this with me as I returned to my job.

*

Working nights and weekends, our Seanad Reform Group prepared to host one more critical meeting in the Central Hotel. The campaign committee had been augmented and included folks like John Dolan, chief executive of the Disability Federation of Ireland, Suzanne Egan, associate professor of law at University College Dublin, Rachel Mathews-McKay, communications expert at Trinity College Library and LGBTQ+ advocate, Derek Mooney, political advisor and communications expert, and Larry Donnelly, law lecturer at the University of Galway. Considerably diverse in their ideological backgrounds, they all shared the same objective: to save the Seanad. Noel Whelan and I met several times around his kitchen table, his son Seamus checking in on us when we took a break, often asking for homework advice after enquiring, 'Are you done yet?' Sinéad McSweeney, Noel's wife and comrade, was also present at times, cooking quietly in the background after a packed day at her own job. The room was full of love.

Noel and I bent over reams of emails and messages from our website, analysing communications from people around the country as they responded to our consultation document on how to reform the Seanad by changing legislation, not the constitution. 'Noel,' I said with a hint of growing excitement, 'most of the messages coming from the ground are positive. People are rejecting the government's "power grab". They want universal suffrage. They love the idea: one person, one vote.'

'This is what will translate to a "No" vote in the government's referendum,' Noel replied with that twinkle in his eye. These views were not yet represented in the polls but our collective intelligence told us otherwise. Something was changing on the ground, reflecting how the focus of public debate had shifted from 'abolition or retention' to 'abolition or reform'. This was a core element of our strategy.

The drafting of the Seanad bill was mostly complete, and we prepared for its publication in May. Its technical title would be simply 'The Seanad Bill 2013'. The media referred to it as 'The Quinn-Zappone Bill' because Feargal and I were its sponsors and initiated its legislative journey in the Seanad chamber. Feargal Quinn was a legend; I was a neophyte. I felt so proud and humbled at the same time. It put a formal stamp on my desire to effect change, to see my name reported in relation to something I felt so passionate about. The biggest reform in the bill was to open up Seanad elections to include everyone currently eligible to vote. And we extended the eligibility to Irish people abroad (who have an Irish passport) and persons eligible in Northern Ireland. Reform, according to this bill, would ensure a fifty-fifty balance of female and male senators, and it also proposed extra powers of legislative scrutiny for the Seanad.

We gathered the troops at the Central Hotel in April. The room was the fullest it had ever been, including political advisors, educators, trade union members, activists, academics and journalists. People had travelled from Cork, Limerick, Galway and other parts of Ireland. Most had been active on social media, local radio and informal meetings and conversations in their own villages and towns, encouraging debate and outlining reform views. It was time to give ourselves a better name than the 'Seanad Reform Campaign'. Noel and I had generated a number of possibilities and presented our top options to the group. 'Democracy Matters' pretty much won outright. It would be known as cross-party and non-party: a group of concerned individuals and citizens who were banding together in an attempt to save Seanad Éireann. We outlined our timetable for the Seanad bill publication and the Democracy Matters launch, and the campaign meeting ended on a high.

Feargal Quinn and I stood in the Seanad chamber the following month. I had asked my close friend and colleague Peadar Kirby to tutor me in some Irish beforehand. I wanted to introduce the bill 'as Gaeilge' to mark its importance. I rehearsed for days. Linguistics is not one of my strengths. As it turned out, my accent wasn't too bad, but there was hardly anyone else in the chamber when I started to speak. It only filled up after I had completed the Irish introduction. So much for the romanticism of it all! While the bill never made its way out of the Seanad because the government did not agree to give it more time, we were able to use it as a central plank of our campaign strategy. It told the electorate what reform could look like.

At the end of May 2013 we launched Democracy Matters and our national campaign in the Davenport Hotel, in front of a packed group of journalists and supporters. Professor Gary Murphy of Dublin City University chaired the meeting. Professor Diarmaid Ferriter of University College Dublin spoke, alongside journalist Una Mullally and Olive Braiden, former chair of the National Gallery of Ireland. We had five months to sway the Irish electorate to our views, still an uphill battle. But we were off. I started to take part in a number of debates and media interviews. I went up against

Richard Bruton, TD, the government's director of elections for a 'No' vote, on *Prime Time*. That one was really scary. I role-played several times before I went out to RTÉ's studios in Montrose. I always felt so nervous going in the gates, and so relieved coming out. I think I gave Richard as good as I got that night. My confidence in media work started to grow.

Ann Louise had finally come home. The MRIs were clear, she had gained more weight, her memory appeared intact, and the only physical loss was her eyesight. She needed a lot of rest still, and spent most of the days over the next five months in our bedroom. My independent, dynamic and imaginative Annie had been stilled. She didn't mind stillness – and had practised it through disciplined meditation over the years. But a big loss seeped in because she had to stop her many interests, hobbies and scholarly projects. While she could still care for herself, most of the domestic responsibilities landed on me, for a long period of time, and I just did the best I could. Exhaustion was a daily occurrence for me.

Our bedroom provided solace, though, because it was a beautiful space, redesigned for us by Dermot Bannon to partake in the television series *Room to Improve*. The bedroom had a small wood-burning stove, and floor-to-ceiling French windows looking down the gorgeous garden Ann Louise had created and cared for. We often used chopped wood from the branches of the hardwood trees that lined our property. Major Gamble had planted them over one hundred years earlier. What foresight, I often thought. He did not live to enjoy the full fruits of his biodiverse practices, but we did. What a gift, especially during those days. Most nights I would sit in a chair at the bottom of the bed, facing Ann Louise, and talk about the day. I often brought our dinner up and once in a while she would join me in a glass of wine. Those were such special, intimate moments. Each day she felt a little stronger.

One night she appeared to be exceptionally alert, so I shared with her one of my biggest worries at work. 'Annie, I have to get back to my bill for trans people. Nothing is moving on the government front.'

She was sitting up in bed at this stage. 'Katherine, this may be one of your most important pieces of work. Their lives can be so hidden. Get back to it, darling. I need to close my eyes now. I'll help you on it, in any way I can.'

The next morning I telephoned Michael Farrell. 'How is Ann Louise, Katherine?' was his first question.

'She's regaining her health each day, Michael. And you'll be happy to know that she's encouraging me to get back to work on our bill!'

'Sounds like she is getting better.' He chuckled softly. 'I'll start to organise our first formal meeting, Katherine, of the people I think may be able to help us.'

Thus began my close collaboration with human rights lawyers and human rights non-governmental organisations who were building momentum to drag Ireland into the twenty-first century. Broden Giambrone and Sara Phillips, director and chair respectively of Transgender Equality Network Ireland, led the charge with such professionalism and bravery, and worked closely with Lydia Foy, Michael, FLAC and its Public Interest Law Alliance (PILA) project. Broden is a young trans man with a softness in his manner and a steely determination in his heart to get justice done. He is Canadian, and shared a migrant status with myself. Sara is a trans woman and has worked as an activist for over thirty years. The three of us established trust easily. I was inspired by their strategic deftness, always practised with respectful, albeit authoritative, ways of speaking and negotiating. Tanya Ní Mhuirthile, a legal expert in transgender issues, and Fergus Ryan, a human rights lawyer in Maynooth with an expertise in LGBTQ+ matters, also joined the extended clan. They are both top-class in their fields and brought personal commitment to the technicalities of law which could be felt in the finished product.

We met together, regularly, to tease out the details we wanted in the bill. David Dodd, a barrister on the PILA pro bono register, led the drafting of the private members' bill, which we entitled the Legal Recognition of Gender 2013 bill. The group fed into and commented on it until we felt satisfied that it was the 'gold standard' for gender recognition. Critical ingredients included allowing transgender individuals to 'self-declare' their preferred gender. Specialist medical evidence was not mandatory for their recognition. The bill did not require married transgender individuals to be divorced before they could make this self-declaration. And we included a provision for people under eighteen.

I launched the bill in Buswells Hotel with Broden, Tanya and others at the top table with me in early July 2013. It felt like a perfect day. We got plenty of media coverage, adding to the mounting campaign of pressure for the government to legislate. Though the bill did not progress any further, we were able to highlight the long delay in producing even a draft of a government bill. And we offered a template for more tolerant and inclusive legislation. I had in-depth discussions with Joan Burton and her civil servants. I respected Joan's political work and through our engagement on this issue came to see her determined commitment to equality and fairness. She was willing to recognise the efforts and expertise of human rights organisations, and this helped our bill towards becoming a powerful proposition. When the government produced its own bill in January 2015, it reflected some of the key elements of ours. With continued lobbying from the NGOs, and the pressure of a further legal case coming down the tracks from Lydia, the government's bill passed all stages on 15 July 2015. The biggest wins were that trans people over the age of eighteen would be allowed to self-declare their gender identity, and a legal pathway was provided for sixteen- and seventeen-year-olds.

When I told Ann Louise about our progress, she was so happy. She loved hearing the stories, especially those of the young trans people. I know that she missed campaigning for change and the hard work to liberate lives. But I could see that even in her tired brain she had started to devise a plot for her next project. Her warrior spirit was never far away, in this instance celebrating our headway for transgender people, small albeit in the right direction, at least. And I feared that if the Seanad was to be abolished, it would make bills like the trans bill much, much harder to create, if not impossible. We had to save it.

*

The day finally arrives: 4 October 2013. Would the citizens of Ireland vote for abolition or retention of the Seanad? The latest polls suggest abolition. Our research points in the other direction, but it feels tight. As the votes start to be counted on Saturday, 5 October, our group stays in touch by text. The count is close in many parts of the country – but not Dublin. We are winning by a large percentage there. Noel, whose sixth sense can feel which way votes are going in most elections, rings me to say, 'Katherine, we are going to win! Start to make your way into Dublin Castle. The count is happening at the Coach House.' It is the most excitement I have felt since before Ann Louise took ill. I find Noel and Feargal and we march through the gates together. Michael McDowell is already inside. As are Senators David Norris and John Crown, who also had conducted their own hearty campaigns with a bill similar to ours, and Micheál Martin, leader of Fianna Fáil and the opposition at the time. He and his party had advocated retention. We find one another inside the Coach House as the result is announced: 591,937 votes to abolish the Seanad, and 634,437 votes to retain it. We win! 51.73 per cent of the electorate have rejected the government's plans, while 48.27 per cent have agreed. We win by 42,500 votes.

As they say in politics, a win is a win. I am euphoric. It feels so good to be high. For this day, most worries leave my body. Maybe Ann Louise will be alright. Maybe all will be well.

CHAPTER 4

Image the Possible

I love the autumn. Ann Louise and I used to call it the fall. It always evokes memories of my first family home in Spokane, Washington, my birthplace. Maple trees in the front garden, pine trees in the back. A little girl named Kay diligently raking the leaves for her mom and dad. Fall meant the excitement of returning to school, first with my new pencil pouch and empty notebooks, later with collegiate dress for university. I met Ann Louise in the fall.

I first saw her in a large meeting room in McElroy Commons on the campus of Boston College in 1981. I was twenty-eight, she was thirty-six. Her green eyes dazzled me, her posture was upright and her gait held a light lilt.

I turned to the person next to me and asked, 'Who is she?' 'I don't know' was the answer.

The induction of master's and doctoral students continued to unfold while the September colours of Massachusetts' trees glistened in the warm afternoon sun. Ann Louise's presence distracted me. This was unexpected. I had ended a thirteen-year relationship with Catherine just months before. I was mourning this relationship, and certainly not on the lookout for another partner, because I was involved with another woman. I can still smell Heather's perfume. There were no promises or commitment. Just pure pleasure and companionship.

Ann Louise and I were thrown together by fate. Theologians and educators from the Jesuit university had chosen us as the only two doctoral students for a particular interdisciplinary programme that year. Their decisions led to our shared destiny. How ironic, because we spent the next couple of years trying to hide that from them.

Ann Louise was staying in a graduate students' residence colloquially named 'Foster Street' because it was located at that address. There was little privacy in that communal life, and any other student residents could see me come and go to Ann Louise's room. I was in the attic of a private home in Newton, a suburb of Boston. It had been renovated for student accommodation, furnished with a double bed and a big desk under a roof window. I could see the stars at night.

Heather called me a few times from New York, not happy with my decision to separate from her. I couldn't say, even now, that such a desire had anything to do with Ann Louise. I certainly did not know that at the time. What I did know was that I wanted a new life, a break from the past, a way

75

of finding myself again. I wanted to concentrate on my professional life and enjoy a new venture with no personal commitments.

One September evening I returned to Boston, after a long car journey from Heather in New York in my orange Beetle. It was still only September. I phoned Ann Louise and she invited me to her room in Foster Street. There she was. It was Sunday, and she had the day's newspapers spread out on a big table. She loved the news, in whatever form. I was so distraught. The weekend had not gone well. Heather had accused me of all sorts of things, some of which I now admit were probably true. I began to tell Ann Louise some of the story, necessarily requiring that I 'come out' to her. I was fearful, of course. She was from Dublin, Ireland. Would she understand?

As the next hour passed, I realised that the trepidation I felt did not surface from a concern about Ann Louise's possible homophobia. (Indeed, as I would come to know, Ann Louise was fearless about everything for most of her life, at least until that first haemorrhage.) No, her wide-open face and intense listening caught my heart, and every other part of my body. I knew she had been almost engaged once to a man. What was I doing? Then she turned to me and said, 'I don't believe in labels. I just believe in love.'

And that was the beginning. We left, shortly afterwards, for my double bed in the rented attic room of my home in Newton.

We attended several of the same classes. Some were interminably long. I was having 'bad thoughts' in theology courses. All I wanted to do was to whisk Ann Louise away and make her naked. Intimacy, of the deepest and most sensual kind, is filled with vulnerability. Deborah Levy describes in *The Cost of Living* (2018) a conversation she had with a man who was crying inconsolably at the funeral of another man. She asked if they had been lovers. 'He said yes, on and off for many years, but they never had risked making themselves vulnerable to each other. They had never owned up to their love.'

With Ann Louise, I learned that baring the soul and heart demands love. Tossing attire aside does not. It is, however, the most exquisite experience when it all assembles together in space and time. Pure joy, again and again, when the physical mingles with the spiritual, and when every part is shown by the self and known by the other. I know it was the same for Ann Louise since she told me so.

*

So fall was a special and blessed time for us. Ann Louise was more and more herself as the autumn after her haemorrhage unfolded. She practised her walk from our bedroom, at the back of The Shanty, to her study, at the front, each day. She did not use a stick, instead memorising the route in her mind. The hallway was wide and I made sure there was no clutter. Gradually her stride improved to one with confident authority. She rediscovered her extraordinary sense of hope: hope that the future would be better than the present and that she had the ability to make it happen, with me. Her attention to the present, courage in doing everyday things and kindness to whomever she engaged with shined again.

She generated a formula for this kind of life, and made it visible, especially during her years of healing.

It was a way of being that enabled abundant and abiding happiness and peace. Waking up next to her each morning, I could feel doubts about my day begin to dissipate. Personal hurts I might be carrying felt soothed, especially as we embraced gently. Other mornings, she simply called me into the present moment. I felt a quiet insistence from her body. Long before popular literature identified the power of now, Ann Louise found and shared it. It is at the root of the best sex. Of the best way to be ourselves. Isn't that what so many of us want?

In 2009 she expressed prescience of this heightened approach during a speech marking her early retirement from thirty-five years of working in St Patrick's College, Drumcondra. We were all gathered in the college's dining area and Pauric Travers, president of the college at the time, invited her up to speak. Years earlier Pauric had advocated for Ann Louise to be treated with fairness and justice when the archbishop of Dublin, as manager of the college, vetoed the decision of the St Pat's Academic Council to appoint Ann Louise as head of the department of religious studies. All those gathered in the room knew that story. Ann Louise had resisted the power of the patriarchy and achieved a partial win in her legal battle against the archbishop, getting appointed for five years to the position (though it was traditionally offered to the successful candidate until retirement).

In her professional life Ann Louise had learned to live with a deep sense of 'outsider' status as a lesbian. Becoming blind brought another layer of alienation, teaching her new things about what 'normal' means while swimming upstream.

She faced this head-on, made it part of her healing formula. She wrote in her journal:

> *Out of nowhere I had to function as a blind academic. To seek its meaning. To retain the fullness of my humanity, to embrace the human losses of blindness.*
>
> *The brain longs for optic stimulation. Part of my brain is dying.*
>
> *If I accepted this thing I would die. Therefore I must resist. There is no escape.*
>
> *The past collapses into nothingness.*
>
> *You find inner resources,*
>
> *Connecting more.*
>
> *Remembering more.*
>
> *Feeling more confident.*
>
> *Blindness will either renew you or destroy you.*

In another diary she described 'the loneliness of being blind in Twitter-land' and noted that she must ask her cousin Dara Hogan if 'there is some piece of software that translates voice to typed text'. Hers was no false hope. She learned how to navigate her world in different ways, as she dealt with her deepening physical limitations. Hers was a true and powerful hope.

She turned all her energies towards healing in a new way. She started reading – through audiobooks – about neuroscience. I went online to find the audio of *My Stroke of Insight: A Brain Scientist's Personal Journey* (2008) by Dr Jill Bolte Taylor. At thirty-seven years old, Dr Taylor was struck down by a stroke. It bathed the left side of her brain in haemorrhaged blood for hours. She spent eight years in recovery, which she went on to regard as a transformative experience. While the left side of her brain was damaged, the unharmed right side set to work through the powers of neuroplasticity – the ability of neural networks in the brain to change through growth and reorganisation. She provided evidence, from her own life, that the human brain has a tremendous potential to heal and change itself.

I read my printed copy of Dr. Taylor's book sitting in my mother's chair every night. After my mother's death, the chair had been transported across the Atlantic from Seattle to Dublin. My oldest brother Bob put it on a boat for me. What enduring hope this book gave me – especially the fact that Dr Taylor eventually recovered. For me, this meant that if Ann Louise did not recover her sight within the first year, it did *not* mean that it would never happen.

I believed that Ann Louise would recover her sight well enough to drive again. *She will be on the road again, driving a new small yellow truck with hen food, hay for their bedding, lots of peat for the garden and new varieties of hydrangea or azalea – maybe even an apple tree – just waiting to be planted.* On the paddock we continued to raise Jacob sheep, using the wool in our Weaving Dreams venture – a high-quality felted craft small business we set up to complement our educational work. Two of our dogs are buried in the paddock. We planted potatoes, carrots, cabbage, broccoli and tried to grow a little corn. Located on what we call 'high ground' in Ireland, it often gets very cold and even receives snow now and then.

'Far from this was I reared,' said the Dublin 4 girl often. Never was she happier, though, than when she went to the field to work on her garden or be with her animals. I put my foot down when she said she wanted bees. 'No way,' I said. 'We could never travel as much if we had bees. I mean, who would mind them?'

So what was this thing called 'neuroscience', and did it have the potential to help Ann Louise to heal her brain? Her doctors didn't talk about it much. When she worked with the stroke team at Baggot Street Hospital after her first bleed, there was little explicit discussion of it. They were great people. Top-class professionals with the patience, sympathy and expertise required to support very slow but substantive change, incrementally over time. What bothered Ann Louise, though, was that if a patient or client wanted to participate further in her or his own healing, there was a paucity of literature on the subject. 'There are so many academic, lengthy texts about brain injury,' she remarked. 'There are basic three-page pamphlets scattered in hospitals or sitting rooms. I am so troubled though, Katherine, that there are no texts of substance, easily read, that could encourage and guide those of us who have had a bleed.'

Aha.

'I will write a book, Katie! It will be my next project. I will use my own experience to offer a "how to heal" manual for those who have suffered brain injuries. I will talk about what I have learned from neuroscience, and how I have applied it in my own life. I will bring in what I have learned from Buddhism, and from my neurologists and doctors along the way. The book will hold a central place for the imagination and how to activate its powers to heal ourselves. I will have meaning again. It will help others.'

Brilliant! I thought. *She has a project that she can sink her teeth into again. This means she's getting better.* In truth, our home life felt as if it was getting back on an even keel. While Seanad work for me was increasing, I felt less guilty about that now because Ann Louise had her own project, one that could really make a difference to many other people's lives. We had worked together on so many undertakings; now was a time when our professional paths diverged. I'd leave the house early and return late most days. We'd share stories about progress or logjams. Just like we used to. Cleaning and a bit of gardening started to fill our weekends, and though she could not help with much of that, every morning she swept the kitchen floor. I can see her still: my brilliant Ann Louise, humbly faithful to an intention to share the housework. When she felt up to it, we'd drive to Johnstown Garden Centre and choose seasonal plants to add to the garden. I always needed her advice for that. She was the natural gardener. I was happy to follow orders. It relaxed me from the intensity of parliamentary work.

In the early period of her writing, she was assisted by her friend Anne O'Reilly. Anne came to The Shanty for their meetings, and sometimes drove Ann Louise to Blessington for lunch. Though she spent much of the afternoon in 'the horizontal position' after her friend left, Ann Louise would rise from her bed in the mid-afternoon and walk the long pathway from our bedroom to her study. Sitting down, she would begin to compose in her big script. She wrote about the 'unfurling of memories' and how these memories can offer 'hope-filled images for coping with the revelations of the present'. Ann Louise was a great philosopher, and that her blindness offered revelations for her, new ways of 'seeing', amazed me. I was in awe of her resilience.

I would come home in the evenings to find the pages of her writings placed on our large antique dining table. Once we ate the simple supper she produced – she had learned to cook again – I would type from her script. While I maintained an outwardly positive spirit during this secretarial activity, my will worked hard to generate it. It was apparent that this process was a Herculean effort for her. And some evenings when there were no pages, I felt so empty.

The ebb in her writings, however, was soon replaced with a new determination to return to work with Quality and Qualifications Ireland (QQI). Her appointment to the board of this organisation by the minister for education, Ruairi Quinn, had elated her. Though medically certified as blind, she could read words sometimes if they were large enough and stayed steady on the paper or screen. We organised a large visual display, and specialised digital equipment to magnify the reading for her. Sometimes it worked – other days the words fell away too many times. Only on rare occasions did she allow the penetration of deep disappointment or frustration.

She wasn't getting enough of the content of the board papers, though, so one day she picked up the phone to call our gorgeous neighbour Ruth. Ann Louise asked if she would be willing to come over to The Shanty once a month to read QQI board papers to her. This would provide her with a better way to understand all the content, and allow her to take her own notes on questions she might wish to raise at the upcoming meetings. And that's what happened. Ann Louise took copious notes as she listened to us in order to strengthen her memory – and she identified points she wanted to make or questions she wished to raise at the board. The QQI staff (particularly Ms Caitríona Lawless and Dr Padraig Walsh) and board chair Gordon Clark accommodated her carefully and creatively. They wanted her wisdom, though they knew it could often be decidedly challenging, proffered in her quiet, determined and respectful way.

One evening while she attended a board meeting, I found evidence of another sign of recovery. In her journal she had logged critical information related to one of the top hobbies (and she had many) that her publican father Arthur had instilled in her,

The Gold Cup
Sizing John,
No. 4, 3/1
No. 9, 4/1

Paddy Power 1 800 721 821   AG 936654

Ann Louise loved going to Leopardstown! Paddy Power's telephone number was always close at hand. The last numbers on her note was from her Paddy Power card and she used it to phone in a bet. At her passing, the winnings on the card amounted to 225 euro. As in so many other ventures, Ann Louise was careful, bold and a winner. We continued to bet on that.

*

I felt so relieved that she was healing. I promised myself that I would not work too much in the evenings, so that we would have more time together. I am a workaholic, so this was not an easy promise to keep, but things had settled into a less frenzied pace in the Seanad because I knew most of the ropes by then. Nevertheless, it was hard to switch off my radar; I was always scanning for the next thing that really needed to be changed. Watching – and listening – to television together at night was relaxing, but it also kept us up to date. One night as I was driving home, I heard an advert for a television documentary about people with cognitive and physical disabilities who wanted to tell their stories about romantic love. A brief reference to the desire for a change in the law piqued my interest. Why would they be talking about laws? I thought maybe Ann Louise would be interested in watching it with me, if she had had a good day and not too much pain in her head.

When I arrived home, she was in the kitchen, potatoes boiling and vegetables on the counter. She had just found the peeler – a great win for someone blind – and was listening to the news. She knew everything that was going on in Ireland, and in many other parts of the world too. She was happy. Happy to feel her mind working again, to be able to follow her interest in the stories of Irish lives – always bringing a philosophical frame to what she heard. She interrogated the meaning underneath what was going on, in the way that the critical philosophers she taught about in St Pat's would ask, 'Why are things the way they are?'

She had heard the advertisement for the documentary, *Somebody to Love* (2014), too.

'Would you be keen?' I asked.

'It might be a little late for me, Katherine, but let's go to the bedroom after dinner and I will put my head down and listen for as long as I can.'

The documentary was emotionally riveting for both of us. There was no question of falling asleep for Ann Louise. All kinds of stories were told, by the people with disabilities themselves. It was not *about* them. It was *of* them. The message was straightforward, yet rarely heard: 'We want to talk about relationships, sexuality and disability.' As the narrator – with a form of cognitive disability himself – said, 'We are all like you. We are people.' Ann Louise and I just looked at one another when he uttered that. Several years ago when we had received our first media training from Michael Murphy (the former RTÉ broadcaster) to talk about our court case and to advocate for the marriage equality cause, he told us our message was a simple one. 'It's this,' he said. 'We are like you. We are like you.' That really struck a chord with us then, and we used it often in our speeches and rallies. Its truth and clarity in common language helped us to speak in a way that people could hear, in a way that would establish an emotional connection with others.

Ours were the hearts opening now. The documentary outlined the legal and practical barriers facing people with disabilities who want to engage in consensual sex outside of marriage. The biggest problem was the law. Tucked into a piece of legislation from 1993, the Criminal Law (Sexual Offences) Act, is a section on the 'protection of mentally impaired persons'. It states that a person who has or attempts to have sexual intercourse with a person who is mentally impaired is *guilty of an offence, unless they are married to each other.* Any sexual relations outside of marriage were technically criminalised!

The law was portrayed as a way to protect those with cognitive disabilities, because lawmakers believed that such people were too vulnerable, or lacked the necessary capacity, to consent to such intimacy. In legal terms, where an individual 'lacks capacity' to consent to sex, the sexual act could be criminalised. However, while it was widely recognised that this legislation had not led to increased prosecutions, it had had a chilling effect on the sexual expression of people with cognitive disabilities. Many were fearful of forming relationships. In addition, it meant service providers were reluctant to give people with disabilities the freedom to have intimate contact. Mandy Finlay, a young woman with an intellectual disability who featured in the documentary, had to wait four years and undergo multiple assessments before she could be supported by staff to go on a weekend away with her boyfriend. The real-life stories portrayed a powerful message, best summed up in the words of the people themselves: 'We just want to be alone, together. This is our story, our need to be loved.'

Ann Louise and I had known nothing of this. We were outraged! How could this be? And how could so few people know about it? It was really hard to get to sleep that night. She finally turned to me and said, 'Katherine, you have to do something about this. Use your position of privilege. I will support you in whatever way I can.'

'I will, Ann Louise. I have to find a way.'

A short time after the airing of the documentary, I saw a blog post written by Dr Eilionóir Flynn, a colleague of my dear friend Professor Gerard Quinn at the Centre for Disability Law and Policy at the National University of Ireland Galway. Eilionóir criticised the current law and outlined possible ways to change it, so that the rights of people with disabilities could be the same as those who were not disabled. I thought, *That's it: I'll contact Eilionóir and ask her if she would help me to develop a private member's bill to address these issues.* People with cognitive disabilities should not be patronised or criminalised. But I also felt a unique kind of solidarity with them. My love for Ann Louise was not recognised in law. Their right to love wasn't either. We might be able to change that, or influence the way it changes. But we'd need the views of the people themselves to tell us how.

Eilionóir responded with enthusiasm and generosity, inviting her associate Anna Arstein-Kerslake to work with us. They both travelled from Galway for our first meeting in Leinster House, and spent the afternoon enlightening me on both the technical legal issues, including the opportunity to design a bill that would be compliant with the United Nations Convention on the Rights of Person's with Disabilities, and the remarkable advocacy efforts of the people with disabilities themselves and the organisations that represented them. Ger Quinn, a soft-spoken, albeit unswerving, advocate and erudite academic, had been one of the authors of the UN convention. Writing it was a mammoth accomplishment. Getting nations to implement its principles and legal commitments in their own domestic law was an even bigger mountain to climb. As a former human rights commissioner,

I loved that challenge. But head stuff is never enough to get this kind of radical change. It requires solidarity, an agreement of feeling and action between and among those who are like us and not like us.

Eilionóir arranged for me to meet with individuals and advocacy organisations several times over the next months. Because I was an Independent senator, it was not likely that the bill we were about to develop would become law. But not unlike the work I did with the gender recognition bill, this was an opportunity to raise awareness, to act from inside the system and to influence the government's law. We also wanted to reform the law-making process. Collaborating with those outside the formal systems of power, but with the life experience that the law encircled, was our magic formula. As long as our houses of parliament did not have public representatives with life experience of cognitive disability, this route offered greater potential for a law that would protect and promote the human rights of people with disabilities. And so we met with the National Platform of Self Advocates (run and controlled by people with intellectual disabilities), the Inclusive Research Network (people with intellectual disability who do research together on ideas and issues that matter to them) and the Community Participation Network (helping people with disabilities to get involved in their local community structures) to ascertain their concerns and hear what legal changes they wanted.

Brave, ambitious and inspiring people blew away my heart and mind time and again. The self-advocates I met spoke their truth. A submission by the Connect People's Network to the Law Reform Commission reads (italics added):

We believe that people with extra support needs have the right to have romantic relationships, just like everyone else. We don't want laws that are about testing us, to determine if we know what it means to consent before having sex. *There aren't laws like this for people without disabilities.* We want proper sex education. Then we can make our own choices. We don't want special laws for people with extra support needs either. The new law should be disability neutral. It should apply to everyone. *We want you to listen to our opinions. We want you to take them seriously.*

Their views, I thought, were eminently sensible, and I felt their sense of urgency. They needed me to shed my prejudices about them and to write a law that reflected what they wanted. We went to work. Our challenge was to draft law that people with disabilities would understand. Legal detail at the best of times is not easily understood by laypeople. So Eilionóir and Anna came up with the brilliant idea to design a summary of our draft law in everyday language, an easy-to-read version of the very technical bill – the Criminal Law (Sexual Offences) (Amendment) Bill 2014 – that had been drafted by the impeccable Dr Brian Hunt (a member of the Oireachtas panel of legal drafters) under our direction.

It contained simple language and images to explain the legal concepts. The summary was so innovative that I decided to circulate it to all members of the Dáil and Seanad. Many of my colleagues got back to me saying that it was the best explanatory memo (the traditional note accompanying bills) they had ever seen. That was a triumph for us.

With agreement from the self-advocates, we finalised the bill and set a launch date for its publication. On 10 June 2014 we headed off to Buswells Hotel yet again. It's where we had held meetings with the advocates, and they felt comfortable with a venue they knew.

The press conference to launch the bill was led by a panel of people with intellectual disabilities who spoke about their own experiences. We were so pleased to have Zlata Filipović, the producer of *Somebody to Love*, join the panel.

We called it the 'Right to Love' bill. That's what I heard the self-advocates tell me: that they wanted a right to love, just like everyone else. And I knew it was a message that could ignite warm sympathy from lawmakers and non-disabled people. Law does not usually do that, but we wanted ours to. It contained two key parts to ensure that people with disabilities would have the same rights as people without disabilities. First, it offered a definition of consent. It stated that both people must consent to sex. That consent means agreeing to have sex with the other person and telling her or him that you agree to have sex with them. If one person does not agree, then it will be illegal for the other person to continue. Both people must understand sex. And understanding sex means knowing what consequences may follow. Second, it offered protection from sexual abuse. The bill indicated that nobody should be sexually abused by someone whom they trust or depend on. This could be a family member, staff or support worker, or employer. The bill stated clearly that it would be considered a crime if someone you trust or depend on pushed you to have sex with them. It was intended to provide more appropriate protection against abuse that could apply to *all* individuals who may be in a position of dependence, including persons with disabilities. I concluded by saying, 'This bill was created in response to a call to action by self-advocates and disabled people's organisations. I've been deeply touched by the rightful anger of those who say their love has been criminalised and who want to make choices for themselves.'

Orla Belton and Brendan O'Reilly, a couple who have mild learning disabilities, were the real stars of the moment. They stood up together, holding hands. Brendan looked straight into the gathering, speaking quietly yet intently as his face slowly coloured: 'People do not take our relationship seriously. It upsets me so much. The law tells them not to take us seriously.' Orla put her hand then on his arm and said to all of us, 'People told us we'd never be able to manage or have our own apartment. But we do. We've been living together for a few years and do lots of stuff ourselves. And it's the best thing we ever did. We should be given a chance.'

Then Brendan spoke again, with more confidence: 'We are planning to marry next summer!'

It felt like an engagement on air! Applause broke out, led by the media folks. When it died down, I ended by saying, 'We still need individuals and civil society organisations to make their voices heard. What really makes the government move is if people express their outrage at what is wrong and unjust.'

Reaction from the media and general public was overwhelmingly positive, the launch and issue covered widely. I brought the bill to the Seanad floor. During the debate, Minister for Justice Frances Fitzgerald said, 'I have no difficulty incorporating a number of the concepts in Senator Zappone's bill into the sexual offences bill currently being drafted by my department, and I intend to do that.' The government was listening. With respect to the minister, it was no longer my bill. It was the advocates' bill. And we all just needed to keep on the pressure, so that the government's bill would indeed reflect their voices.

CHAPTER 5

Marriage Equality

On 1 July 2014 Taoiseach Enda Kenny announced that the marriage equality referendum would take place in the spring of 2015. Ann Louise was having a cup of tea in the kitchen when she heard the news. I was out in the garden. I had returned from an early run to the garden centre and had a boot full of begonias, impatiens and petunias, according to her instructions. The Shanty garden held hundreds of feet of border along the long drive up from the road to our home, so bedding plants were a must. Geraniums filled the back seat (with plenty of protection for the car's fabric underneath them!). My mother loved geraniums, of every type. So I love them too. They are easy to care for, have a hearty character and flower from spring to at least late autumn. A worn conservatory fronted our home. Upon entering, our guests were immediately met with a concrete tub bursting with geraniums, and big reddish-brown clay pots always filled with the royal geranium type, usually pink. It was glorious to sit there on a warm, sunny summer day.

I was trying to decide if I had bought enough compost for the planting when Ann Louise told me the news: 'Katie, Enda has called the referendum.'

Knowing she could not see my face well, I embraced her quietly for a moment and said, 'I think our time has come, Annie.'

'I want to be well enough to participate,' she replied.

'Ann Louise, you just have to be, to participate. Your vision and wisdom for our marriage equality comrades is plentiful. You must take it easy for the next number of months, though, until the campaign takes off properly. Then we will need to hear your voice. Ireland will need to hear your voice.'

She nodded and whispered, 'I am so happy to be alive for this time.'

It had been a decade of struggle to get to this point, and the Marriage Equality organisation shifted up to high gear. Ann Louise and I continued to attend the board meetings. Eventually a decision was made for the three national organisations – Marriage Equality (ME), the Gay and Lesbian Equality Network (GLEN) and the Irish Council for Civil Liberties (ICCL) – to work together as one collective voice under the banner of the 'Yes Equality' campaign, launched in March 2015. We decided that we needed to have one voice and agreed messaging in order to win. Not an easy decision because of some deep differences between ME and

GLEN. GLEN believed in an incremental approach to change, supporting the enactment of civil partnership legislation on the road to marriage equality. We believed in the direct line of action, that there's no half-equality. You are either equal or you are not. Civil partnership did not provide equality. Lawmakers had followed GLEN's route, and this still did not sit well with us. But we acceded that – with a referendum in sight – working together would provide the best chance to get this over the line. I was invited to join the campaign's steering committee – effectively as a public representative to help keep the lines of communication open between the inside and outside of Leinster House – and it met weekly or bi-weekly in the early morning. The 107-day campaign had begun. An account of its strategies and tactics is well told by its leaders – Gráinne Healy, Brian Sheehan and Noel Whelan – in *Ireland Says Yes: The Inside Story of How the Vote for Marriage Equality Was Won* (2015).

It was painful for Ann Louise not to be included in the steering group, but we were not in charge of decisions in the Yes Equality campaign. At this point the march to marriage equality had widened way beyond us, as we had hoped it would. That was always the intention. Leadership in burgeoning social movements and national campaigns usually does raise strong feelings about who is in charge, and who is perceived to be the person or persons that might get the job done. We resisted these feelings as much as we could but there were some days when we got lost in them. Ann Louise had to keep a lower profile because of her blindness and reduced energy, and this exacerbated her feelings of vulnerability.

We talked about these issues a lot.

'I feel sidelined, Katie. I've worked every day for years to get to this point. I put my job on the line, risked our financial security. And now, for the final stretch, the organisation that we helped to set up seems to be asking me to move aside.'

I didn't know what to say to her. There were days I thought she was right. Her pained face broke my heart. But I could also understand that a successful social movement needs a tight strategy and the discipline to enact it. For the last stretch, part of that strategy was to get the faces and voices of ordinary couples into the public arena. Let their stories move the heart of a nation. This is what I tried to explain to her.

'Well, okay. So be it,' she replied.

What helped us to carry these conflicted emotions was our deep trust in the Yes Equality leaders: Gráinne Healy, Denise Charlton, Noel Whelan, Orla Howard, Mark Kelly, Brian Sheehan, Moninne Griffith, Andrew Hyland and Adam May, among others.

*

With Marriage Equality preparing to merge into the Yes Equality campaign, Ann Louise and I were looking towards the future. We saw an opportunity to form a team to canvass for the referendum vote in Dublin South-West. We could bring our story, our national profile and our intense desire for a win to the communities where we had spent the last twenty-five years supporting adult educational opportunities, and children's learning and care. Our discussion did not stop there.

'Ann Louise, I've loved my time in the Seanad. And I always said I would never run for the Dáil – too daunting a prospect. But I think now that I could get more things done, bring about change more directly, if I were in the Dáil. My work in the Seanad has received relatively good media coverage. And we certainly are known nationally for our advocacy on marriage equality. So I might have a chance. But it would take me away from you more, especially during the evenings. What do you think?'

I will never forget her response that day. 'Katie, I am getting better. I am building a new life. You must do what you want to do. I will support you in whatever you choose.'

'Darragh Genockey might agree to be my campaign manager,' I said. 'We'd have to raise some money. It's a lot, Ann Louise.'

Her face broadened into the biggest smile since her haemorrhage. 'Katherine, I think you could win.'

'Will I ask Darragh, then? If he says "yes" Darragh and I could test the waters – for both of us – by asking him to lead the Dublin South-West marriage equality campaign.'

'Yes. Ask him, darling,' she said, looking straight into my eyes. Maybe she saw my forever love looking back.

I first met Darragh Genockey when he was an older teen. He was with his mother, Anne, in their Jobstown home to discuss something related to our Shanty educational work. Anne had been one of our first learners, a total star, and also worked closely with us on managing the project in the early years. Darragh – tall, dark-haired and muscular – stood practising an electric guitar in the dining room, while we were trying to talk! A talented lad, I thought. He was all on for the chat that day too. His interest in music prepared him for the role of entertainments officer in Trinity College Dublin, where he studied a few years later. The job was an elected position; the voters were Trinity students. Darragh cut his teeth on directing his own winning campaign. I met him again during that period in the early summer of 2014, when he was going door to door in the Tallaght South constituency, campaigning for his sister Martina to be elected to South Dublin County Council. As I accompanied him, I witnessed how strategic and clever he was in his choice of what doors to knock on, what to say on the doorstep and how to record the data when moving from street to street. He was bright, positively engaging and unflappable, regardless of the resident's response. *If I ever run for the Dáil, he'd be fantastic as my campaign manager*, I thought to myself that day.

Darragh was keen. He had wanted to do something for the referendum and was intrigued with the further opportunity if all went well, if we got on, if it really did look possible to build a Dáil campaign. In October Darragh emailed Moninne Griffith and Andrew Hyland at Marriage Equality to say that he hoped to work with us to gear up for a campaign in our constituency. He wanted to check in on how the national campaign plans were going, and to ensure that we would work with them as closely as possible, indeed be part of Yes Equality once it got going, to receive and offer support. Ann Louise, Darragh and I were eager to work in sync with the national plans. We knew it would be some time yet before it launched, though, and we wanted to begin to prepare the groundwork. We got Marriage Equality's blessing to start, and Darragh initiated his work to devise the strategy.

In January 2015 we kicked off our social media recruitment drive for Dublin South-West volunteers to canvass for the referendum. In February, Darragh, with the support of two students from Tallaght's Institute of Technology, filmed a recruitment video of myself and Ann Louise in the library of An Cosán. We even put out a few local press releases at the same time. Just after Yes Equality launched the national campaign in March, we had our own local launch ready to go with a 'Pledge to Vote' event in Rua Red – the beautiful arts and cultural building envisioned by my friend Joe Horan, county manager of South Dublin County Council – just opposite the back of the Square shopping centre. Over fifty people attended and we were ecstatic. I had only canvassed at doors once before, a few years earlier for one of Ivana Bacik's campaigns. At the time, though, I was afraid to speak, and very conscious of my American accent, so I doubled up with Ann Louise and let her do the talking. Now I just had to get out there and start talking for myself! Of course Ann Louise and I often canvassed together, but this was a new challenge for me to overcome. She was the pro. Though blind, she had no qualms once she arrived on the doorstep. She was my teacher once again.

Campaigning is hard, though. It is tiring. It requires a big tank of energy as one leaves the starting location, which is usually next to the campaign leader's car boot. That's where all the buttons, stickers and clipboards to record the household responses are lifted out early each evening and put away later that night. Darragh would welcome campaign volunteers by name and give them time to catch up and chat before the work of the evening began. The pep talk then ensued, and Darragh (or another leader) would talk through the latest messages from Yes headquarters. These were refined a number of times each week, as intelligence from the ground throughout the country was sent in. Each evening bonds were built between the small teams of canvassers and this enabled us to listen intently, and for positive dialogue to happen on the doorsteps. At the end of the night, there was genuine jubilation when one of us told a story about how potential voters changed their mind from an adamant 'No!' to a faltering 'Maybe' – and sometimes to a 'YES!'

Once in a while those conversations were awful, especially for some of the young gay men who accompanied us. They were scowled at, sometimes spat at. One constituent shook his head and said, 'You are dirty – you will go to hell.' Ann Louise was always one of the first to put her arm around our volunteers, and then push them back gently, ask them to stand straight up, and look directly into their eyes and say, 'You are extraordinary. Thank you for doing this. We will win. Only good will come from what you do.'

One evening, alone, Ann Louise called on a house that was dark and dilapidated. As the door was opened by a timorous Spanish au pair, a voice boomed up the corridor from the back kitchen. The interrogation that ensued was peppered with shouts of condemnation and threats of hell for all who were campaigning for marriage equality. During this time, I realised she was gone longer than she should have been, so I clipped back to find her, anxiety rising in my chest. I saw her at that doorstep and I could feel her fear. I rushed up, took her arm and hand, stood straight up with her and we walked steadily out into the street so I could scout out where the others were. We saw them, they came running to us. We were safe.

We all loved working with Yes Equality. They provided campaign materials, the 'how to' manual for canvassing, training in the messages and a steady stream of national or local events to keep people energised. We appreciated that they gave space for each group to 'do their own thing', to bring their own local approach to the canvassing. Headquarters acknowledged that constituency leaders knew their areas best: they held the maps of how households voted and what kinds of messages would do well on the doorsteps. It was a huge learning experience and a once-in-a-lifetime campaign.

The referendum date steadily approached. We received an invitation from local LGBTQ+ organisations to speak at an event in Galway city in early April. Ann Louise felt up for it, enlivened by the opportunity to speak again. We discussed what each would say. The organisers asked us to galvanise the crowd before they took off for a friendly demonstration throughout the town. By the time we arrived, Ann Louise wasn't feeling her best. But she sat down and wrote out the themes of what she wanted to say on large five-by-seven notecards. Then she reviewed those cards for the next several hours, peering at them – trying to read what she had written, though the words kept falling away. That's what her eyes saw: words falling away. Nevertheless, she reviewed, memorised and sweated.

Marriage Equality

A Time for Confidence. Life is a gift. Let's use it to create the possible. The will to change.

Some of her notes for that speech. I look at them now with sadness and immense inspiration for my life without her. 'I know we will win, Katie,' she said. 'I can see it.' Though she could not see physically who was in the crowd, she connected deeply with everyone there.

We received one more opportunity for a public speech together. On 10 May 2015, twelve days before the vote, the independent, youthful and exceptionally creative voluntary group LGBTQ+ Noise held its last of six marches to advocate for marriage equality. With uncommon energy and logistical talent, they planned marches that always gathered large numbers of people with hopeful faces, vibrant 'Equal' placards and an unmistakable determination. This time comedian Tara Flynn presided over the event in Dublin's Merrion Square where an estimated 3,000 campaigners turned out to show their support.

To conclude the event, Tara invited Ann Louise and me onto the Mack-truck low-loader stage. We were exhausted, but it was not the time to give in to that. Ann Louise had the microphone, and with every fibre of her petite body she looked out at the crowd and spoke from her big heart. She began by proclaiming that it was a joy and privilege to be with them on that day, and immediately called on their powers of creativity and imagination. I can still hear her beautiful Irish voice say, 'Katherine and I have been together since 1981, and I love her more today than I did then, if that is possible.' She recalled the day we came out of the

High Court in 2006 having lost our case. A woman had sent her a card that said, *Never give up*. Again, I hear her voice: 'And we are all here now because none of us has given up. We could have given up. We could have given in, but we haven't. And from now on – and there are twelve days left of this campaign – I beg and plead you to keep up the motivation. You might ask, "How?" Because sometimes it gets a bit tiring out there and we all know that. But the way I suggest, and the way that helps me, is this. Hold an image of one person in your life whom you know. If we can get this over the line, it will change their lives for ever.'

Ann Louise, great storyteller that she was, then spoke about someone we had met in a town in County Kerry. We were in the public library, having just launched our memoir. There was a man walking furtively up and down the stacks of the library. Ann Louise went over to talk to him, and heard the horror story of his life, as a young boy growing up in rural Ireland, knowing he was gay. This forty-year-old man continued to motivate her fight so that some day, as an older man, he would know that finally he was an equal. He would know that Ireland now recognised him and gave him back his dignity for the very first time.

'So, each one of you, hold an image of someone in your mind who will be freed by this change. Let that motivate you to get out and make a final effort. This referendum is different to any referendum previously held in Ireland. It's all about love. And so, when we go in to vote, feel full of love. This referendum *is* about love. And when you come out from your poll, come out singing, singing *yes*!' God, she was on fire! And my face, as I stood beside her, was filled with love and joy. Nothing could be better than this . . . I let that joy seep in, once again. Ann Louise looked vibrant, powerful and happy. I could not wish for anything more than to be by her side, urging the nation to do the right thing.

*

In early May something else political started to happen for me. I was in my beautiful, albeit small, Georgian office with its high ceilings and draughty window, on the ground floor of Leinster House, opposite the back of the Dáil bar. I was reviewing my next speech for the Seanad, to take place during the 'order of business', a time allotted at the beginning of each morning's proceedings. Senators view it as three minutes to make their mark on a topical issue and maybe get media coverage later in the day. Sometimes it worked for me, especially when Jimmy Walsh, Seanad correspondent for *The Irish Times*, was covering the upper house. My phone rang and it was the Independent TD Stephen Donnelly. We had been exchanging papers on developing new policies for childcare and the early years. I had approached him because I liked his speeches in the Dáil. He sounded like a progressive thinker and was solid on economic matters. Ever since finishing my MBA at Smurfit Business School, University College Dublin, I loved the macroeconomic stuff. And high-quality childcare has a lot to do with macroeconomics. Stephen asked, 'Katherine, can you meet me in the restaurant of the Department of Agriculture later today?' Many Independent TDs had been allocated offices there as a sign of their 'low on the totem pole' status because it was outside the Leinster

House cut and thrust. 'I have something I'd like to discuss with you – a proposition of sorts.' Intrigued, I told Magdalene Hayden, my assistant, that I would be meeting Stephen, and we both just assumed it was about childcare. She offered to prepare a synopsis of what we were working on. As a skilled policy analyst from Finland, her knowledge of early years and childcare services was formidable. Just what I needed.

Leinster House has a small back door, just off the members' dining room. It opens onto a laneway towards Merrion Street, where ministerial cars are often parked. There is a smokers' hut of sorts on the right, adjacent to a big iron gate that opens to the car park for the Department of Agriculture building. That was the way Stephen told me to come the first time, and I often used it after that. As soon as I came in, Stephen said that he, Catherine Murphy and Róisín Shortall were in conversations about forming a new political party, social democratic in nature. 'I'm wondering if you would be interested in joining us to form the party,' Stephen said. 'I need to talk to Catherine and Róisín to see if they would welcome you, but I think you are someone who could add a lot to what we are trying to do.' I was stunned. I hadn't made it public that I was considering a run for the Dáil. Stephen insisted, further, that if I were to join, he would want me to co-lead with himself, Catherine and Róisín. Another shock. The women are both heavy-hitting speakers, prodigious in their workload and effective constituency politicians. I had respectful awe for them. The opportunity felt scary, but nonetheless tempting. Better to acknowledge fear and move through it, rather than pretend it is not there. Ann Louise had taught me that.

So I spent the next two months participating in several meetings in Agriculture House and one full weekend in Róisín Shortall's home. We deliberated at length about the new party's core values of 'progress, democracy, equality and sustainability', all things close to my own political identity. The four of us, along with our assistants, Councillor Jennifer Whitmore, Niall Ó Tuathail and Magdalene Hayden, developed policy papers on 'Deepening Democracy', 'Community First: Communities at the Heart of Development', 'Early Childhood – An Equal Start', 'Tackling the Mortgage Crisis', 'Planning for Pensions', 'The Future of Work', and many more. We invited experts to provide us with their intelligence, all in the context of top secrecy – a new political party was brewing. Each day I felt full of a new future, while being thoroughly exhausted at the end of it. Politics can be a drug. And it was all happening in the midst of the run-up to the constitutional referendum on marriage equality.

*

I have one more media outing for the referendum just two days before the vote: a debate about the issue on RTÉ's *Prime Time* with Labour minister Alex White and head of Amnesty International Ireland Colm O'Gorman, against my senatorial nemesis Senator Rónán Mullen and *Irish Times* conservative columnist Breda O'Brien. It is an incredibly heated exchange. For myself, the climax comes when I look straight at my opponents and call out their cheap tactics of using posters which claim that *Children Deserve a Mother and a Father*. I practically roar, 'I have dear friends with two beautiful young children, *who can read*, and every day they have to pass by that poster!' One of the viewer tweets that RTÉ put out at the end of the programme says, 'Katherine Zappone brings the debate right back to earth with the last words: "All we're looking for is equality."'

By the time the Irish people go to the polls on a glorious sunny day in May, Ann Louise and I have knocked on thousands of doors in South-West Dublin, and have held hundreds of conversations with people in the Square (Tallaght) and other shopping centres. Our Dublin South-West Yes Equality team has covered many miles in snow – we started in early February – sleet and sun until we have knocked on every door, at least once.

We go to bed on the eve of the 22nd after the citizens have cast their votes. I turn to her and say, 'Ann Louise, I am still not sure. Is it really possible that we could win? I have never felt so nervous in my life.' I am starting to spiral.

She responds with gentle insistence, 'Katherine, we have done enough. Rest easy. We have done enough.'

She's right. I give her a kiss. I turn the radio off; there's little news anyway. We are both exhausted. Sleep comes easier than anticipated.

I wake early, grab the radio, turn it on just as the announcer says, 'Yes is winning!' She hears it too. Our bodies feel jubilant next to each other.

'Let's go! We need to head to the count centre as soon as we can. No time to eat. We'll pick up something down below. What will I wear?!'

Ann Louise had prepared her clothing the night before, so she's all set. Thirty minutes later we are in the Citywest count centre, surrounded by Darragh and our team. A joyous bedlam sets in. And once we've kissed each of the team on the cheek, we say goodbye and head to Dublin Castle. Results from count centres around the country will be fed in to the national count there.

And so, when we enter the Castle courtyard on 23 May 2015 it is a moment of pure jubilation. Two thousand people have gathered to witness one of Ireland's most historic moments. 'Equal' signs are everywhere. Rainbow flags are flying. The final county result is called. We have won! Some 62 per cent of the Irish population have voted 'Tá!' And 71.3 per cent of Dublin South-West have also voted 'Yes!' This is the first time that a country or state has legalised marriage equality by popular vote. Being in the courtyard and being able to go onto the stage with Ann Louise, to lift up our arms together, to look at the crowd and to feel that we have all achieved this – we are euphoric.

I bring her down to the crowds and move close to the stage. Miriam O'Callaghan, RTÉ broadcaster, wants to interview us – and it is then that I turn to Ann Louise and say, 'Ann Louise, will you marry me?'

She says, 'Yes!'

We kiss – on television – and that kiss goes around the world – to 12.5 million viewers online. Pure joy again.

Ann Louise and I continue to walk through the thousands gathered, kissing so many, hugging and shaking hands. Tears streaming from all eyes . . . It is then that I see she is exhausted. A raw, heavy sadness starts behind my breastbone. She has expended almost all her energy; her head hurts and we still have a huge party to attend later that evening.

I turn to her and say, 'Ann Louise, let's go back to the hotel. You can rest. We don't have to go to the party. I'm pretty tired too.'

She is so relieved. More tears, this time ones of sadness, not delight.

'Ann Louise, we made it. You are getting better. But it has been a very big day.'

We walk slowly down Parliament Street and look up. On a balcony is Una Mullally – the *Irish Times* journalist – she is recovering from cancer at the time. She runs down to give each of us a glass filled with champagne. We toast our victory, full of joy – while grief hovers in the distance. All three of us are aware of the personal cost. Radical social change is filled with stress that can take its toll on one's body as well as one's mind. Yet we must keep going, with as much protection as we can muster. Ann Louise and I spend the celebrations in our hotel room: Ann Louise asleep, her energy levels depleted, me beside her with a cup of tea, the adrenaline of the day subsiding, watching the revelry unfold on television. There's nowhere I'd rather be.

*

The following week I returned to my Seanad work and the preparations for a new political party. Towards mid-June, however, I became much less comfortable with the idea of four people leading it. Three would be more than enough.

Trust was an issue too. Building it with people I did not know well – for such a big venture – was not easy. And the others had been elected and were TDs, while I had not yet faced a public vote. I finally decided that my time and focus really ought to be on 'just getting elected'. I asked for a special slot in the next meeting of our group and formally confirmed my decision. Stephen was deeply disappointed. Catherine and Róisín understood and, I think, might have felt some relief. Too many leaders was not a good thing. While I had been involved passionately in good faith, and had learned a lot, it just made more sense to wish all three well and turn my energy towards a seat in Dublin South-West. The work with my colleagues to establish the Social Democrats, however, confirmed that I was being viewed as a seriously active political figure. On 22 June I announced that I would be standing for election as an Independent candidate for Dublin South-West. In July Stephen, Róisín and Catherine launched the Social Democrats. That same month I voted in the Seanad for the bill on gender recognition. It contained enough of the 'gold standard' gender recognition bill, developed by the advocates and myself several months earlier, for me to support this to become a landmark act.

*

It was time for a break. August at The Shanty – if the sun shines at least half the day – is paradise on Earth. Ann Louise and I started to gear up for a staycation and to host a few small dinner parties to celebrate our great win and her ongoing recovery. We looked forward to spending more time together and to strategising about the upcoming general election, which we thought would be six months away. On the first Saturday in August I opened *The Irish Times* to read various articles to her. We enjoyed this special Saturday ritual, having begun it a few months before. Ann Louise was my wisest political counsellor and she consistently offered me opportunities to analyse in a deeper way what was happening in Ireland and our world.

I turned to the opinion page and a headline took hold of me: '*Government should back inquiries into Halawa case. The trial of innocent Irishman Ibrahim Halawa, who has been held for two years, starts tomorrow in Egypt.*' Authors Caoilfhionn Gallagher, Katie O'Byrne and Mark Wassouf, barristers from Doughty Street Chambers in London who act for Ibrahim and his family, were telling Ireland that '*an Irish teenager lies abandoned to his fate in a Cairo prison, cut off from the world . . . He was arrested as a child, at age 17, one of a group of 494, rounded up and charged with crimes that carry life imprisonment or the death penalty. In the two years since his arrest he has been severely mistreated . . .*'

We were both horrified. 'Ann Louise, listen to this . . . his trial starts tomorrow . . . and the authors say that it will inevitably be unfair. And then they write that, while Ibrahim has been receiving important consular support from the Irish embassy in Cairo, "it is not enough. Why hasn't the Irish government – at the highest level – been more outspoken in supporting its citizen and in condemning Egypt's grave disregard for international human rights?"' Ibrahim's sisters

– Omaima, Fatima and Somaia – were holding a photo of him in the centre of the 'Opinion and Analysis' page. I cut it out and, eventually, taped it onto the bookcase in my Leinster House ministerial office a year later, looking at me every day, reminding me to act as often as I could, believing that someday Ibrahim would come home.

*

And that was it – the end to my break. Three days after reading the opinion piece, I am standing on the beautiful breezy grounds of Dunboyne Herbs in County Meath. I am waiting to see Seán Boylan, the legendary GAA football manager of the senior Meath team for twenty-three years. He also happens to be an extraordinary healer, trained in the art and science of traditional herbalism practised within the Boylan family as far back as the fifteenth century. My friend Senator Mary Ann O'Brien introduced Seán to Ann Louise after she got ill. Seán's training, and spiritual character, allows him to assess energy flows and blockages, muscle ailments and tension, as well as mental distress, almost as soon as he looks at you. He's helping me cope with our new circumstance. My body and spirit require regular restoration now.

My phone rings. It is Colm O'Gorman. 'Katherine, thank you for your interest in Ibrahim. Amnesty International has been following his case since his arrest, and we have prepared a briefing in advance of appearing before the Joint Oireachtas Committee on Foreign Affairs and Trade.' We continue to talk – and within the next thirty minutes Colm outlines the background to Ibrahim's case, a human rights analysis noting several significant concerns, and the kind of response they hope for from the government. He's brilliant at what he does, I think. I am so grateful. Human rights intelligence is crucial for me right now. I feel much more confident about contacting Ibrahim's London barristers to see what I can do to help.

I email the Doughty Street barristers soon after, asking them for a copy of the legal opinion they have written to the Irish government regarding what it can do for Ibrahim's release. I also let them know that I will be in London in early September, chairing a session at King's College on the parliamentary oversight of human rights. I conclude with a request for us to meet when I am in London.

Thus begins my extraordinary relationship with the people of Doughty Street (where Charles Dickens lived) – internationally renowned human rights lawyers – and their colleague Darragh Mackin of KRW Law in Northern Ireland (who also successfully represented the families of the Stardust victims). Mary Lawlor, director of Front Line Defenders at the time, is also exceptionally helpful. Though I am an Independent senator, I feel accompanied by all of them as we seek Ibrahim's release. I may not have a political party, but I am not alone.

Before the Seanad term resumes properly, I travel to London for a meeting at Doughty Street. The briefing provided is both masterful and shattering, the details stark, horrific. I am shown some of Ibrahim's letters from prison. In a letter from 3 June 2015, he writes:

We were sitting down chatting and suddenly the cell door opened. 'Get out. Get out.' Personally I was dragged, then beaten by sticks, then I was told, 'Lay down on your stomach with your hands behind your back.' We were stripped naked, one by one. Then we were left to wait.

Caoilfhionn, Katie, Mark and I start to think about how I can raise my voice as an Irish senator to add to their remarkable lead. Part of the plan includes a visit by the three of them to Leinster House, to testify in front of the Foreign Affairs Committee. This does not come to pass; the committee vote against such a meeting. The chairman indicates that he prefers holding an 'informal' meeting with the lawyers (which means it would not be placed on the record). We try to plan a visit to Ibrahim in his Egyptian prison, but the government refuses to provide us with visas or for us to apply for prison access. Eventually, and much later on in the year, I am able to join them for a public briefing, alongside Colm O'Gorman and Ibrahim's sisters, on Human Rights Day, 10 December 2015, in the Royal College of Physicians on Kildare Street, not far from Leinster House. I conclude my presentation by calling for the Irish government to apply a law that would allow Ibrahim to be transferred to Ireland, and in the meantime to press for bail to secure his release. I feel colour rising in my cheeks as I urge them to act immediately, my heart racing as I say, 'Now is the time to secure his freedom. Now is the time to bring Ibrahim home.' I can only hope that the passion I feel about it has come across in my presentation, and that I have successfully managed to impress the urgency of Ibrahim's situation upon them. But all I can do now is wait.

*

By mid-September 2015 I was caught up in the intensity of plans for my general election campaign. Darragh did amazing research on the constituency, and was joined by Claire Murphy, our sterling volunteer and committed comrade. Claire – from Tallaght, with a mother who had attended courses in The Shanty – was taking a break after completing her Maynooth University master's in 'design thinking'. So my two key people were the children of Shanty learners. Noel Whelan and Brian Murphy agreed to be roped in to provide counsel to ourselves and the campaign, and the first cut of the 'Zappone Plan' was drafted by them. What a 'leg up' from two of the greats! Everyone agreed that I needed to establish a physical presence in Tallaght. An office became available on Main Street, opposite the Dominican priory. *How appropriate*, I thought. 'Perfect,' says Darragh. 'It's where it all started.' The adult education centre, on the grounds of the priory, was where I had met many of the women who would come to form a management committee to help us establish The Shanty Educational Project in 1986. They had invited me to give a lecture on feminist theology to their women's studies course one evening. I'd been delighted to do so, had a great time and at the end of that session I had said to them, 'Ann Louise Gilligan and I have a home in Brittas, just a few miles up the road. Would you be interested to come up to us some weekend? We will teach a little more about feminist theology, but we also want to tell you about a small dream we have – sharing our home as an educational space for women who have left school early.' They had accepted our invitation and became an integral part of the work. So, in the autumn of 2016 I felt like I was completing a full circle. We signed the lease and set up what we dubbed 'TeamZappone HQ'.

By October 2015, back at the Seanad, the marriage bill was ready to come to the upper house. After the people voted for equality in the referendum, the houses of the Oireachtas were obliged to pass an act that would allow same-sex couples to marry and would allow for the legal recognition of the foreign marriages of same-sex couples. This was the category Ann Louise and I fell into. The *Zappone and Gilligan v. Revenue Commissioners and Others* (2006) case had argued that our Canadian marriage in 2003 ought to be recognised in Ireland. While we did not succeed in the courts, we 'won in the court of public opinion', as Gerard Hogan, one of our senior counsel (and future judge of the Supreme Court), said to us at the time. Now indeed the full impact of that win would come to pass. Never did I anticipate in 2003 that one day I would have the privilege to vote for a government bill that enacted our desire and struggle.

As I rose to give my Seanad speech on the bill, my body felt as if it might not be able to contain all the emotion. I took a breath, the feelings settled, and I began by paraphrasing a line from William Butler Yeats: 'change comes dropping slow'.

I took another breath.

When Ann Louise and I first imagined this change over thirteen years previously, a change for ourselves, other LGBTQ+ people and Ireland, we never thought it would take so long. It is the politics of change that throws up the contestations, conflicts, resistance, and the prison of prejudice that must be overcome to unleash freedom for an oppressed minority. Before the referendum vote, I often said it was the people who would have the power to banish inequality between a majority and a minority and that such an opportunity did not come often in a lifetime.

So, how did the people rise up for this?

The politics of change became personal, especially for the young.

The personal is political, as the elders know. But it was the young who invented #Home to Vote, coming home on planes, trains and ferries from everywhere, to vote YES!

My closing remarks referred to the power of memory and imagination, inspired of course by my lover, my partner, my spouse. The marriage equality law will always carry the memory that citizens, by collaborating, can bring about fundamental change and enable a cultural seismic shift for the good. I believed then, and still believe now, that the memories this law embodies provide touchstones for citizens to imagine other changes that are necessary to bring about a 'Republic of Equals' for all.

As I write now, I read Ann Louise's card to me for that day. It contains a quaint Irish phrase that she used often when addressing me, from the earliest years of our being-in-love.

Marriage Equality

To the LOVE of my LIFE
Me ould segotia . . .

My heart still flips as I hear her beautiful Irish voice say those words, as she looks at me with such glee and mischief in her eyes.

CHAPTER 6

Facing Forward

A reservoir of energy from the marriage equality win boosted us on the campaign trail. Darragh worked the phones and the laptop non-stop, and ran each canvass with me and our team. He was a taskmaster! In early November we met at headquarters and he laid out the final timeframe, the tasks leading up to the February 2016 election date.

He said, 'Katherine, we need to sharpen our focus at the doors. No Independent has ever won in this constituency. And we haven't had a woman in any of the five seats since Mary Harney contested a newly created constituency in 2002.'

He reminded me that many of our volunteers for the marriage campaign had been really nervous at the beginning and experienced it as a bit of a roller-coaster. They were scared to go to the doors because they hadn't ever done it before. But they'd become engaged and eventually had fun. 'They want to deliver another change and you have a track record for doing that. But it would be great if we could get them some additional training from a professional.'

'Have they all come back and stayed with us?' I asked.

'Most of them,' Darragh said. 'I'm just looking ahead. We're getting into the bad weather; exams will be coming up for those still in third level. They want to be here for you.'

'We need to harness their energy, then,' I said. 'How about a canvass boot camp? With a real pro.'

'Who?' he asked, with a touch of incredulity.

'My friend and colleague from the Save the Seanad days, Michael McDowell,' I replied with a playful look.

He was no longer a politician at the time, but Michael was political to his fingertips. As a former attorney general, minister for justice and leader of the Progressive Democrats, he had run many a campaign. He was bigger than life, a character, committed to the art of politics. And he had campaigning down to a science. He *relished* doing the numbers and analysing the history of a constituency. Darragh loved the idea. A pro to help review strategies and tactics would be brilliant. But could we get Michael?

'I'll ask him tomorrow. Michael and I may not agree on all things political, but he's a man of considerable integrity and he is my friend. I think he would do it.'

Relationships of trust and affection are rare in politics. I had that with Michael. 'Katherine, I'd be happy to help you,' he answered, with a little mirth in his voice when I asked him. We scheduled the training for the following Saturday. There was not a moment to be wasted. Volunteers responded with a 'yes!' at high speed, from ages twenty to seventy, women and men. 'Do you know how to get to Main Street, Tallaght, Michael?' I asked in all seriousness. 'Of course I do, Katherine. It might not be my usual stomping ground, but I am familiar with it.' He even knew that there were parking spots across from us in the priory lot.

Approximately thirty folks gathered. Our office was packed. Michael brought constituency maps, a soft manner and a big smile. We were happy to sit at his feet. He raised the issues of messaging, my profile and record, ways to approach the doors and the importance of knowing the political allegiance of the households, if we could get access to that information. Harder for an Independent to do, especially one who had not run in the constituency before. Through informal networks, though, we managed to acquire sufficient intelligence. We studied the maps, engaged in some role play and reviewed the strategy. Michael thought we had a good shot. His parting words: 'I'll be watching!'

The team felt recharged at the end of the day. Darragh, Claire and another steadfast volunteer, Ellen Tanam, stayed back to brainstorm about how my messages as an Independent voice for Dublin South-West could be fine-tuned. We had very clear policy positions, formulated with the help of Brian Murphy and Noel Whelan. I laid out plans for 'An Equal Start in Childhood' – with high-quality early education, after-school care and one-stop shops for family services as the best way to cut poverty and inequality. My policies to 'Champion Women' focused on decent working conditions, including a living wage and abolishing low- and zero-hour contracts, which affect women disproportionately. 'Fairness in Housing' emphasised protection for tenants and a community-based model for housing those who were homeless or seeking refuge. Now we just needed to paint my portrait so that the voters would get to know me.

So often Irish people vote for a party. Since I was running as an Independent, they would need to vote for me, the person. At the doorstep we would ask often, 'Who is the person you want to represent you in parliament?' We leveraged my experience from the years of community education work in the constituency, and my national work for marriage equality. We wanted them to get a taste, too, of my work for the issues that matter to constituents, and developed YouTube videos presenting clips of my Seanad voice. In the chamber debates I had said:

'They are sleeping in tents in Tallaght! So we have a shelter crisis here.'

'Inequality of wealth and income are not good for any society.'

'Irish Water has been an unequivocal failure! On 11 October I marched peacefully alongside thousands in Tallaght.'

On social welfare benefits for lone parents, I would often demand, 'Will the government please invite lone parents to the dialogue?', and I finally declared in the Seanad that I would set up my own working group to produce a report on what lone parents said they needed to live a good life for themselves and their children.

As all that work filtered through to the volunteers on canvass duty, the young people spread the message. I had name recognition, not so much through marriage equality, but more through The Shanty and the An Cosán educational project. Constituents said, 'Oh yes, my mam went to The Shanty', or 'That started in your living room!', or 'I love my classes in An Cosán and try to get others to go.'

We didn't have a lot of money and we didn't have the support of a big party, but we had the energy of our volunteers and the significant number of lives that had been touched through my work. We listened to what the people said on the doorsteps. We rebuilt our messages and went back out on the doorstep. We engineered a data-driven approach. And we learned to ask directly, 'Will you give her your number 1? If not, how about your number 2?'

During this period Ann Louise and I tried to find time for ourselves as often as we could. She had good energy, was focused on writing her next book and canvassed with me periodically. The pains in her head had softened. Her much-improved form opened my mind to imagine something I had always hoped for. An Irish wedding! Of course our Canadian marriage was now recognised as legal in Ireland, but I felt deeply that something was missing for us. We had had a life-partnership ceremony in Boston in 1982 when there was no possibility of marriage anywhere on the horizon. We married each other legally in Vancouver, British Columbia in 2003. We had nothing in Ireland, though, and this was our home, and where we had fought the good fight. At the first ceremony we had friends, not family. At the second ritual had family, not friends. Let's have one more ceremony with family, friends and colleagues.

'Why not an event to renew our marriage vows?' I asked Ann Louise one day.

'That sounds too much like something that would happen in a church,' she responded with slight disdain.

'Yes, but we can't marry here because we are already married. And Irish people – being the Catholics that they are – would understand vow-renewal, Ann Louise.'

It was not imaginative enough for her. That just did not represent the jolt to the imagination that she wanted people to experience – it carried too much nuance of the past and did not capture the extraordinary newness the marriage equality movement had ushered in.

'Why don't we invite people to an event that Brings Our Marriage Home? I will organise the cake!'

What great fortune to marry such an incredible chef! Ann Louise loved her cookbooks and had hundreds of newspaper recipe clippings that would fall out of them. I would find her reading them at all hours. She had the entire collection of Darina Allen cookbooks, and indeed had attended her famous cookery school. One time she came back from Ballymaloe with a cock for our hens, and she dubbed him 'Mr Allen'.

I digress. It is not hard to do so. Ann Louise was always imagining and doing something new, something different, something that no one else could see. This often resulted in the most delicious dinners that I had ever eaten. My father especially loved to eat at her table. He used to say that she had every pot from the cupboards in the sink before she was finished. It was true. I was very happy to wash them up, and indeed to play the role of sous chef. Coming from

America, we had one plate for dinner. Not good enough for Ann Louise. She was at her happiest with a table of at least 6–8 people, and a four-course meal would be followed by a cheese board and delicious coffee or tea. I am still digressing. Or am I? This is Ann Louise. I want her to be seen in all her *jouissance*. Our table, set with so much love-filled nourishment, was bound to produce stimulating, lively conversation and debate. Hearts, minds and bodies were filled.

She set about her mission to find the best cake-maker in Dublin. And she did. Her favourite photo at the time was the two of us laughing as we cut it up. Not that she could see much of it. My job was to organise the venue, music, readings and invitations. Much easier to do if one has eyes that work. But, politically, I was in the midst of devising a campaign plan, drafting letters to potential donors and preparing campaign speeches at the same time as sending out wedding invitations, choosing readings and music for the ceremony. My campaign manager Darragh lent me a big hand. Making arrangements felt possible then. Against many odds I managed to hire Dublin City Hall – adjacent to Dublin Castle, where seven months earlier we had been lifted in a sea of glory. Usually they accepted only people who were 'getting married' – but they were gracious enough to make an exception in our case. My family flew from Seattle – most of hers were already here. Neighbours from our road in Brittas, friends, colleagues, a third of the Irish cabinet and the president of Ireland with his wife Sabina filled the hall. Róisín O and Brian Kennedy, two of Ireland's prominent musicians, sang gloriously. Miriam O'Callaghan led the ritual and blessing (one of her most unusual and stellar roles!). We proclaimed vows to each other that we had said thirteen years earlier in the hospitable and generous land of Canada. Eternity rings were exchanged. Bliss.

Michael Murphy concluded the event with another apposite poem, 'A Vote for Love'. He wrote it after a meal we shared with himself and Terry O'Sullivan, his husband, in the Dáil members' restaurant one evening. He wrote to me several years later that Ann Louise's discussion of Julia Kristeva and the French philosophers that night had inspired it. 'Indeed the line "Not to be erased by a knowing consensus" is quoting Ann Louise directly. This country owes you both so much.'

A Vote for Love

The floodgates of Dublin Castle opened after the
    vote

It was a Katherine and Ann Louise day
Who asked to have their Canadian marriage
Recognised by Irish courts a decade ago
A love they both proclaimed and named
A life they proudly lived out loud
They asked just to be included
Not to be erased by a knowing consensus

On that joyous Saturday all the people approved
The two women threw their open hearts to the
    audience

And we caught them gratefully
Overturning years of hurtful judgements
In the stroke of a pen

Today the red and black sparkled gowns that we wore for the Irish marriage event are in Collins Barracks, one of Ireland's national museums, as part of the LGBTQ+ collection of memorabilia from the movement days. It feels somewhat strange to know that my 'Irish wedding gown' is in a museum. But the director of the National Museum of Ireland, Lynn Scarff, and her team believe that museums ought to hold collections from the present as well as the past. They have a vision that museums ought to represent the achievements of those who are living, especially those who have been hidden in history. In this way, they posit that museums contribute to continuing cultural, social and historical change. I agree. So would Ann Louise.

My American family, who had travelled so far, joined us with Ann Louise's family for an intimate dinner after the champagne and cake reception in City Hall. The momentous occasion had been duly celebrated. Throughout the afternoon and evening my feelings moved from ebullience to a profound and quiet peace. This peace, after such a lengthy and immense struggle, infused my whole body. A part of this has never left me, even in my darkest days.

The following week I put my family to work. Our father was a salesman, one of the best. We brought Lucy, my goddaughter, Suzanne, my sister, and Philip and Mark, my brothers, to the Square shopping centre in Tallaght. Darragh gave them a pep talk, outlined the messages, told them they know me better than anyone else on the campaign trail, and set them loose on the second level of the Square. Phil had been mentored by our dad on how to sell, but didn't know much about Irish policies or politics. It didn't stop him from turning on his colossal charm and getting at least fifty votes that day. The others did well too, even with their American accents. I felt so proud.

*

After we brought our marriage home, I had one more month to put myself before the people of Dublin South-West. My team donned the rain and snow gear every day of that month, canvassing home to home. Ann Louise put on her wool cap (her head was still sensitive to the cold) and the TeamZappone jacket and went out every day or night with us, no matter what the weather. It was such a long shot, running as an Independent candidate, regardless of electoral experience or profiles. I was running against candidates from Fine Gael and Fianna Fáil, and there were increasing numbers of other candidates on the far left, Sinn Féin and Solidarity. They all had so much more money. But we managed to keep the energy up and flowing, especially when our volunteers bore witness to Ann Louise's determination. If she could do it, they certainly could too. I loved her more then than ever. I felt so grateful to Darragh and the rest of my team. We would return to headquarters some nights frozen, but not daunted. They knew and I knew that this election would be my best shot at political power.

Would my policies and vision of a 'Republic of Equals' – grounded in my experience of working with the people of Tallaght West and the marriage equality movement – be enough to get me over the line, though? Every day Ann Louise looked at me and said 'yes'. The people went to the polls on Friday, 26 February. The next day we spent hours waiting for results in the Citywest count centre, just a couple of miles down from The Shanty. Four of the five seats had been filled by late afternoon. My team and I had held our breath each time the surplus votes of a successful candidate transferred to those still in the running. But each time the news was bad and it really was difficult to sustain hope. We had worked so hard and had run such a long campaign. I was exhausted and tried not to show on my face how crest-fallen I felt. There was just one seat left. It was the fifteenth count. I had been trailing behind five other candidates all day and I was still behind by 1,577 votes. It looked like it was all over.

Ann Louise and I decided to go to Citywest's hotel for a cup of coffee. The centre was too tense and, frankly, some depression was beginning to set in. Just as we received our order, the waiter turned to me and said, 'Are you Katherine Zappone? I'm watching the tallies. You'd better get back over there.' We looked up at the monitors, and the final count was about to be announced. Another Independent candidate, Peter Fitzpatrick, had a significant sum of votes that would be transferred to candidates still in the running. I grabbed Ann Louise's hand, and we dashed over to the centre, to arrive just before the announcement that, on the sixteenth count, I had taken the fifth seat! Our team erupted with a roar. I grabbed Ann Louise and kissed her. I was unreservedly jubilant. I had won by 152 votes, receiving most of Peter Fitzpatrick's transfers.

Immediately Fine Gael called for a recount. In their view, Anne Marie Dermody, their candidate, who had been ahead of me all day, should have won. The party prepared to bring in some of their big guns to oversee the review. New to politics, I was initially confused, but we copped on pretty quick that these were standard tactics to impress those tabulating votes that the results needed to be perfect.

'Is there anything I can do, Ann Louise? Are we okay?'

She looked at me and said, 'Why don't you phone Michael McDowell and see if he will come to the centre to supervise the tally with you.'

'Brilliant!' I said. I phoned Michael immediately and he came right away. The cameras turned to us. Great drama unfolded as Michael went over to the other side's lawyers and all the fine gentlemen looked over the tables together, as the counters continued their work. Later that evening, I was confirmed as the fifth elected representative of Dublin South-West. It was time to go home.

*

My scrape to success in the general election moderated any feeling of glory. Nevertheless, it just felt so cool to walk into Leinster House, to be greeted by the ushers with 'Good morning, deputy!' rather than 'Hello, senator!', and to find a seat in the sizeable, handsome, wooden-panelled Dáil. It is a hallowed setting. Only deputies and civil servants can enter the seating area. The public views proceedings from a third-level, half-circular corridor framed by glass, above us. The second level holds individual chairs for senators so they can witness debates, and also contains a special box for VIPs.

Magdalene and I set about moving offices to Leinster House 2000, and Darragh and Claire joined the two of us to view the lie of the land for the immediate work ahead. Governing power did not belong to any political group after the election. A coalition needed to be formed because no party had secured enough seats to rule on its own. Both Fine Gael and Fianna Fáil wanted to talk to the Independents and Greens to try to form a government. Most of the momentum was in the Fine Gael camp, though, where I spent the majority of my time. I did attend some of the Fianna Fáil meetings, and I met Micheál Martin and Deirdre Gillane (his chief advisor) in his Leinster House office one afternoon. I enjoyed very much our intellectually robust discussion, especially on the future of educational policy. I left that meeting, however, feeling that opportunity was in the other direction. It did not appear that Fianna Fáil could make up the numbers.

The meetings with Fine Gael in Government Buildings were intense. I had a hefty team of generous advisors helping me put together a policy document that contained my political priorities: Dr Tom McDonnell, co-director of the Nevin Economic Research Institute, Dr Micheál Collins, economist and assistant professor in social policy at University College Dublin, and Dr Mary Murphy, professor of sociology at Maynooth University. These progressive public intellectuals continued to assist me with the work ahead. The stimulation of the negotiating days kept me on a sustained high. It's part of who I am.

I also asked for advice from several non-governmental organisations that I trusted, such as the National Women's Council, Focus Ireland and The Wheel. The brilliant education journalist of *The Irish Times*, Carl O'Brien, gave an expert hand in the background too. It was imperative, for me, to have a robust place to stand as I called for this or that change to the heavy discussion document Fine Gael put before the Independents and the Greens. Having never done this before, and without any party to show me the ropes, the advice and expertise I received boosted my confidence to speak with an authority I often did not feel deep down.

I can fully understand, now perhaps better than at the time, why Shane Ross and Michael Fitzmaurice formed a political grouping of Independent TDs, the Independent Alliance, in March 2015. Shane emerged as the realpolitik leader, though, especially since he decided to go into government with Fine Gael and Michael did not. In my view, they often acted as a political party. Interestingly enough, the gentlemen never invited me to join, though in his *In Bed with the Blueshirts* (2020) Shane remembers that he did ask me and that I did not answer. My memory is that he did not ask, and that I did not offer. We're agreed on one count, at least!

As the days passed, however, some of the Independents not associated with the Independent Alliance formed smaller groupings to get some solidarity and a little more negotiating power. Denis Naughton (an Independent Roscommon TD) invited me to work with him but not in any formal alliance. He had also initiated a Rural Alliance of Independents and was smart in the ways he tried to get all Independents to work towards similar strategies in negotiating with Fine Gael. I deeply appreciated Denis's reach out to me. It was the beginning of a respectful friendship, solidified further during our shared time in cabinet. We had some serious policy differences, but that did not deter us ever from 'having each other's backs'.

I gained confidence as the weeks went by. I met regularly with Andrew McDowell, Enda Kenny's economic advisor. I made notes in those meetings and sent them back to Andrew, outlining changes to the Fine Gael document that he had agreed to make, including details related to my priorities on further, adult and community education; urban regeneration through investing in communities; childcare and early years education; women's equality related to the gender pay gap; the removal of the 'baptism barrier' for primary school entry; investing significantly more in education; and taking a quantum step up to reduce child poverty. Some of the changes were minor, others more significant.

Perhaps surprisingly, negotiating is a heart thing for me, as much as a head thing. I really try to connect with the other person – and endeavour to hear their concerns and commitments. In the process, bottom lines sometimes shift. The question 'Can you live with it?' often comes into play. If one is open, and I strive to be, that question touches one's moral fibre. My conscience is activated, as is my head and heart. It's hard work. I think, however, it is the kind of work that ought to demonstrate respect for the other. It is not a game for me. And I did not always get it right. My days got longer, and while exhaustion was almost a nightly occurrence, I was never too tired to share my day's adventures with Ann Louise. It brought a fullness to her day, and big love and wise counsel to mine.

Independents and Fine Gael spent more than two months negotiating a programme. Two moments stand out. One was a compromise of sorts. The other, a 'walk away' issue. In the early days, we consumed an enormous amount of time grappling with a draft chapter initially entitled 'Public Finances and Expenditure'. I was keen to get agreement on a 4:1 ratio split between government spending on public services and spending on tax reductions. I knew that was absolutely not part of the Fine Gael conservative agenda (their document stated forcefully 2:1) but I argued with great fervour about the importance of progressive values. I talked about my work in communities of exceptional disadvantage and why we needed a social economy model to guide Irish public income and investment. Intransigence arising from both sides clouded the air. I felt as if I was probably failing.

The next day we had to agree on this part of the document. We were all sitting around the big tables on the third floor of Government Buildings. The Sycamore Room was the location, with its high ceilings, lush carpets, long windows. I must admit to feeling very important every time I entered it. I was seated opposite several Fine Gael politicians, including the man who would eventually become minister for public expenditure and reform, then finance, and much later on, president of the Eurogroup. The distance between us felt enormous.

At one stage Paschal Donohoe looked straight at me and exclaimed, with a sense of impatience and distress, 'But you don't understand! You think that we don't care about the poor! We want to invest more money in business and the economy so that we can use the income from increased tax revenues to pay for the needy' (or something to that effect).

I retorted, 'I hear that you care. I am not disputing that. But the best way to care, in my view, is to make a greater initial investment in those living in disadvantaged conditions, so that they are empowered *to help create the wealth*, rather than need more of your wealth to be redistributed in ways you see fit.'

If a pin had dropped . . . The meeting's chair said, 'Let's take a break.'

The next morning, Fine Gael advisors talked me through a new draft of the chapter, now entitled 'Towards a Social Economy'. That title remains in the published document to this day. Words matter when negotiating a programme for government. New words were also included: 'economic repair must be complemented by social repair'. The amended document outlined a commitment to spend a significant sum of additional money to deliver public services in 'child development and care'. A nascent sense of the centrality of care for a productive economy and inclusive society – in a way that ensured gender equity – was now a commitment. The ratio of 2:1, however, remained. I knew this was as much as I was going to get. The mindset was shifting, though, I believed. As it happened, the next Irish budget after the government was finally formed – Budget 2017 – delivered a package of spending that 'favoured expenditure increase over revenue reductions by over three to one' ('Statement of the Minister for Finance, Michael Noonan, TD, 11 October 2016'). I was part of the cabinet that agreed on this ratio.

My other prime 'red-line' issue was reproductive freedom and healthcare for all women, inclusive of access to abortion. Before the 2016 general election, Enda Kenny promised a 'citizens' convention', if elected taoiseach, to address the divisive issue of the eighth amendment to the Irish constitution, which gives equal status to the rights of the mother and the unborn.

*

When the original draft discussion document for negotiations to form a government lands on my desk, it is entitled 'Building a Strong Economy for a Decent Society'. On page 120, it reads:

B) Constitutional Reform
We propose that a number of referendums be held . . .

[followed by a list of four]

We will *look to establish* a Citizens' Assembly, without participation by politicians, and with a mandate to look at a limited number of key issues over an extended time period . . . we will ask the Citizens' Assembly to make recommendations to the Dáil on further constitutional changes, including on the Eighth Amendment [emphasis mine].

Am I the only one who notices the future conditional form of the language, not the declarative? The words mean that the establishment of a citizens' assembly, inclusive of consideration of the eighth amendment, *might be possible* for the future. They do not mean that it is our absolute intention to establish one in the future. I circle the three words in the text. I need them changed. I need it to be absolutely clear that this is what we *will* do when a government is formed.

A citizens' assembly is a deliberative form of democracy. A randomly selected group of citizens deliberate on important public questions, with access to experts in the process. Conclusions and recommendations are offered to government and parliamentarians, usually through a form of voting. The constitutional convention on marriage equality was an earlier experiment in this for Ireland. As a political tool, it demonstrated enormous value (and not just because of the result). It helped us, as a society, to push through a long-standing contested issue. Of equal importance, I think, is that it provided us with an extension of democracy, another way for the people's voice to influence the direction of law and policy. The power of an organised voice of the people, in my view, helps to ensure greater accountability from elected representatives. I want to see the experiment codified into an assembly and to take on an even bigger challenge.

*

Another day in that beautiful room in Government Buildings begins. And this time, I sit opposite some of the rural

Independents. When we get to page 120 of the text, I raise my hand. There are only 122 pages to the document, so all of us are getting very tired, even though it's just the beginning of the day.

I decide to be brief. 'Chair, my understanding of Enda Kenny's previous commitment on these matters is that he *will* establish a citizens' assembly to consider the eighth amendment. May I request, then, that the language on page 120 under the "B" section be changed to represent this promise more clearly?'

That's it, but I don't get away with a brief discussion. Some of the rural Independents shoot up their hands immediately and tell us all how they are absolutely not in favour of repealing the eighth amendment. An argument ensues, for a long time, with no genuine movement one way or the other. Its tenor and content are familiar.

'Deputies,' I say with steel in my voice, 'we have been having these kinds of debates in the country ever since 1983 when the eighth amendment was inserted into the constitution.' My voice raises. 'No one's going to *win* here. It's *not* the time and place to get into these arguments.' I am as fired up as they are. Not my best moment and I regret letting my composure slip. I manage to pull myself together, though, and say, 'It is not the issue we need to resolve in the government programme. All we need to do is to agree that we will ask the citizens to consider it.' I finish by stating with as much respect as I can muster, and without pounding my fist on the table as much as I'd like to, 'I cannot, will not, sign up to a programme that does not include this agreement, this promise.'

I don't know what happened in the backrooms after that.

But I do know that the text was changed. The final published 'Programme for a Partnership Government' reads:

> We will establish a Citizens' Assembly, within six
> months . . .

> We will ask the Citizens' Assembly to make
> recommendations to the Dáil on further constitutional
> changes, including on the Eighth Amendment.

On 10 March 2016 the first vote for taoiseach takes place in the Dáil and no one is elected. Negotiations continue. The second vote takes place on 6 April. Again no one is elected. Anxiety in the country builds. We are still negotiating.

The public is waiting. I review where things are at. I talk to Ann Louise. I talk to my team. I talk to myself. I can see that we are moving towards voting Enda Kenny in as taoiseach. *Too slowly*, though. I believe it will happen eventually. So does everyone else. But seven weeks is enough. I make my decision to tell him. My people ring his people and a meeting is set up. On the morning of 14 April I pass the majestic fountain in front of Government Buildings – it always lifts my spirit – and walk up the marble steps. That night, deputies are to vote for a taoiseach for the third time. I walk the long corridor towards what I think is Enda's office. Very Irish and very gorgeous pieces of art hang on the walls. I pause to look at one or two, because I love art, and because I am nervous. Stillness filling this powerful physical space is abruptly interrupted when Andrew McDowell pops out from nowhere to greet me. He brings me to a room I think is his, and asks me to wait.

After a few minutes, Enda walks in and sits at the small table where I am seated. I tell him that I have decided to cast my vote for him. He is genuinely over the moon. No Independent (apart from Michael Lowry, a former Fine Gael minister) has yet promised their vote. I go through a few reasons for my decision – I am hardly even listening to *myself*, let alone Enda listening to my rationale. The room is electric, joyous. But I have one more communication I want to offer to him in this moment. 'Enda,' I say, 'I have a poem for you. From one of my favourite living Irish poets, Brendan Kennelly.' I read him some of the lines.

Yes

I love the word
And hear its long struggle with no
Even in the bird's throat, and budging crocus.
Some winter's night
I see it flood the faces
Of my friends, ripen their laughter
And plant early flowers in
Their conversation.

You will understand when I say
It is for me a morning word . . .

I am always beginning to appreciate
The agony from which it is born.

Clues from here and there
Suggest such agony is hard to bear
But is the shaping God
of the word that we
Sometimes hear, and struggle to be.

Quietly I fold the paper that I have written the poem on, and I give it to him. A wide yet pensive smile fills his face. He stands, shakes my hand. Asks Andrew to come back in . . . and then dashes off.

Andrew escorts me down the same hallway, this time headed in the direction of Leinster House. He, too, is smiling. We share no words. We arrive at the end of the hallway and he places his magic pass on the fob receiver of the door to the ministerial corridor. We nod to say goodbye, and I slip past him and head towards Leinster House 2000, a building on the opposite side of the Dáil.

Denis Naughton has texted to say that he wants to meet me. I look around and see him in the lobby. 'Katherine, some of the rural Independents called a meeting this morning of all the Independents who are negotiating with Fine Gael. I went, looked around and saw you were not there. I asked if you had been invited. They said no. I tried to stall the meeting so that you could attend but that didn't work. The group came to a consensus that they would *not* vote for Enda tonight.'

I am very taken aback. 'Thank you for telling me, Denis. I cannot believe I was not invited. Well, I have made my own decision, nevertheless.'

I say no more. We part.

Later that night as I enter the Dáil chamber and descend its steps (made for men's shoes, not for the heels of women's shoes), Deputy Michael Healy Rae (one of the rural Independents) sprints up to me to apologise that I was not invited to the meeting. He doesn't know how it happened, but, anyhow, they had all decided not to vote for Enda that evening and asked if I would conform.

'Thank you for the apology, Michael. You will see my decision at the time of the vote,' I respond.

A few minutes later, it begins. Pressing a 'tá' or 'níl' button at your designated seat is the usual way to indicate your choice. Once you press, your selection flashes up on a screen behind the Ceann Comhairle (chair), so all can see who it is and your decision. Tonight, however, we are instructed to use the 'walk through' procedure. The vote is called, and deputies ascend the stairs to turn left for 'tá' and right for 'níl'. I ascend, not being noticed much, and I turn left. Several of the journalists are a bit stunned as they look on from their sacred spot above the Ceann Comhairle. The news goes out that I have just voted for Enda Kenny. Michael Lowry, Independent and former Fine Gael minister, also votes for Enda (and did so the week before). No other Independents do. Enda still needs a few more votes. He is not elected, for the third time.

A fierce national drama continues to play out. President Higgins, reflecting the nation's impatience, issues a warning to the major party leaders on 19 April. He says that if they are unable to reach an agreement, he is 'very, very well aware' of Article 13 of the constitution which gives him the 'absolute power' to decide whether the Dáil should be dissolved if the taoiseach tells him a government cannot be formed. No one wants to go back to the country. Too much time has passed without a government and there is no guarantee that the results would be much different. So, on 29 April, Enda Kenny and Micheál Martin agree on a Fine Gael-led minority government, paving the way for Fianna Fáil members to abstain from voting at the next sitting. On 6 May, the fourth and final vote takes place. Enda Kenny acquires seven additional Independent votes and he is crowned taoiseach, for the second time.

Enda Kenny's cabinet includes three Independents as senior government ministers: Denis Naughton as minister for communications, climate action and the environment, Shane Ross as minister for transport, tourism and sport, and I am appointed minister for children and youth affairs. I become the first Independent public representative, and newly elected TD, in Ireland's history to become a minister. I am the second American citizen to take a seat in the Irish Dáil. Éamon de Valera held the honour ahead of me, both of us being dual citizens. I certainly did not anticipate this distinction, nor a ministerial position upon winning my seat. I felt elated; Ann Louise was ecstatic. Never had I had so much responsibility, nor so much influence to enact change.

The next week I stand to speak from a minister's seat in the Dáil – usually one or two rows up from the floor to the left of the Ceann Comhairle as he or she faces the members. I am responding to the opposition's commentary on my portfolio as minister for children. First I look up to the public gallery and locate Ann Louise. She has waited a long time to hear me speak. She is holding her head, but she is there. Most of what I know about public speaking comes from watching her over the years.

Scribbled notes form the basis of my remarks.

I want to begin with some optimism and hope for the Irish people. I have an ethical obligation to do so as the new minister for children, so that we can, in the words of our Sinn Féin colleague Deputy Martin Kenny, 'allow our children to raise our grandchildren'.

Or so that we can find, in the words of Deputy Micheál Martin, 'a new direction' for the way of conducting our country's business, or so that all our children can grow up in a country that supports, in the words of our taoiseach, their 'psychological and emotional well-being' as he has pledged.

One of our collective tasks is to end child poverty. Several colleagues have identified and spoken about this as a critical task for us all to engage in. If the programme for government in its current form does not have enough on that – only the seeds of it perhaps – I ask them to work with me and other colleagues to do that once and for all. I know a little about attempting to end child poverty. It comes from the ideology that I carry. For want of a better word, I use the word 'progressive' too. Some of the people who have informed that thinking may be political theorists such as Jürgen Habermas or radical educators such as Paulo Freire.

It has also been informed by the practice of my work as a community educator in Jobstown, west Tallaght and the wider Tallaght area. There, my spouse, Ann Louise,

who is still with us in the visitors' gallery, and I set up
one of the first crèches in Jobstown community centre
thirty years ago. We invited twelve women from the
Jobstown community to come to our home. That is where
we started our educational project. We invited them to
take the brave step to get back on to the learning path
so that eventually they would either become leaders in
their own communities or get jobs. If the jobs were not
good for them, eventually their children would get good
jobs, because their children were well-educated. This is a
little of the practice and experience that I pledge to bring
to bear on the leadership of my new ministry.

This is just one of the many collective tasks we must
engage in so that we, in 2016, can garner all our efforts,
our imagination and our skilful use of our resources to
cherish all of the children of the nation equally and
provide every child with 'an equal start' in life. This is
what I called a set of parental, preventative and early
intervention supports that should be delivered in one
place for the child and his or her parents.

I, therefore, begin with that hope and identification of a
couple of key collective tasks. However, how will we be
effective in the delivery of these and other collective
tasks? Several colleagues have referred to the very
difficult birth of this minority-led government. I agree. It is
not perfect. It was far too slow . . . It is true that we must
get better at this. It is true that more trust needs to be
built. It is equally true that constructive opposition, radical
left opposition, left opposition, Sinn Féin opposition,
Labour opposition, Green Party opposition, Social

Democrats opposition, indeed, all this opposition, is
required to stop us when we are not doing what is
required to cherish all our children equally or to transform
opposition towards creative proposals that all of us would
welcome for our people.

How is it that we will be effective? Each one of us has
to ask that question. I imagine other deputies have done
so, as have I. How will we use our power? I define power
as the ability to get things done. How will deputies use
their power in opposition? I respect their choice, whether
party or non-party. The same applies to party, non-party
and Independent deputies in government. Clearly, I have
made my choice. I have discerned, after much reflection,
that I will attempt to get things done over here rather
than over there. ['Over there' refers to where members of
the opposition sit; 'over here' refers to seats for members
of the government.] I believe I bring to the table my
progressive approach, my practice and experience with
the people of Tallaght, along with my practice and
experience as a feminist, educator, former chief executive
of the National Women's Council, human rights advocate
and marriage equality leader.

Therefore, I know what people power is like and what
it means to mobilise the people to get things done and to
bring about effective change. Moreover, I know how long
it takes to do that. Some of this was brought into this
programme for government document. It is not perfect or
complete. It is simply a guide for the action plans,
strategies and budgets that we will and must create
together.

I wonder now what my fellow TDs thought. It sounds somewhat naïve, many years later. I had so much to learn. I meant every word, though, and tried to be true to the ethos of collaboration with all sides of the house. I endeavoured to open a corridor for voices from outside too, including them in private and public deliberations. Ann Louise smiled softly after I sat down that night. It was enough for me then.

I spent the next two months learning the content and political priorities of my ministerial portfolio, getting to know my departmental staff (headed by Fergal Lynch as secretary general). Fergal had started in the department about eighteen months before me. I liked him immediately. I trusted his guidance always, but especially in the first year when I had so much to learn about being a minister. We would have our disagreements later in my term, though not often. I appreciated his careful leadership, systematic approach to policy and warm heart. In July I decided to work from home for a couple of the summer weeks. I wanted the quiet and warmth of The Shanty to surround me as I prepared for one of the biggest challenges the cabinet would face during my term: how to steer the process of asking the people to reconsider the eighth amendment to the Irish constitution.

I come into our kitchen one morning in mid-July. The day before, the government had moved a resolution to hold the citizens' assembly on abortion. Ann Louise is preparing our breakfast. 'Katie, I want a Repeal sweatshirt too!' she says. Mine has arrived. A few weeks earlier, while surfing the Net, I had come across a new website selling sweatshirts designed by Anna Cosgrave, the young human rights and abortion activist. The black jumper has six white capitalised letters on its front – REPEAL. I thought it was gorgeous and ordered one straight away. I don't know why I didn't walk down to the other part of the house and ask Ann Louise if I should order two. No worries, I'll order another, now that I know she wants one. By the time I go to the website again, the stock has vanished, and a message says, 'Come back when we have more inventory.' Later there are media reports that the jumper has sold out in one day.

'Something's going on,' I say to Ann Louise. 'The undercurrent of a long, long movement is making waves. It is the young. They are taking the torch.' That afternoon I tweet 'Women are moral agents.' Several people tweet back, 'What does that mean?' My response: 'Women hold the capacity to make ethical decisions.' I tweet another message: 'Our laws must allow women, indeed support women, to exercise this.'

I continue to make preparations for 25 November 2016 when the citizens' assembly will sit for the first time. Our government programme had promised that we would establish it within six months. And this we do. I flesh out some of my arguments on a type of notebook that Ann Louise always used for speeches, ever since her studies for a master's degree in Paris, long before we met.

I feel her by my side when I jot down:

Women are embodied moral agents, not simply disinterested and detached observers. Women's knowing through their bodies is a prime source for ethical decision-making. It is not the only source but it is indeed the prime source.

No culture has yet been found in which conscience is not recognised as a fact, and it has always been viewed as integral to ethics — a functional guide for action: a capacity for ethical evaluation. But it is not enough to invoke 'conscience' simply because one feels strongly about something or spontaneously judges that a certain action is the morally correct one. Sincerity alone is not sufficient.

The conscience which most fully carries moral authority and to which one can appeal is the conscience which is continually self-critical, aware of the dangers of ignorance, bias, prejudice, selfishness, arrogance and self-sufficiency.

Pregnant women have such a capacity and can and do exercise this capacity in the process of human reproduction.

Pregnant women are 'embodied moral agents' — their life circumstances, social and economic conditions, as well as physical and mental health, are key sources for an ethical, that is, a good decision. Why won't our laws allow for this now?

There is great irony, I believe, in politicians arguing that they must follow <u>their</u> conscience in legislating (which, by the way, I agree with) but they want law that prohibits a pregnant woman to follow <u>her</u> conscience.

In August 2016, my human rights legal advisor, Professor Fiona de Londras, and I begin to discuss what should happen *after* the citizens' assembly had concluded its work. Fiona is another generous powerhouse, exceedingly bright, intellectually speedy and has a wry sense of humour. She is always looking around the next corner. We often do it together. How do we move from a citizens' assembly to a referendum if the citizens recommend doing so? And what is the best wording to put to the people in that referendum? We examine this at length, analysing documents and having long telephone conversations *three* months *before* the assembly sits for the first time.

We presume, because we feel that the hand of history is finally with us, and because I always 'image the possible', as Ann Louise has taught me to do, that the assembly will recommend a referendum and will itself be in favour of repeal. So while we thought that the citizens' assembly would come down on our side in general, we didn't expect it to so forcefully recognise that limited change wouldn't do. It enables us to start talking about wholesale constitutional and legislative change. The focus of our considerations at this stage, though, is on the nature, membership and terms of reference of the Oireachtas committee that will receive the citizens' assembly recommendations. Will it be the already constituted health committee? Or will it be a special committee? We develop arguments that it should be a committee that is solely dedicated to this issue – and I put this forward informally. It would ensure a tight focus for experts to present evidence and committee members to debate and negotiate among themselves, and it would help to increase public awareness through media coverage. The job would be done as quickly as possible, because no other issues would come before the special committee bar citizens' recommendations.

We expect that the citizens will be able to deliver their report to the house of the Oireachtas sometime in June 2017. By the time this happens, Leo Varadkar has been elected taoiseach, and he chooses to establish a special Oireachtas committee to receive the report. Its formal work commences in September, so we weren't too far off.

*

Once September arrives, I need to get to work on the upcoming budget for the children's department, my first. Increasing investment in childcare will be central to my efforts. An enormous responsibility for someone with little experience. While I feel a certain amount of intimidation, passion for the work increases my confidence in squeezing as much juice out of a tight budget as possible. I have worked for years in the field of children's early learning and care. Determined attempts to collaborate with the sector on public policies for childcare marks my ministerial time, with highs and lows from start to finish. The genuine affirmation and anticipation of 'one of their own' becoming minister feels a light burden to carry in the beginning. Early on, the Children's Rights Alliance invites me to open their AGM. Tom Costello, with whom I had worked closely during the years of Atlantic Philanthropies, investments in Ireland, chairs the opening session, and Tanya Ward, the Alliance's chief executive and my former comrade in human rights work, welcomes me to the podium. I speak, with an open and expectant heart. The meeting receives it, with affection and joy. Tom tears up. All stand. Yes, it feels like joy. While we grasp the vast challenges ahead, our collective hope diminishes the heaviness of our past toil.

My technical experience in both its theory and practice supplies no background, however, in the bargaining skills required to lift the profile and importance of childcare and early learning in our government work. While some understanding exists around the cabinet table, it is a 'women and children's issue', thus way down the totem pole. The department was assigned a trifling budget of €260 million for childcare when I took over. We had 331,500 children aged 0–4 in 2016, so that budgetary sum was not going to spread too far!

How can I change this? The childcare sector itself is becoming more savvy. I am determined to find ways for us to work together. But I also suspect that a strengthening of their collective voice may not always be to my personal advantage. I am a member of the government, often perceived in the past as the enemy. I might become the target in their meetings and in the media. I begin, slowly, to fold a shield around myself.

Nevertheless, I work with my political team to communicate in ways that invite collaboration from them to arm me for the money fight. I have chosen Patricia Ryan as my policy advisor and Jerry O'Connor as my communications advisor. Both came with top-class experience. Patricia is incredibly astute on policy, even in its most technical detail. Her solutions to policy problems are second to none. Her kindness and interest in people, an exceptional gift in politics, earns the respect of all. Jerry is a master at any kind of media, and I love watching him type away at my next speech. He prepares me for media engagements, with role plays and lengthy Q&As. If I go wrong, it is my fault. My team calls him the 'magic man'. We all have so much fun together. One day early in my ministry, a Fianna Fáil TD stops me at the bottom of the Dáil stairway. He leans over to congratulate me – on the team I had chosen! He is so right.

I am new to the 'game' of politics, however. My civil servants want to do the initial budget negotiations. I look at Dermot Ryan, a clever and careful assistant secretary general, and Fergal Lynch and say, 'I'd like to give it a try first.' Surprised – yet smiling, genuinely – Dermot responds, 'Okay, minister, why don't you give it a go? We are here to help you, if you need us.' And they are. And the meetings and notes are extensive, as are my questions to them. They get used to the fact that I read the detail.

The 2017 budget negotiations intensify. I am Independent, not a member of the minister for public expenditure's political party. Media coverage of my efforts amplifies the fact that all sides in politics accept that the current system of childcare must change. The public wind is with me.

I sit down with Paschal Donohoe, minister for public expenditure, twice, in his grand office in the Department of Finance. While I wait for him to arrive, I glance at his bookshelves (a habit of academics) and notice that many of his economics books are written by authors I have read. I find this surprising. I thought he was a conservative, though there are a few of those authors too. I feel a little more confident to be persistent in my negotiations. At the end of the second meeting, he does increase his offer, specifically for the childcare and early learning element of it, but I think *that is still not enough*. There is no way that what's on the table is going to signal a new direction in childcare, and certainly not a path towards appropriately valuing the workforce and professionalising the sector. *This is not what I signed up for*, I believe. It is the first time, as a minister, I feel my Independent status being put to the test.

I take some additional advice on budget talks. Then, I hand-write a note to Paschal saying I need 'x' amount, or I will offer my resignation. Fear, turning to panic, builds in my body. I leave my Mespil Road office and go for a short walk along the Grand Canal. I breathe and breathe again. I sit alongside Patrick Kavanagh on the bronze bench, sculpted by John Coll as part of Dublin's 1991 European City of Culture celebrations. I am calmed, and begin to feel the freedom that I ought to feel as an Independent. If I ever lose this, I think, I know it will mark a loss of my integrity and I will need to stop practising politics.

Once I feel steadier, I phone Eugene O'Sullivan and tell him we are going back to the Department of Finance. Eugene – a great Kerry man, impeccable ministerial driver and former courageous garda – collects me along Mespil Road, drives swiftly and safely for the next five minutes, and pulls up outside the finance offices. I go through the glass entrance doors, hand my note to the person at reception, and leave. We drive back to my department and wait. My advisor receives a phone call within the hour. Another meeting is scheduled, just between the minister and myself. While I do not get the full 'x' amount, it is much closer to a meaningful shift in direction. We shake hands.

The next morning the cabinet budget meeting is held (where all ministers are told what the full budget will be, as well as their own share). I walk into the room as the others gather and Enda Kenny stops me as I pass by him. He declares with a twinkle, 'You did the best of all the ministers!'

Later that day childcare is front-page news – in a positive way. It is a good day but I know that it will not always be like this. In my four years of serving as minister, I am able to increase the childcare budget by 145 per cent, from €260 million to €638 million. The highest increase by far, though, is in my first year, after the deal with Paschal.

By mid-October, post-budget, I turn my attention to repealing the constitutional ban on abortion, and consider the question *What type of constitutional change should we seek?* Fiona de Londras drafts an extensive human rights analysis of six options; for example, to remove the eighth amendment without replacement, or to remove the eighth amendment and replace it with an abortion-related provision. The best option, I decide, is this: *Remove the eighth amendment with a promise to introduce legislation, a draft of which is available in advance.* While some 'left' members of the opposition argue that we need a clean repeal, I believe that we need to advocate for repeal and offer the people some kind of amendment to replace Article 40.3.3, which states that the Oireachtas has the power to determine laws related to termination. And that it is part of the government's responsibility to put out to the people an example of the type of law that regulates the termination of pregnancies, so that the people know how the state will protect in new ways the rights of the pregnant person.

This is all background work by an outsider on the inside, remaining connected to human rights expertise to keep things moving in the right direction. This is what I am attempting to do. While I go about this, an enormous civil rights movement roars past on the outside. Warrior women and men, young and old, rich and poor, those with homes, those without, those with children, those without, all our races and ethnicities represented, led by some of the most strategic feminists of the era.

*

In mid-January 2017 my private secretary, Lisa Hughes, came into my office one morning, concerned about a phone call she had just taken. The office of the minister for health had phoned her, requesting that she contact Mrs Lorraine McCabe. Mrs McCabe, wife of the garda whistleblower Maurice, had phoned the Department of Health to request a meeting with the minister about a very disturbing matter related to her husband and Tusla (the Child and Family Agency). Lisa phoned Mrs McCabe, confirmed that the matter was related to our department because I am the minister with responsibility for Tusla, and set up a meeting with Maurice and Lorraine McCabe for the following Wednesday, 25 January. I thanked her for doing so and asked her to contact Patricia, my advisor, for us to begin to prepare for the meeting. A very slight foreboding began to rise in me, though I had confidence in my political team and department to resolve any difficulty.

*

On 24 January I phoned Frances Fitzgerald, out of courtesy because she was the minister for justice, to let her know that I would be meeting the McCabes. That same day my advisor,

Patricia Ryan, met with an advisor from the taoiseach's office to tell him about my upcoming appointment. Given the history of Maurice McCabe's engagement with the state, we believed that it was important for both Enda and Frances to be informed. On 25 January I met Maurice and Lorraine McCabe in my departmental office. Patricia Ryan and Michele Clarke were at the meeting. Maurice was holding a bulky file of papers from Tusla. Lorraine was clearly distressed. Maurice, with the heavy history of being a prime whistleblower in 2014 on corruption within An Garda Síochána, described his present discovery that a counsellor – an agency worker, not a direct employee of either the Health Service Executive or Tusla – had 'mistakenly copied and pasted' allegations of the rape of a child by digital and anal penetration into a file that Tusla had created on him in 2014. This file, containing the false allegation of child abuse, Tusla subsequently sent to the gardaí, without Maurice's knowledge. Furthermore, the names of four of his five children were listed in the file. Maurice then recounted how his papers indicated that Tusla admitted the 'clerical error' of what they had done in 2014, but that he first heard of these allegations only in 2016. Lorraine expressed how they both felt devastated about these revelations, especially their deep concern about the names of their children being placed in Tusla files.

I was so shocked about what the McCabes were telling me, I could not respond immediately. Then I expressed my utmost concern for what they had experienced over the past years, and more particularly since they had received Maurice's record from Tusla. Those words, however, felt so inadequate.

I was deeply conscious of all they had been through. I promised them an urgent report from Tusla, indicating that I would share the findings with them as soon as possible. After everyone left the room, all I could think of was that I was determined not to cause them any additional hurt. I knew that I was in uncharted territory politically, and we had to be as careful as we could to try to do the right things without adding to the couple's burden.

The following Tuesday Frances Fitzgerald brought a memorandum to cabinet recommending the establishment of a commission of inquiry to investigate an alleged smear campaign by senior gardaí against Maurice McCabe at the time of his whistleblowing. I went to the cabinet room early that day, looking to have a word with the taoiseach before cabinet to tell him about my meeting with Maurice and Lorraine. I indicated that we had discussed false allegations of sexual abuse made against Maurice to Tusla. Enda turned to me and said, 'Katherine, this will be covered by the commission of inquiry that we will be discussing this morning.' I said no more about it, not even during the cabinet's discussion of the terms of reference to establish a commission of inquiry. A trend of leaking information from cabinet had been developing over the past couple of months. The information that the McCabes had shared with me was not in the public domain at the time. I did not want to risk it getting there. I also believed that it would have been inappropriate for me to brief cabinet on confidential, highly sensitive and personal information, which one could reasonably assume was the subject of a protected disclosure (a formal complaint about the belief of a wrongdoing) that was leading to the establishment of the commission. I had spoken with the taoiseach and trusted what he had told me: the Tusla file on false allegations would be included in the inquiry's work.

Later that afternoon I was thinking about my youngest brother, Mark, who is an exquisite ballet costume designer. 'Mr Z' they call him. My parents had always attended the opening night of any ballet he had costumed. Since their passing, one of Mark's siblings tried to be there for him. A big opening night was approaching soon and I decided it was my turn to be 'our family's ambassador'. *Looks like it's going to be a quiet time*, I thought to myself, and I can fly out on Thursday and return on the Monday. On Fridays the Dáil is not in session, so I should be clear to leave. I asked Paudie Sheehan, my other driver, to bring me to the airport. Paudie is also a former garda and a great gentleman. He holds confidences impeccably. Little did I know that my first grave political crisis was about to explode. I would be thousands of miles away from Ireland. Ann Louise would have travelled to Paris with her niece Hilda. It would be a final visit to her beloved city, unbeknownst to both of us at the time.

*

On Thursday I took a flight to America to attend the opening of my brother's ballet. During my short lay-over in Chicago, I received urgent texts from my advisors about a *Prime Time* broadcast. I opened my laptop, clicked on RTÉ Player and watched the latter half of the show. All the information I had received from the McCabes was now in the public domain. I was aghast. Early on Friday morning

I spoke with Patricia and Jerry. The media wanted to talk to me. We agreed that they would put out a press release of my initial response, and then I could take further engagements on my return on Monday. Part of that release said that I had informed relevant government colleagues about my meeting with the McCabes. My department was subsequently flooded with questions from the media. Why hadn't Tusla been mentioned, then, in the terms of reference for the commission of inquiry? Surely it would be a big part of the work.

I barely managed to see the ballet that evening. I was non-stop on the phone talking to my advisors, the taoiseach's advisors, the minister for justice and my departmental officials. The taoiseach was denying that I had given him details about my meeting with the McCabes. That was wrong. I did give him details. And various media had reported that many of my ministerial colleagues (no names were cited) were furious with me because I had not spoken up in cabinet. The Independent Alliance did not accuse me in public of anything but said they wanted an urgent meeting with me. I was wrecked. I was not sure how this was going to go. Perhaps I should have spoken up at cabinet. I learned from that. But how did the crisis get so intense? I had been a minister for only seven months. I felt everything was slipping away, and I wasn't really sure why.

When I arrived back on the Monday, I feared being mobbed at the airport. Eugene was there, ready to defend me, but no media in sight. He whisked me away to the department, where the media was stationed outside the main entrance. We went in the back. I huddled with my advisors.

I would have to meet the press. We had to get our messages straight. I rehearsed as much as I could, trying to remain calm. Eugene drove myself, Patricia and Jerry to Leinster House. I entered on the Merrion Street side, walked through the back door to the front door to the plinth. Every media woman and man must have been there. Multiple cameras and microphones. *How would Zappone get out of this one? She's really under the bus now!* was in the air. Jerry calmed everyone down and said I would make a statement. Which I did. Later, one of the journalists wrote that I had 'danced like a boxer'. (I considered that a compliment. My dad was a boxer.) I told them that I had spoken with the taoiseach about my McCabe meeting before cabinet. At that stage, the taoiseach was denying this. And, on weekend radio, he had said that I met him *before* the McCabe meeting and that he had advised me to take a good note of it. That never happened.

I left the plinth and went quickly to my ministerial office in Leinster House. My private secretary phoned the taoiseach's office to ask for an urgent meeting, which was granted. I went to the taoiseach's suite and waited. We had to discuss this on our own. When he was ready, I went into his office, sat down and said, 'Enda, we did *not* meet before my meeting with the McCabes. That never happened.'

He paused, looked me straight in the eye, then slapped his hand against his forehead and said, 'You are right. That did not happen. I am so sorry for not remembering properly.'

'Thank you for your honesty, Enda,' I said.

The drama did not end there. The next day, Enda admitted in the Dáil that his initial statements were not correct. Opposition members interrogated the 'who said what to whom and when' sequence, calling out at times what appeared to be some further contradictory statements from the taoiseach. I gave my statement and answered their questions. Several members of the opposition affirmed my contribution. The political and journalistic attack began to shift from me to the taoiseach. Though the government survived a motion of no-confidence the next day, several journalists started to nail Enda's coffin. *Fateful events that led to the fatal undermining of the Taoiseach and shredded his authority* (Pat Leahy, *The Irish Times*). *Enda the Road: Nine Days that Toppled a Taoiseach* (Gavan Reilly, 2019). I am told that some of the Blueshirts blamed me for the taoiseach's resignation six months later. And that some still do, asserting that I, and my advisors, acted with insubordination throughout the crisis.

I didn't see it that way. I don't think that Enda Kenny did either.

CHAPTER 7

Two Clouds Descend

As minister for children, one of my responsibilities was oversight of the mother and baby homes commission of investigation. It had been established in 2015 by the previous government to investigate eighteen institutions throughout the country, many run by nuns and other members of the Catholic Church, others the responsibility of local authorities, Protestant leaders or institutions of the state for almost eighty years. The last home closed as recently as 1998. These were institutions where women, unmarried and pregnant, were sent by family members, priests, state authorities and others to deliver their babies. Some of them acted as adoption agencies. The commission worked independently of government, though it was required to provide periodic reports to myself as minister.

On 21 February 2017 I was called to an urgent meeting. In a small room just off the ministerial corridor in Leinster House I met with Judge Yvonne Murphy, chair of the commission, Professor Mary Daly, a member of the commission, Ms Ita Mangan, director of the commission and Dr Marie Cassidy, the chief state pathologist. They came to inform me that their excavations on land adjacent to the location of the Tuam, County Galway mother and baby home had revealed significant quantities of juvenile remains, individuals with age-at-death ranges from approximately thirty-five foetal weeks to two–three years. Some were discovered, as the commission noted later, in 'a separate long structure . . . appearing to be related to the treatment/containment of sewage'. Catherine Corless, a local Galway historian whose advocacy on behalf of 796 children whom she believed had been buried there, had brought us to that moment. The women showed me photographs of some of the remains.

I could not utter a word. I was dumbfounded. It felt impossible to take in the gargantuan scope of the horror contained in the photos. The violence, disrespect, unfathomable silence and hiddenness of lives just beginning. I knew this would be the start of a long journey, perhaps of a battle, to get government agreement for justice for these children. It would take a considerable time, so something should be done as soon as possible. I needed to process this though and, honestly, I cannot remember what happened during the rest of my workday. I postponed a couple of evening meetings to get home as soon as I could to talk with Ann Louise.

She knew something was terribly wrong as soon as I entered The Shanty. She could feel my distress and placed her hand on my cheek. 'Katherine, what is wrong? What could have you this upset? Has someone died?'

'I have seen photos of the children's remains' is the first thing I uttered.

'Oh no. Oh no,' responded the greatest lover of children I have ever known. And we both just held each other and wept.

Ann Louise agreed later that evening that I should go to the children's burial site first thing in the morning. I did not want any public attention, or any press. If I rose early enough, Eugene and I could make it to Tuam before dawn.

The next morning we woke at 4 a.m. to the dark. I had forgotten to set the correct timing for the furnace to fire up, so it was exceedingly cold. Brittas was always a couple of degrees cooler than central Dublin. I dressed quickly, started a fire in our small wood-burning stove and sat down in the chair just across from the bed's end. As she sat up to look at me, Ann Louise said, 'Take some snowdrops from the garden. And go to my desk, third drawer down on the left-hand side. I have a small bottle of holy water from a long-time-ago trip to Lourdes.'

I felt I had to do something. To be present for the deceased children *themselves* and to acknowledge that this was a terrible wrong done to each of them. I knew that a political response of new plans, policies, perhaps even law would be required, but I knew that this would not be enough. I wanted to honour and respect these babies who had been discarded without a funeral or a prayer, and without even their own graves.

When Eugene and I arrived at the Tuam site approximately three hours later, I was surprised and dismayed to see fences erected to barricade the memorial garden on the grounds. They hadn't been there on my previous visits. I had written some words in the car on the way, and I wanted to get close to where I imagined the remains to be. Eugene offered to help me stand on top of a stone wall, so that I could see over the fence, toss the snowdrops and the holy water over, and recite my words. Up I went. I spoke as the dawn broke.

A Burial Ritual

AFFIRMATION AND MAKING VISIBLE
As the minister for children of the Irish government,
I come to acknowledge and affirm your short life.
I come to acknowledge now, what should have been
    yours long ago,
Recognition that you are *imago Dei*.

APOLOGY AND BEREAVEMENT
As the minister for children of the Irish government,
I come to offer you an apology
For your hiddenness
For your silenced life
For the terrible manner in which you were buried.
Your families and the Irish people are bereaved,
Because you did exist.

167

BLESSING

As the minister for children of the Irish government,
I come to bless you, to acknowledge the goodness of
    your life.
I come to bless the ground where you have been
    buried.
I come to bless the memory of your mothers.
    Amen.

On 28 February I informed my government colleagues of the Tuam findings. I had already spoken with the taoiseach to inform him, and my departmental officials had worked with me day and night to prepare the communication of this information. I spontaneously decided to tell them about my early-morning visit. I concluded with the words I had read over the children's burial ground. I just felt it was the right thing to do. For most, it felt like poetry. Speaking in the Dáil six years later, Taoiseach Varadkar stated that it was this moment that 'convinced' the government to act on the mother and baby homes.

It was such a solemn moment, as each member took in the gravity of the discovery. We all knew that this news would rock the nation. It would bring a dark, dark part of our past out into the light of truth, though only a partial truth. Who were the children? Who had buried them there? Why did they do it? How can we, how *should* we respond? The news to my colleagues, once they had digested its meaning, sparked quite a reaction, and along with my officials I knew a significant amount of work lay ahead of us. We had to figure out how to communicate the news to the rest of Ireland, and indeed to the rest of the world. But the last thing we needed was for this news to go out haphazardly to journalists. I was adamant that we must let survivors and family members of the mother and baby homes know *first*, and that we must have some idea of what response we would take to this devastating news.

On 3 March my department and I called a press conference. We had done our best before that to inform the various survivors, their families and their advocates. I met the press, informed them of the discovery, and indicated that we were making our best efforts to respond sensitively and respectfully to the situation, and that we were bringing together all the key administrative departments and agencies to set out a way forward. The most important thing for that day, however, was to remember and respect the dignity of the children who had lived their short lives in the Tuam institution. I concluded with the determination that 'we will honour their memory and make sure that we take the right actions now to treat their remains appropriately'.

The news exploded in Ireland, and went around the world.

So much inestimable grief, mixed with horror and shame. And though I started on a ministerial path to attempt ways to respond to all the dimensions of this appalling experience – accompanied by Ann Louise, my counsellor and personal bulwark – within a month the greatest loss of my own life had begun. If there was anything good about my deepening grief as Ann Louise began slipping away, perhaps it was this: a quietening of my soul that allowed me to hear the voices of survivors and their families in a profoundly different manner than I might have otherwise. Much of the time I was able to hear their fury, their anger at the state that it had happened, that it had been covered up, that the discovery of the truth was coming only because they and their advocates had campaigned for years. And I had to accept that, while I was minister, I *was* the state and the subject that had caused their distress. Hate, fury, grief, anger all thrown at me. It was horrible, and I was often wrecked emotionally. I heard it, though. I took it in.

But it wasn't always wounding personally. It did not always feel as if a shovel was pounding against my chest and heart. The public and private meetings I held with survivors and their families, and my conversations with adult children who had spent their earliest years in Tuam, were filled with a mixture of gratitude that the state was finally listening and near despair that the survivors might die before the full truth would be uncovered and officially acknowledged. One gentleman, in his seventies, told me how he – and other children in the Tuam institution – had to wait until the 'normal, acceptable, legitimate' children had walked to school each morning, and then they would follow, heads bowed.

I delivered three formal public speeches within four months of the Tuam findings, two of which I gave in the houses of the Oireachtas. My advisors, Jerry O'Connor and Patricia Ryan, worked tirelessly with me to ensure that the tone and content was appropriate to the profundity of what had transpired. I also wanted to offer some kind of vision for moving forward. Professional conversations and ongoing consultation with two remarkable human rights lawyers, Professors Fionnuala Ní Aoláin and Fiona de Londras, assisted greatly. Fiona was working with me on repealing the eighth amendment. Fionnuala and I had been friends and colleagues since we were appointed to the Irish Human Rights Commission in 2000. She is one of the founders of the Transitional Justice Institute at Ulster University. They both talked to me about the concept and practice of *transitional justice*, and its potential to be applied to these circumstances.

Ann Louise taught me always to look forward, especially in the practice of remembering. She spoke often about the intertwining of imagination and memory, and this concept became embedded in the practice of her own healing. Transitional justice appealed to me not just at a conceptual level. It sat easily with all I had learned from Ann Louise. And so, when I went to speak to senators in early March 2017, it was my first effort to 'image the possible' of what the state ought to do by way of response to such an appalling period of Irish history.

I was mindful that, by design, the commission was largely concerned with questions of legality, legal liability and compliance with the laws of the day. These are important questions. They are, however, not the only issues we had to consider. What happened in Tuam is part of a larger picture, part of a tapestry of oppression, abuse, repression and systematic human rights violations that took place in Ireland for decades. I put forward the idea that we must not treat these as isolated incidents, but rather confront what was a dire period in the country's history in an honest, mature and reflective way. We must acknowledge that what was happening in these institutions was not unknown and not without the support of many pillars of society. And we must acknowledge that sometimes it was fathers, mothers, brothers and uncles who condemned their daughters, sisters, nieces and cousins and their children to these institutions. As the representative of the state, I insisted that we must listen to, record and honour the truth of people's experiences. I acknowledged that it would not be easy, but that we must do it, for those who had suffered and for future generations.

As a feminist, Independent minister and Irish woman, I felt a moral compulsion to reach beyond the legal questions of what happened in Tuam and elsewhere. I insisted that we make sure that, while we still have time, we look to those who are still alive and accept their accounts of what was done to them and the wrongness of that. My remarks concluded by putting forward an image of what I thought would be possible.

In the coming period I promised to start a conversation with advocates, historians and scholars specialising in transitional justice, defined by the United Nations as the set of approaches a society uses 'to try to come to terms with a range of large-scale past abuses'. Transitional justice puts survivors and victims at the heart of the process. It commits to pursuing justice through truth. It aims to achieve not only individual justice, but a wider societal transition from more repressive times, in order to move from one era to another. It means that we ought to find out and record the truth, ensure accountability, offer redress and make reparation, undertake institutional reform, achieve reconciliation and guarantee that it will not happen again. Especially, in this historic case, for women and their children. It was a mammoth, complicated and painful task. Such an undertaking, I knew, would be difficult for the state, given the habit of legalistic approaches to 'historical wrongs' and over-riding concerns about cost and liability. But we had to move beyond this, I believed, if we were to transition into a different kind of space to bring our reckoning with the past into the present.

*

On 22 March 2017 I had just returned from a long week in Boston, representing Ireland as minister for the St Patrick's Day celebrations. I was in my office, exhausted from the trip and bent over a new bill on adoption legislation, preparing to lead a second-stage debate in the Seanad.

At approximately the same time, Ann Louise entered the Alliance Française, about a minute's walk from the Dáil and Seanad Éireann, and took the lift to the second floor. Room 25 beckoned. It was her favourite space in the entire building, and she always found a spot to sit close to the bay window, overlooking the Pavilion of Trinity College. Others wandered in for the class in conversational French – the Alliance's most advanced course – taught by Véronique Glenat (who recounted this story). Ann Louise was a fluent French speaker, learning the language in her mid-teens as an au pair, later taking a master's degree through French in L'Institut Catholique, and over the years returning again and again to the Paris she loved. The course offered her an opportunity to converse with others, in French, about current affairs, literary interests and other matters. It was a joyful part of her week, even more so subsequent to her blindness after her first haemorrhage.

But this day was different. Véronique noticed a certain distress in Ann Louise, her 'hands were walking on the desk'. She was nervous, obviously trying to steady herself, moving her body on the chair. She spoke at a rapid pace. Véronique requested that people leave the room. 'Go down to the café, now,' she said. While they were all very surprised, they filed out, except Ann Louise.

'I need a drink,' Ann Louise said.

'I think we need to call a doctor,' Véronique replied.

Ann Louise nodded and said, 'I need to go to the bathroom.'

Véronique went around the table to assist her. As she got up from her chair, Ann Louise stumbled and indicated that she had a pain at the back of her neck. She walked a few metres and then collapsed. Thankfully, Véronique caught her – she knew what she was witnessing was a stroke, so she called 999 immediately. Ann Louise was getting weaker.

Ann Louise took it with such dignity, as she did everything. She asked that Véronique phone me, and then the full bleed came on and Ann Louise lost consciousness. Véronique was on the mobile at this stage, the emergency responder providing her with instructions as to what to do. She held Ann Louise's hand. She phoned reception to say that an ambulance was coming and to send them immediately to Room 25. A colleague joined Véronique. Ann Louise was fading, her anima slowly absenting her body.

Véronique kept speaking to her, though there was no reaction. She was convinced that if she continued to speak to her and hold her, 'she would stay on this side'. The French language flowed non-stop as they waited for the ambulance.

Véronique pleaded, 'Please think of Katherine. You can't leave like this, Ann Louise. You cannot leave. A Parisian lady like you cannot leave. Katherine is here. You have to come back. Please stay with me. Katherine does not want you to go.' But she was leaving. At a certain point, Véronique and her colleague both thought Ann Louise was dead.

Then, like magic, she came back.

Véronique testified to me: 'It was a moment; for the first time in my life, I witnessed something beyond the natural occurring. I am not a believer; I am a humanist. But I saw some vision of a miracle. Or the powerful force that Ann Louise was, of such great intelligence; even when she was on that road, she was able to stay. Because she was leaving us . . . I had no doubt about that. And then she came back. I had kept kissing her forehead. I said, "Women need you. You are such a mentor. You can't leave Katherine."' And all of a sudden, in Ann Louise's typical beauty, her voice came back. And she said, 'Oh your kisses on my forehead brought me back.' That's what she said. In French. If she wasn't the powerful, optimistic person she was, Véronique believes that she would not have come back. She heard my name and came back.

They accompanied her to the ambulance and as she was carried into it, Ann Louise said, 'You have to tell Katherine,' in English. She had come around; her mind was fully there. It was just her legs that could not move. 'Katherine is in the Dáil, you have to go and tell her.'

And that is what Véronique did. She ran all the way up to Leinster House. The guards let her through when she mentioned my name. They got word to me in my office through my private secretary, Lisa Hughes. Lisa told me, 'Ann Louise has had a stroke, but it is a mini stroke. She will be okay.'

When recounting the story, Véronique indicated that she never diminished what had happened. She knew that it was a major stroke and that Ann Louise would no longer, never, be the same.

I cancelled my time in the Seanad chamber, called my driver and walked slowly to the lift that brought me down to North Road – a back alley, really, where ministers' cars are perched for quick take-off. I was in rote mode and then the shock started to travel slowly through my tired body. Eugene greeted me with a sombre, respectful nod and took off with a mission to get me to St James's Hospital as quickly as possible. I just tried to stay in the present and prepare myself for the unknown.

I thought we had more time. *Stay in the present* says the Buddha. *Image the possible* says Ann Louise.

I walked through the Urgent Care doors of St James's Hospital and followed long corridors to the stroke section. There she was. In one of the single rooms, with a plethora of doctors surrounding the bed where she was propped up. Ann Louise was in full flight, conducting a seminar on neuroscience and how to heal the brain. She had them all on their toes, quizzing them about what part of the brain controlled memory, sight, imagination. They did not know the answer to the last one. Her laughter could be heard by nurses beyond the room. She was in her element. I texted family later: 'Her mind is crystal clear! Just the left side not cooperating. Yet!'

She was a teacher to her fingertips. I felt so relieved. Her female imagination recreated her self.

Why wouldn't I believe, then, that Ann Louise – with the professional support of the best doctors in Ireland – would push through this second major setback? Alone, again, I tried desperately to muster an image of her being with me at home. I met Dr Joe Harbison in a consultation room across the corridor from Ann Louise. He had reviewed the medical reports from Professor Delanty in Beaumont with the first haemorrhage. While it was very troubling that she had experienced a second major bleed, his optimistic temperament discerned that rehabilitation was possible. She would require an extensive regime in the specialised Mercer's Institute for Successful Ageing (MISA) in the hospital, but recovery was on the horizon. My memory now sees Joe Harbison saying that small and erratic bleeds also appeared on some of Ann Louise's tests, but it was way too early to say if they had any pernicious significance. A junior doctor had mentioned this to me three years earlier. I just ignored it then. I dismissed it now again.

I walked back to her room. She was on her own now. She looked at me with her beautiful green eyes and they started to tear. 'Katie, why did this happen? I tried so hard to get better. I thought I was getting better.'

My vocal cords couldn't move. A whisper then came finally, 'Joe says you are going to get better.'

I leaned down to kiss her on her mouth. She received it gratefully. I was stirred.

*

After two weeks in James's, her medical review was very positive. The consultant on call named it a 'settling period, with energy levels improving (but unpredictable), blood pressure satisfactory, no blockage in neck vessels' and said that she was ready to transition to 'planned activity' of physiotherapy, wheelchair trips to the coffee shop downstairs, sitting up in a chair throughout the day, and eating in the common room instead of her own. We started that routine. And, as the days passed, often she was crystal clear, sometimes whistling, and could not wait to head to physical therapy.

During these early days of progress, I allowed my mind to wander more to political concerns. I was distracted and very troubled by the continuous unlawful imprisonment of Ibrahim Halawa, a young Irishman, in the notorious Egyptian prison Wadi el-Natrun. I had been advocating for his release since his arrest in August 2013, following a protest at the Al Fateh mosque in Cairo. The protest took place in the aftermath of the ousting of the Muslim Brotherhood government in Egypt. Ibrahim was being prosecuted as part of a group, along with 493 other defendants, and the trial process had been subject to many delays over the four years. He was on hunger strike, and his letters from prison indicated that his health was deteriorating significantly. In late March his family reported that Ibrahim had lost consciousness and was in a very serious condition. I asked Dónall Geoghegan – the political coordinator for Independent ministers – to help me think about what to do. Dónall's sensitivity and political savvy was always impressive.

Back in 2016 I had drafted a paper entitled 'A Vision for Equality in Ireland' to use in my negotiations as an

Independent TD with the Fine Gael party to form a government. The paper concludes with the words 'Bring Ibrahim Halawa Home'. Towards the end of March 2017 I finally felt I had the opportunity to make an impact on an issue that I felt so strongly about. I met with the taoiseach subsequent to the family's report and raised the matter of Ibrahim's declining health. I reminded him that to 'Bring Ibrahim Halawa Home' was one of my priorities in joining his government. I insisted that he must communicate again with President el-Sisi and call for Ibrahim's immediate release. I also indicated that this matter was core to my membership of his government, painfully aware of the risk this held for my position and for Enda's government. Enda looked at me and asked: 'What if I send an Irish doctor to Egypt to assess Ibrahim's medical condition? Wouldn't that be the best step forward right now, before us sending any ultimatums to the president?'

I was pleasantly taken aback. My nerves started to abate slowly as I responded, 'I think that is a most creative idea, taoiseach. It would offer some consolation to his sisters, father and mother, and give us an accurate read on Ibrahim's condition.'

'Let's wait for the report and then I will consider writing another letter.'

I nodded. He subsequently received government approval to proceed. No one stood in our way.

Addressing the Dáil the following week, Enda Kenny said that the government had arranged for an Irish doctor nominated by the chief medical officer to go to Cairo. He had participated in a consular visit to Ibrahim Halawa at the

Wadi el-Natrun prison on 29 March with the ambassador. Dr Mark Rowe, a Waterford GP and expert in men's health and mental well-being, recommended that specialist medical evaluations take place and that Ibrahim be returned to Ireland for these assessments. The taoiseach concluded by saying that he had sent an urgent letter to President el-Sisi to release Ibrahim on humanitarian grounds.

Later that evening in hospital, I fell asleep as I sat beside Ann Louise. I was so drained. Sometime later, I opened my eyes in the quiet of her room. No one had come in to take her blood pressure or to turn her over. We were alone. I loved her so much. I breathed when she breathed. Conjuring her warrior image provided a modicum of relief. If anyone could recover, it would be my Annie.

Some days her face broadened with joy as I walked through the hospital room door. 'Hello, my darling,' I would say. I would bend over the bed to kiss her. When she was awake and smiling, I could have lingered on her mouth for ever. Other days I felt cheered in the early-morning visits when I arrived and she was dressed and sitting in her wheelchair, wondering if the next physiotherapy session might begin soon.

'Katie, I want to get out to go walk in the Slievethoul forest as soon as I can. I know that will heal me. I know it will.'

At other times her visage wore distress and distraction. One morning I arrived and looked into vacant eyes. This could not be! The doctors had said she could get better with enough physiotherapy, good food, proper medication, occupational and speech therapy, and rest. What was happening now?

Another bleed, but this time it was a major one. Was I the only person who could see the bleed? Had anyone else noticed? She was in her wheelchair, so they had dressed her and got her out of bed. Well, maybe the bleed had happened after that. Regardless, in that moment I was the only one who could see it. A scan soon after my arrival confirmed what I already knew. I was heartbroken. This was a turning point. Maybe things would not get better. I was not prepared for this.

What else was going on in her brain? Why did it continue to bleed? Did she know this was coming? Not just the bleed that morning, but all the ways in which her body was being injured. Did she know that her time was short? And if she did, why didn't she talk to me about it? She never once spoke about her fear of dying. She had knowledge, I think now, but she had no fear.

At the end of that week I arrived a little later than usual on the Friday evening. As I entered the ward, I heard Ann Louise screaming my name.

I rushed down the hall to her room. I was exhausted – from the day, from my grief and sadness. I felt embarrassed, too, that the whole ward could hear her. And I felt awful that I should feel embarrassed.

Ann Louise's brain was bleeding, and her placid, wise and authoritative spirit had left her body that evening. She just wanted to see me. To tell me how she was being fed poison, and that the hospital was filthy, and that she needed to get out. She would be okay if she could just get out.

I looked at her beautiful green eyes. They contained a terror and anger that I had never seen before. I fixed my eyes on hers and spoke slowly, with as much calmness and authority as I could muster, and told her that everything would be okay. I reached for her left hand – the one that could not move, even after days of physiotherapy, and I rubbed it. I had to take deep breaths to find the stamina to do so. I don't know where it came from. Maybe the years of love between us ensured that some energy was always somewhere and could be found, no matter what. Finally, she settled.

How could this be happening? It was not supposed to be this way. I could not take my gaze away from her. As I witnessed the threads of vulnerability spreading upon her face and neck, I felt so lost. I had come from a day of heavy responsibility. I had been minister for children for eleven months, and the learning curve had only just begun to plateau a bit. That day, however, stress was spreading throughout sections of my department because we were formulating policy and legislation that was radically new, and the public had to wait longer for it than initially had been anticipated. My job was to sustain departmental energy, while calming the public's nerves. It had been a day of leading, chock-a-block with meetings and media conversations. I would have loved to come home to Ann Louise, with dinner on the kitchen island where we often ate, the wood-burning stove throwing its warmth towards us. I would have told her the details of my day. That's what we did almost every evening. And she would listen. She loved how I appreciated every mouthful of her meal. She often said I was like my father in that regard. She knew him well and they had a very close relationship.

I closed my eyes. None of that happened that evening in St James's Hospital. I tried to prevent the feeling of its loss from paralysing me. One of us was enough. I managed to calm myself, though not until every nerve of my body had been touched. The experience of extraordinary loss had started with a vengeance. I knew it would grow, deepen and become a part of every moment of my life from then on.

I looked at Ann Louise again. She was sleeping. I was in the presence of one of the greatest warriors I had ever known. All her life she had been a champion of justice and equality. The only thing that changed was who or what the fight was for. Underneath her formidable and plentiful crusades lay an inextinguishable hope for the positive.

So did her healing practices work? Did her brain 'change itself' as the neuroscientists asserted it could? Yes. This is what I now claim. I did not think so at the time. My grief and devastation, my intense focus on getting through each day – in the hospital, then in the corridors of power and back again in the hospital – did not allow me to see what I now see. I thought she had finally lost the good and valiant fight.

What we know now, however, is that Ann Louise was not simply unlucky with two brain haemorrhages. I met Joe Harbison in the coffee shop of James's early one morning in April to review her case. 'I see some dispersed black spots on the images of Ann Louise's brain,' he said. 'This may – or may not – indicate the presence of something much more sinister than a stroke or a discrete brain injury.'

My heart really did stop as he spoke those words. 'What do you mean?' I asked.

It was the first time he had uttered the words 'cerebral amyloid angiopathy'.

I hated those words. I could not say them together without tripping over my tongue. And I hated the acronym 'CAA' even more. I chilled every time I heard it. 'What the hell is that?' I asked Joe.

'Amyloids are a type of protein,' he said, 'that sometimes deposit within the blood vessels of the brain. They don't break down as quickly as other types, and their build-up in blood vessels can be overwhelming. It can produce small or larger bleeds in various parts of the brain. Martin McGuinness died of a similar disease, amyloidosis, deposits of abnormal protein in tissues and organs throughout the body. There is no cure for it.'

Martin had died the day before Ann Louise was admitted to James's. Memories of sitting next to him in the Áras after Michael D.'s first inauguration, telling fly-fishing stories, flashed in my mind. Another memory was our chat after a long lunch at the North South Ministerial Council when he looked so exhausted and pale, saying he was supposed to go to China the next day. He did not make that trip. I would have travelled to his funeral in Derry had Ann Louise been well. The fluidity between politics and sickness was my life now. I flipped back and forth, desperately trying to be present where I was. Sometimes I was. Sometimes I was not.

Cerebral amyloid angiopathy is a horrendous disease that is almost impossible to diagnose until the end is nigh. Brain scans over weeks and sometimes months eventually reveal different bleeds in different places, not just in one blood vessel. CAA, in laywoman terms, is the bleeding of the brain. Once diagnosed, it is a death sentence.

Joe merely intuited it that day. He also said, 'It may not be the case. We'll just have to wait and see. And, until then, I will treat her as a patient who can and is recovering.' He finished by saying, 'If you expect a patient to do badly, they will do badly.'

Ann Louise had the perfect consultant doctor. Their temperaments matched. Healing is relational, as Ann Louise believed. In the 'healing journal' we kept as we cared for her, her friend Gráinne Dowling wrote:

> *Dr Harbison (AL said) is a deep listener . . . AL wished me to put into the diary that he was <u>without arrogance</u>.*

My precious Annie.

*

I did not have very many close friends at the time. Ann Louise did. I witnessed her fidelity to these friends time and again, especially after her first haemorrhage. She would sit in my mother's chair in our open-plan kitchen/dining room and telephone one or another friend to check in, to hear their news, to tell them 'Well done!' or to offer whatever the circumstance required. She practised the habit of friendship better than anyone else I knew. Her days over the last four years of her life brought this to the fore. She would plan lunches with them, write birthday cards to them, meet them for a cup of coffee whenever they needed her wise counsel.

Gráinne Dowling asked Ann Louise to sit for her portrait, and every week Ann Louise obliged. I would come into our kitchen and there they would be: Ann Louise seated in one of our dining-room chairs, Gráinne sketching, rubbing it out, sketching again. 'I have always found myself resourced, excited by, and engaged in any creative project,' another notation found written amid Ann Louise's papers.

Those were precious times. Ann Louise's friends from earlier periods of her life began to accompany her in a different way. It was she, however, who initiated this different journey with them. Anne O'Reilly was called on to partner her in writing a book. Another friend was coached as she planned a change of profession. Toni Ryan talked often about the remedies of nature complementing traditional medicine. And there was always something discussed about her goddaughter Caoimhe Kirby: a worry or the celebration of a recent academic achievement. The daughters of Mary McEvaddy, Clodagh and Tara, were never far from Ann Louise's thoughts and conversations too. Noeleen Quigley's photography was encouraged, this encouragement interspersed with stories of Ann Louise's gratitude for the friendship of Noeleen's late husband, Frank.

These friendships formed the backdrop to one of the most significant decisions I made during Ann Louise's illness in St James's. After many days of going to the hospital every morning and every evening, bookended time with my beloved during days fraught with one government issue or another, I was frantic. While she was in the best place for her condition, I wanted her to be accompanied every moment by love. As one who had given so much to so many, this she deserved more than anything else. I also believed that it would enable her to heal so that one day, soon, she could stand up straight, take both my hands in hers, and we could walk together away from that nightmare.

I decided to assemble a healing team, close friends who would act as a relay of companions. Ann Louise agreed. I knew I was asking her to track new territory in vulnerability; I was desperate, and she could hear this in my voice.

'Well, if you think it will help, Katherine.'

'Yes, I do, Ann Louise.'

I phoned Hilda McEvoy, her beautiful red-headed niece, her friend and the second daughter of her sister June. Hilda had spent mornings, afternoons and weekends with Ann Louise since her first brain injury. She would telephone, set a day and time, and arrive to assist with a household project, or speed off to the bookstore in Blessington for tea and a chat. Hilda unfolded love around Ann Louise and made her glow. A month earlier they had spent four precious days in Paris together. Ann Louise, determined to see one of her oldest friends, Mme Eglin O'Rourke, did not let blindness deter her. I used to say that Ann Louise had been French in one of her past lives.

Nothing consoled me more than to walk into the hospital room to see Hilda, with her MRSA-protection apron on, helping Ann Louise to brush her teeth or clean her nails. They had several routines. Some days Hilda would sit quietly in the room while Ann Louise slept. At other times they would whisper French to each other. Hilda brought an abundance of dignity, practicality and adoration into the room several times a week. I know that this made it easier for the great orator, educator and impeccably dressed Dr Gilligan to allow her private world to be seen.

Hilda's eloquence and profundity at Ann Louise's last ritual captured so much of those precious hospital days. Her tribute to Ann Louise at the funeral included how her aunt had ignited a passion for *la France* et *la langue française* in her own life. She said how affirming Ann Louise was of her, at every important moment of her life, and that she always encouraged Hilda to be her best self, to be fearless. She acknowledged Ann Louise's formidable character.

Hilda joined the healing team not out of duty, but out of gratitude. Every day she was with Ann Louise, she was present to the person Ann Louise was, not someone who was in need because of sickness. In my exhaustion, as I witnessed their relationship, I too caught some of the healing power between two women.

After Hilda took up her station, I phoned Ann Louise's closest friends. Each time I would say to Ann Louise: And is it okay if I contact Noeleen (Quigley), Gráinne (Dowling), Mary (McEvaddy), Anne (O'Reilly), Toni (Ryan) and Anne (Genockey)? Each time she would look at me, quietly, then nod her head.

I felt so relieved after all the phone calls. I was less alone. Ann Louise's friends brought a blanket of compassion and comfort and wrapped it around me. I felt I could now bear what was to come.

There is a small meeting room just on the left as you enter the George Frederic Handel Ward of Mercer's Institute of Successful Ageing in St James's Hospital. It has windows, a small round table and chairs, and is situated over the entrance. The healing team met me there periodically. We brought our calendars, and Claire Murphy, my constituency manager and friend, would work patiently with us to develop the roster of time with Ann Louise. We reviewed her progress (or lack of it) too, discussed the opinions of doctors and nurses, and called into being our collective determination to heal Ann Louise and bring her home.

Other friends would drop off a hot meal for me and I would go to meet them in that room. Gráinne Courtney and Orla Howard, Ellen O'Malley Dunlop, Gráinne Healy and Trish O'Connor, Denise Charlton, Paula Fagan. I was starved for good food, friendship and conversation. The presence and gifts of these women kept me going. No food or friendship could fill the void that was opening, but my physical and spiritual energy managed to be sustained, as I took on the task of my life. Luce Irigaray said, 'Whoever is capable of providing in oneself a place not only for the other but for the relation with the other is human.' She was one of Ann Louise's prime muses. She inspired not only Ann Louise's philosophy of education (that she taught to thousands in St Patrick's College, Dublin City University over the many years she worked there), she also filtered into our work with other women, and some men, to end poverty through education. Love can do so much. It can form the basis of a shared life. It can inspire us to joy; it can unite us in grief. We had found this in our working lives too. Setting up The Shanty, a programme of community education in our home, had been an act of social change, but it had also been an act of love. We were so full of our 'in-loveness', we believed we could do anything together.

The love generated in the small meeting room of the hospital ward felt the same as in the circles of women we had gathered in our home and in Tallaght West communities over the years. A member of the healing team (and poet), Anne O'Reilly, captures it this way:

Spinning Women

The tapestry was a
reproduction
but the scene was old
two women spinning
and I thought of both of you
of how you weave together
the very stuff of your lives
and ours
we women whose paths
crisscross with yours
you pattern us too
spinning a new story
as you turn an ancient wheel
and we rock
to the steady rhythm
of an old, old memory.

In your spinning circle
we are held together
by threads of infinite tenderness
tying us to origins and futures
where women's hands

190

touch and celebrate
spin and weave
and make all things new.

Now, they were holding us in threads of vulnerability.

My sister Suzanne and brother Mark wove into the tapestry too. Dublin is 4,500 miles from Seattle where my siblings live, a thirteen-hour journey by air at the best of times. This did not deter Suzanne or Mark from coming to assist us in Ireland when Ann Louise was ill, time and again. Mark looked after The Shanty and cooked meals for us at home. He would spend time in hospital too, quietly, in the common room, nipping in and out of Ann Louise's room when required. Suzanne joined me in hospital each time and often talked to me about how she felt being with Ann Louise. When she entered her room for the first time, she could only say to Ann Louise, 'This is horrible.' We all cried and Ann Louise responded with, 'I thought we had more time.' The sadness of these moments fills me as I write these words. But then I remember Suzanne's stories of how every night I would come into the room and say, 'Hello, my darling,' and Ann Louise would reply, 'Hello, Katie, darling.' And we had parties as often as Ann Louise was able for them. Me with the contra-band wine, Suzanne with a candle that probably should not have been lit. It made Ann Louise happy. My sister and I were happy with her, laughing, staying until very late. Sometimes not leaving till the early morning.

I do not recall, now, when Mark and Suzanne first met Ann Louise, or what the circumstances were. Nor did we share with them the full intimacy of our life-partnership in the early years. I carry sadness about their absence from the first of many commitment rituals Ann Louise and I held.

*

It is 16 October 1982; in Rockport, Massachusetts we rent a summer home during the winter months. It is the only way we can afford it – the rent quadruples in the summer. The house is built on stilts and provides panoramic views of the Atlantic. Though the cold freezes our toothpaste on some mornings, it does not bother us. We have found a place of beauty, a hideaway from the eyes of Boston College. Every weekend we drive down Route 128, merge into 127 and slow down to view the expansive sea vista before we enter the quiet New England resort town.

We cannot get out of the car fast enough. Yet time goes into slow motion as we step over the entrance. Youthful exhilaration descends on us both. Doctoral students should not be having so much fun.

Dan Fogelberg's song 'To the Morning' plays in the background as the bright mornings come and as we watch the sun rise. Ann Louise loved how the song celebrated a resistance to the word 'no', marking that the morning would always happen. The song suited her. And me. And those days of *grá go deo*.

*

One year and two months after we met, we declared ourselves life-partners in front of a group of a dozen friends in our

Rockport home. I don't think anyone else had used that phrase then. We just made it up.

Every moment of the ritual and meal exuded joy, having been planned so carefully. Photos taken, wine poured, food relished, prayers said, songs sung.

Wherever you go, I will go.
Wherever you live, so shall I live.
Your people will be my people,
and your God will be my God too.

Wherever you die, I shall die
And there shall I be buried beside you.

(Song of Ruth, Hebrew Scriptures)

No family were present because we were too afraid to tell them. I take responsibility for that now and I regret that decision. Our bravery reached only as far as our cool friends.

It was my sister Suzanne who wrote to me in the thirty-fifth year of my life and encouraged me to tell our parents about my sexual identity. She was prompted by Mark's similar declaration to our parents earlier that year. He was the youngest sibling; I was the eldest daughter. That just did not seem right. So I took up my pen and sent a long letter across the Atlantic. My father responded (on behalf of them both) with a letter that began with the words 'Dear Daughters'. We are a close family. It saves my life time and again.

Suzanne and Mark had manageable work and family obligations in the last five years of Ann Louise's life. They each stretched that liberty way beyond the normal boundaries of familial generosity, though. I sit here trying to add up the number of months each of them lived in our home during that time. My persona as the 'eldest sister' had to be laid down. I became the one cared for.

Mid-April held mixed progress for Ann Louise. Sometimes she fell asleep in the therapy room and was wheeled back with no exercise taken. She was so disappointed when she awoke later in her own room, feeling as if an opportunity had been missed. And different kinds of pain began to layer her daily experience. A terrible discomfort in her left shoulder, consistent soreness at the site of her cannula, ongoing constipation, a sizeable swelling of her left hand and headaches.

Good Friday morning 2017 came and, after returning from the coffee shop, she wanted to stand up and walk. I did not think she had the strength, and her left side was still paralysed. But her will was as dominant as her imagination.

'I don't want people to tell me I cannot walk to the toilet. That is *not* the way to get healed. If I don't take risks, I won't heal. And I *hate* the hoist.' (With her paralysis, the medical team ascertained that it was the only way for her to get out of bed.) 'It is so painful. Excruciating for my shoulder. I feel so undignified.'

I certainly knew that her spirit was indomitable. 'Okay, Annie,' I said as I looked around to make sure that no nurse was passing the room, 'let me help you sit on the side of the bed. Pull yourself up first. Then we'll get your legs on the floor and I will place my arm around your waist to walk you to the bathroom.'

We got as far as her legs on the floor and she collapsed in my arms. Terror shuddered through my body. I frantically lifted her back into bed. Thank God she was so thin, she would have been on the floor otherwise.

Saturday was a quiet day.

But Easter Sunday we broke all the rules and brought our beautiful dog August in to see her. Mark took such lovely photos. He brought Ann Louise some fillet steak and fresh vegetables that day. Though a vegetarian for years, Ann Louise knew that protein was what she needed, and she thought the steak was delicious.

*

The citizens' assembly on repealing the eighth amendment has been meeting throughout Ann Louise's stay in MISA. On 22 April, 64 per cent of the citizens who deliberated in the assembly, with the best of expertise presented to them from both sides, vote in favour of 'terminations without restrictions'. Some 57 per cent of the assembly members recommend that the eighth amendment be replaced with an amendment to the constitution that explicitly allows the Oireachtas to legislate on the issue of abortion. These results are far more liberal than many seasoned observers expected.

My comrades, on the inside and the outside, are ecstatic. The wave towards women's reproductive freedom continues to build. But my emotions are deferred. I do not remember any of this. I know it from public records and from talking to colleagues later on in the summer. By the time the citizens' assembly votes, Ann Louise has been in St James's Hospital for a full month. While we still believe that she will heal herself, there are many days when that does not appear to be the case.

The end of April and the month of May become filled with paradox and confusion, yet hope lingers. Some days she is better and takes great delight in teaching the nurses *un peu de Français* if they have time to engage. Other days pain wracks her diminishing body and agitates her wandering spirit. Delusions of our dog August or Ann Louise's parents, Arthur and Imelda, drift into the room. She finally gives in to the build-up of anxiety and requests a pill and a psychologist to calm her. Ann Louise becomes convinced that Alzheimer's is settling on her and wants it confirmed. The kind and competent psychologist talks to us about Ann Louise's 'mild delirium' and how she is 'popping in and out of it'. I ask her, 'What is delirium?' and she responds that 'Perception is affected, reasoning and consciousness are altered by it.' As I take this in, she then says, 'It means to lose one's furrow.' A perfect metaphor. Ann Louise loves metaphors, and this resonates. The psychologist describes how anxiety lives behind delirium, and that this is understandable when one suffers brain injury as Ann Louise has. It eats at your essence, your existence. She turns to Ann Louise and asks, 'Shall we do something about your anxiety? We can prescribe a tiny dose of medication.' Ann Louise just nods, not in a way that is giving in. Rather, in a way that is willing to accept additional support so that she can heal.

Still not much progress on walking. Often Ann Louise falls asleep while being taken to the physio room. Her blood pressure drops and she cannot be woken up, so she is returned to the bedroom without any exercise.

And yet on a visit to the hospital on 30 April, Anne O'Reilly told us that she had some news. Immediately Ann Louise said, 'Brian!', and she was right. Ann Louise had known Anne's son Brian since he was a small child, and he was now thirty-seven years old and awaiting the arrival of his second child. Anne told us that they had had a baby boy, and Ann Louise was delighted for them.

'You'll never believe what they've called him,' said Anne. 'Albus!'

'White: Albus/Alba/Album,' replied Ann Louise, perfectly declining the Latin.

'They probably don't know much Latin,' said Anne. 'Albus is the name of the wizard from *Harry Potter*. Imagine calling your son after a wizard. Remember how we believed that we had to be called after saints?'

To this Ann Louise smiled and said, 'Wizards and saints, Anne – I don't know if there is all that much difference.'

*

Later that day Ann Louise faints. Fainting comes to be a consistent feature of these days, with significant loss of blood pressure. An intravenous tubing filled with fluids brings her back, sometimes slower than other times. 'I want to walk, Katie. I know I will get better if I can walk.'

On 29 May she is crystal clear again. She begins to speak from the bed. Her manner – authoritative, regal and quietly contemplative – descends on her frail body, and my presence recedes. I grab a sheet from the healing journal, and a pen – I know these words will be weighty.

Myself and Katherine

Accepting, certainly not wanting.

Neither of us want this.

If what we understand is going to unfold here, we would never choose this.

Katherine is and has been my beloved partner since we met in 1981. I have adored her all my life and it has been my greatest privilege in life to have loved someone as much as I love Katherine.

Little did we ever anticipate that as this moment of our life is unfolding, that all our beautiful commitments since 1981 would end in this way.

A life commitment – but this is much shorter than any life commitment we anticipated (by about 15 years).

But! we might make it to be 'ladies in our eighties' – we don't know that yet.

A new focus for me would be a very healthy thing.

A new deadline!

I return to Government Buildings the next morning. I arrive in the cabinet room early and stand at one of the large Georgian windows. I stare out, feeling so lost. An arm comes gently around my waist. Leo. We both look out. We say nothing. His touch makes me feel accompanied; and understood. I turn to look at him, his compassionate, albeit shy, eyes meet mine. I smile a little. We return to the table. Business begins shortly thereafter.

*

'Hold hope no matter what because hope is at the heart of human existence,' says Ann Louise the following morning after I ask if she has a thought for the day. She is listening to the radio, a commentary on Seamus Mallon, the great SDLP leader in Northern Ireland, and she says, 'Pursuing justice has results. Where should we go, Katie? Where should *you* go? March up and down the streets? Or enter the political process . . .'

She speaks again, directing her comments to me, though it seems also that she is simply thinking to herself, out loud.

They are going to tell you that our status is changing.

The other day I slipped to the ground — try not to talk about slipping — they all get very excited. And then move you to another status of care.

I tried to indicate that my memory is fading — I have tried to keep going as long as I can. 'What day is it?' they ask. Monday is the wrong answer. And I rallied and asked, 'What day is it?' and I could see something going on for them — that I didn't know it was Saturday.

I have shifted almost 'out of the normal' — it is like standing on something that is slippery. This word is appropriate for Alzheimer's. My memory has become more slippery. I don't have a firm grasp on events. Where are *memories stored? They slip away at a much quicker pace and to retrieve them out of boxes of memory, makes it more difficult.*

This struck me strongly after thinking through — how memory has changed. This is how it has changed. The boxes become way less certain and much more slippery.

I don't know how long this clarity will last. But I can tell you, this is what is happening. We all know that memory changes, once Alzheimer's dawns, in this process of ageing. All I can talk about is the little I know. One of the things I read said that we could stop the onset of Alzheimer's by our diet and by our exercise. Whereas what I think is happening is exactly the opposite. Breakfast is protein every day. No change — porridge with oats. But I love porridge. Every day is lovely.

And then I quietly go out for a walk —

Ann Louise reaches for the journal that I am recording her words on. She takes my pen and writes, in a style that demonstrates the slipperiness of which she has spoken:

Shhh . . . Shhh . . . it is too soon to tell . . . We'll talk later . . . it is much too soon to tell . . .

I tell Joe about this the next day. He insists that Ann Louise does not have Alzheimer's and outlines the various technical reasons to give grounds for his assessment. We discuss how her recent scans indicate more and more smaller bleeds.

*

On the first day of June, feeling more lost than I ever have in my entire life, the professional and personal clouds of this time mesh together. I have to spend a lot of the morning in Leinster House, even though I feel I do not have much time left with Ann Louise. I need to announce that I have made a very significant decision about Tuam.

I enter the Dáil and go to the ministerial seat. The Ceann Comhairle calls on me and I stand to say, 'We have made too many decisions in the dark in this country, but we are not going to do it again in Tuam. We need the experts to tell us what is possible. We need people who have done this type of very specialised work before.' Then I announce the appointment of Dr Niamh McCullagh, forensic archaeologist, to lead the work. I have asked her to bring together a team of international experts in juvenile osteoarchaeology, forensic anthropology, DNA analysis and archaeology. The government needs this expertise to identify and consider the options we have in front of us for Tuam. Will we look for a full or a partial excavation of the Galway site? Is it technically possible to exhume the remains of the children, so that they can be identified? What are the logistical and technical challenges involved in this work? What are the costs and timeframe?

I specify that they must offer us technical advice in layperson's language so that we can all understand the options for the site and what each such option would entail. Information is power and I want the expert reports to be available to everyone. When we are all speaking the same language, there will be a much better chance of reaching a consensus.

*

On the hospital ward and in Ann Louise's room, my face and demeanour are visible to the staff, to other patients and their visitors. Privacy is shared with people I do not know. I am vulnerable. I am dependent on Joe Harbison, Ruth McDonagh and Roisín Kelly, Ann Louise's primary medical team. My moments of intimate conversations with my partner and spouse are shared with the male night nurses. It is all sacred time because each member of Ann Louise's medical and hospital team holds me in different ways. The grace of being held while being vulnerable breeds resilience in me.

CHAPTER 8

In Beauty It Is Finished

Professor Joe Harbison summons me to St James's on 9 June in the late afternoon. Ann Louise walked earlier this morning. She always believed that she would walk again, and so she has. *Does he want to talk about progress?* I wonder. I cut short a meeting in my offices on Mespil Road. It takes twenty-five minutes to get to the hospital. I walk into the lift and press the button for the fourth floor as I have done countless times in the last months. I push through the ward's big doors. Joe and his medical team are waiting for me in the meeting room. We huddle around its table. It is such a familiar space to me – it's where the healing team meets, and where I come to be on my own when Ann Louise is being attended by nurses in her room.

Joe says, 'Katherine, I am so sorry to have to confirm that

203

Ann Louise has CAA. And the disease has accelerated. She is in her last weeks or days.'

I just stare at him.

He continues, 'With the deposit of amyloids, neurons die. She does not have Alzheimer's. Her brain is very well preserved. She has extraordinary cognitive reserves. But what I can say is that her brain has bled on one side, and then has bled on the other. So she could not compensate for the dead neurons, no matter what she did. Yet she has lived beyond what, medically, we might expect. And she has not gotten the cognitive effect of difficulty in speaking or understanding.'

He pauses, and then offers the option of moving Ann Louise to a hospice or to request that the team at MISA begin palliative care. I immediately choose the latter and express my gratitude for their exceptional generosity.

I can't feel at all. I turn to practical matters and ask, 'When will we tell Ann Louise?'

He responds, 'Why not now?'

I nod. We enter her room. She is already dressed and sitting in her wheelchair. We arrange chairs to sit with her. Joe then gently describes his recent prognosis and why it had taken him so long to be accurate. He affirms Ann Louise's exceptional fight and acknowledges her brilliant intellect and courage. 'We will do everything we can for you to be with less pain, Ann Louise. We are here for you, the whole team.'

Ann Louise nods, pulls herself up from the waist as best she can and graciously thanks them for their support to her and to myself. 'I need some rest now, gentlemen and ladies.'

The team silently leaves.

After the nurses put her to bed, I move to sit next to her, as close as I can get. She asks, 'Katherine, did Joe tell me that I am dying?'

'Yes, Ann Louise.' I pause. 'Are you afraid, Ann Louise?'

Without a moment of hesitation she answers, 'No. I was not afraid to enter the world and I am not afraid to leave it.' She closes her eyes and falls asleep. We never speak about her dying again.

I remain in the quiet room with her. I don't remember how much time goes by. I still cannot feel the exceptional gravity of our circumstances. How could she be dying? Not part of the plan. Not now. Not for years. I begin to feel completely alone and that a part of her is already passing.

I go to the common room to tell Suzanne and Mark and ask if they can hold watch for me. Their eyes show more pain than I have ever seen. I phone June, Hilda, Ann Louise's brother Arthur and, one by one, the healing team. Each listens quietly and starts to plan when they will next come in. They all shift up a gear for these last days. As do the medical and extended hospital team. All envelop Ann Louise with love. The staff of MISA have very poignant and respectful routines once a person moves to palliative care. The hospice sign is placed at the entry of the room, signalling a request for quiet in the hallway as one walks by.

I return to the Department of Children and Youth Affairs and phone my private secretary, Lisa Hughes, asking her to organise a meeting immediately with Fergal Lynch, my secretary general, Patricia Ryan and Jerry O'Connor, my advisors, and herself. We sit in a circle. I tell them the news. Patricia gasps. Fergal speaks first. 'Minister, we are so, so sorry. We will shoulder all departmental responsibility for you, in the background, for as long as you need.' No words come; I just nod. I place my trust in them. The meeting ends.

Family and members of the healing team visit Ann Louise over the weekend. She is quieter now, though rallies at times to engage in conversation, often in French. I go to her room on the Saturday evening. No one else is there. She says, 'Hello, Katie,' and I think, *Maybe this is my chance.*

'Ann Louise, do you have any thoughts on your funeral?'

Several minutes pass. Then she responds, 'I do not want a church. No church. Maybe a civic space, like the Mansion House, across the street from my dad's pub [the Dawson Lounge]. I do not want a Catholic Mass. No priests. Some Christian element is fine, though, Katherine.'

She slips back to sleep. That's all I get.

*

My mind turns to politics. I must go into Government Buildings on Monday. It is a very significant week politically. Enda Kenny has signalled his intention to resign as taoiseach on the Tuesday. Leo Varadkar has been elected the new leader of Fine Gael and is preparing to take over the reins. If elected by parliamentary colleagues, he will become the first gay taoiseach. He has the votes of his own party members and needs a number from Independents too. I decide to give him mine. I negotiated hard to be a member of this government and expect that my support means I will be reappointed a minister under his leadership. There are many things I still want to do. And, in the early days of Ann Louise's time in St James's, we agreed that I should stay on.

On Monday morning Eugene drives me through the gates of Government Buildings. I get out of the car and phone Leo.

'How is Ann Louise?' he asks.

'Close to the end,' I reply. 'I am not certain how long.'

Then I tell him that I may not be present in the Dáil on Wednesday, when he puts himself forward to be voted in as taoiseach, but that he will have my vote if I am able to attend. He thanks me and assures me that I remain in his thoughts.

I am exhausted. I hold a few meetings with my team and return to the hospital. On Tuesday, 13 June, Hilda records 9.45 in the healing journal, and nothing else. The rest of the page is empty. Ann Louise sleeps the entire day. Not a stir. Another type of commotion does happen, though, later that afternoon. At one stage my phone rings, and the name 'Paschal Donohoe' flashes up. I click the button and it is Enda's voice.

'Katherine, how is Ann Louise?'

I say, 'She is sleeping peacefully. She is in her last days.'

He asks, 'May I come to see you both?'

'Of course,' I say. 'Thank you, taoiseach.'

He responds, 'I will come after I resign.'

I am stunned.

He joins us in her room a few hours later. We talk quietly while she sleeps. He acknowledges her leadership and contribution. He offers me sympathy and support. He shakes hands with the staff who have assembled in the hallway. Photos snap. And then he leaves.

My phone rings the next morning at five. I am in our bed, but not sleeping. It is the hospital. Ann Louise has had a major bleed. They ask me to come. Too early to ring Eugene to collect us, I jump out of bed, wake Mark and Suzanne, dress quickly and drive us into St James's. We race to the ward after parking the car, and she is not in her room. They have taken her down to the MRI room for the scan. We wait, in shock, though we are grateful she is still alive. Ten minutes later, the doors burst open and the medical team, headed by Joe, take her down the hallway to Room 2. She is unconscious. They do not look at us. She is their patient and they are in charge. They pass us, rolling the stretcher with dignity and authority. Mark, Suzanne and I bear witness to an extraordinary medical and spiritual moment.

I phone Ann Louise's family, the healing team and other close friends to tell them what has happened and to invite them in to say goodbye. There is a steady and peaceful stream all through the day. Ann Louise is no longer in pain. She breathes with tranquillity as the blood washes over her brain.

Later that evening, on 14 June 2017, Leo Varadkar is elected taoiseach of the 33rd Dáil. Mark, Suzanne and I watch the television in Room 2 to view the proceedings. Ann Louise is with us, though unconscious. Leo Varadkar announces his cabinet and invites them into the chamber. After the last minister walks down to be seated, he says, 'And I appoint Katherine Zappone as minister for children and youth affairs. Our thoughts and prayers are with her.' Ann Louise waits for this moment and is here with me, for me.

In Beauty It Is Finished

In the early hours of 15 June, Mark sets down the final note of our healing journal:

Ann Louise has left us in body.

Who will help me choose my wardrobe?
Who will I read my drafted speeches to first?

*

Later that afternoon our neighbours – adults and children – wait for the hearse to arrive at the bottom of our driveway. They greet her as our gates open and follow slowly up to The Shanty. No words are spoken. It is simply the rhythm of the Irish as they walk behind a coffin in the country.

I come out our front door to welcome Ann Louise home, for the last time. She is laid out in our sitting room, in front of the wood-burning stove. August, our beloved golden, comes to pay her respects. Over the afternoon, the first wake begins. Family, friends, neighbours come from all around. Tánaiste Frances Fitzgerald and Minister Simon Coveney are some of the guests. My brother Bob has travelled from Seattle. He brings his best suit. I love him for that. Friends arrive from Boston, Australia, London and all over Ireland.

Ann Louise is waked again the next day in Jobstown, Tallaght West. An Cosán was a second home to her. She was the primary architect of this building, the one with the vision and drive to put it up, with and for the people. And the people come to mourn her, sitting side by side with ministers Richard Bruton and Regina Doherty, former minister Mary Harney and senior civil servants from the Department of Children.

I return home early in the evening to meet Ann O'Reilly. She has agreed to be the creative director and celebrant of the funeral. My neighbour Ruth organises the most exquisite and appropriate civic space. Dr Brian MacCraith – president of Dublin City University – offers the Helix (DCU's Centre for the Performing Arts) as the venue, to pay tribute to the passing of their great educator. It is an appropriate, albeit magnificently generous, act.

*

We are travelling down the mountain road from Brittas on our way to DCU the next morning, and Ann O'Reilly rings me. 'You didn't tell me that this would be a state funeral!'

'What?' I exclaim.

'The new members of cabinet have arrived, the taoiseach is on his way. Enda and Bertie are here too. The president is just turning in and it feels like all of Dublin is here.'

She actually sounds elated. And she would properly rise to the occasion.

*

We enter the arena. Ann Louise is brought in by the seven women of her healing team. A thousand people stand.

The music of Zrazy fills the air.

Be-love-ed.
Take me to your room, and feed me with your
mind.
For here are jewels and precious stones, for those
who seek to find.
Be-love-ed.
Take me to your heart, enclose me with your love.
For I have wandered far and wide, the case of love
to prove.
Be-love-ed.
Be-love-ed.
Be-love-ed.
Take me to your bed.
And take me where you will.
For I have only one desire, your hungry heart to
fill.
Beloved. Beloved. Beloved. Beloved.

Several friends and colleagues speak. The music of the Laetare Vocal Ensemble, conducted by Dr Róisín Blunnie, fills the hall. I close this tribute to Ann Louise by an attempt to articulate what she represented to me:

How do I love thee, Ann Louise? Let me count the ways.
    I love your fearlessness, especially when it was mixed with your great sense of fun. Ann Louise drove a bright red BMW motor scooter for years, and stopped only because of blindness after her first haemorrhage. It was one of the hardest 'letting-go's for her. Prior to that, however, several times a week, she would gear up, put

on the big helmet and drive the bike out our gate. I would often watch as she left, bless myself and try to celebrate the freedom she felt on that bike.

I love your extraordinary sense of hope, that fuels your positive approach to all things in life, especially its greatest challenges. After her last visit to the eye specialist in Beaumont, a number of months ago now, Ann Louise wrote in her journal: My sight has not improved – but my capacity to use what I have left has improved.

I love your wisdom and depth of acceptance of what is given. I love your beautiful mind, your brilliance, creativity and the ways in which you thought deeply about everything.

I love how you loved me. Ann Louise was so proud of my appointment as an Irish cabinet minister. She waited for my reappointment and passed away quietly and peacefully only hours after it happened.

And now, in the presence of all gathered, I have to let you go. Beloved.

She was my beloved, of course. Nevertheless her horizontal County Wicklow granite tombstone commences with the line 'OUR BELOVED ANN LOUISE'. Her public achievements were multiple as educator, philosopher and social activist. She spoke often about love as the foundation of learning, knowing and acting. In each realm she loved and was loved. In the educational arena, Ann Louise's love of her students in Dublin City University manifested in countless ways. At the time of her passing there would have been thousands of primary school teachers throughout Ireland who had been taught by her. I lost count of those who wrote to me, emailed me and stopped me on the street to tell a story of how she had changed their lives.

Dublin City University has honoured her by naming one of its lecture theatres at the Drumcondra campus the Ann Louise Gilligan Lecture Theatre. It is located in the same building as the Seamus Heaney Lecture Theatre. She would be chuffed by that. At the launch of its naming, I told a story of how she started teaching at St Pat's in her early thirties, as a petite, gracious and very polite woman. She would enter a big hall and begin her lecture, one that she had prepared with great commitment and creativity. Five minutes into the lecture she would notice some of the lads at the back of the hall – they would be carrying on intense conversations with one another or spreading out the daily newspaper to read. And so she would stop, stand her full five feet two inches tall and stare at them, until they noticed that the lecturer had stopped speaking. Once she had their attention, she would say, 'It is your choice to be here or not. If you choose to stay, I need your full attention.'

Well, that would settle them. Most anyhow. A few days after the naming of the lecture theatre, I was visiting one of the primary schools in Dublin South-West and, as I was leaving, the principal proudly told me that her husband had been taught by Ann Louise. That morning he was recalling the day that he had misbehaved in her class, and she asked him to leave the lecture theatre!

Dr Paul Downes, her friend, DCU colleague and current director of its Educational Disadvantage Centre, hailed one of Ann Louise's educational legacies as helping 'dissolve the silent tremor of thwarted hope in Irish society by converting people's hope into expectations – and expectations into entitlement and rights'. This she did by becoming the founding director of St Patrick College's Educational Disadvantage Centre. Integral to its mission was to ensure the mainstreaming of attention to the socio-economic conditions of pupils' experiences in the act of teaching and learning. Children's experience of poverty demands that we teach teachers how to take it into account. This now happens. Together, Paul and Ann Louise published *Beyond Educational Disadvantage* (2007), a collection of essays from over forty leading educationalists in Ireland, giving voice to the reality that the education system needs to change in order to meet the needs of a high proportion of students at risk of early school-leaving. Operating in a similar educational territory, Ann Louise was appointed by the minister for education, Dr Michael Woods, in 2002 to be the founding chair of the National Educational Welfare Board, a statutory agency established to ensure that every child in the state either attends school or otherwise is given an education.

In her philosophical work, Ann Louise 'exemplified the ancient tradition that sees philosophy as a way of life', as her friend and colleague Dr Aislinn O'Donnell recalled at the Helix tribute. Aislinn, now a professor of education at Maynooth University, described how Ann Louise's philosophy 'challenged individualism, sought to dismantle patriarchy and refused to accept that to be human meant to be in endless and relentless competition and conflict, or that we humans have the right to destroy the Earth'. Ann

Louise's philosophy, as outlined in her posthumously published book, *Reclaiming the Secret of Love* (2021), places the faculty of the imagination at the centre of what it means to be human. The ethical imagination allows us to imagine the possibility of things being otherwise and to imagine the world from the standpoint of another. In her own words, 'Our hope for a new future lies in an imagination rooted in love.'

Ann Louise's contribution as a social activist is immeasurable. Her loving toil continues to have an impact on people through the organisation of An Cosán. Darragh Genockey, my former campaign manager, spoke eloquently at her funeral about the intergenerational footprint of Ann Louise's social activism. He began by saying that he wanted to 'acknowledge the impact which The Shanty and An Cosán had on the children of those who had been educated there over the last thirty years'. He knew Ann Louise understood 'that when you educate a woman, you educate her whole family', and referenced his own experience:

'The children of An Cosán alumni are the proof of this. I grew up watching my mam studying in the evenings for her Montessori diploma, attending courses at weekends, and adding even a master's degree to her haul. I'm just one of thousands who had opportunities, thanks to the community education provided by An Cosán. The An Cosán alumni and their children include a senator, a deputy mayor, councillors, educators, psychotherapists, actresses, artists, entrepreneurs . . . and the list goes on.'

Ann Louise's social activism also displayed itself in her life-long commitment to trade unionism. Séamus Dooley,

Irish secretary of the National Union of Journalists, put down his salute to her on the *Irish Times*'s letters page (20 June 2017):

> One aspect of her vast contribution to Irish society that has been overlooked was her commitment as a trade unionist.
>
> Ann Louise was a former vice-chairwoman of the ICTU Women's Committee and, as a member of the Irish Federation of University Teachers, she rightly took pride in the work of that union's equality committee. Her trade unionism was an important part of her battle for equality.
>
> 'Holistic' is a much over-used word but it describes well the vision of a woman who will be greatly missed.

Perhaps what she is best known for, however, is her marriage equality activism. It is true to say that Ann Louise did not think up the idea to rush to the courts. As a well-bred, middle-class Irish woman, it would not have been in her nature. Instead, it was my American 'up-front' character that tilled the ground for our legal battle. When I asked her if she would do it – would she go public about our private lives – she did not hesitate, though.

'If you really, really want to do it, Katie,' she said one day.

'Yes I do,' I responded.

That's not the end of this story, however. The morning before our initial court appearance, I was struck with terror.

I don't know where it came from but it sure was a bolt that filled my whole body. Perhaps it was always there and I had just managed to keep it hidden, from myself as well as from others.

We sat on our high chairs at the kitchen island in The Shanty that morning and I said, 'Ann Louise, I don't think I can do this.'

She looked at me and said, 'Yes, you can.'

She had the same effect on countless others throughout the social movement campaign for marriage equality. Denise Charlton, former co-chair of the Marriage Equality organisation, paid homage to this dimension of Ann Louise's character: 'The gentle hand to our face, the quiet word of support and affirmation – those two words that we gently teased her about but lifted our spirits and resolve every time – "well done". Without her tenacity and fighting spirit – and her fundamental desire for justice – we would not be the country we are today. Our children would not be equal to other children, our families not equal to other families.'

Gráinne Healy, our other co-chair, acknowledged Ann Louise's 'model of feminist leadership' and said that 'many of the messages that emerged as winning messages of the Yes Equality campaign in 2015 were messages of love – parsed and honed by Ann Louise'.

And Moninne Griffith, co-director of Marriage Equality, spoke about Ann Louise's 'superpower' to make each volunteer feel appreciated and special. She was, indeed, a 'gentle radical whose elegance, sensitivity and deep spirituality were matched by her quiet but fearless dedication to the creation of an equal and fair society . . . she leaves a rich legacy for future generations' (*The Irish Times*, editorial, 24 June 2017).

*

We lay her to rest in Manor Kilbride Cemetery. The nation mourns with me. I am held and comforted by the deep sympathy of the Irish people. I am also terribly alone.

I return to The Shanty. August is in her bed, but she comes over to me and brushes against my leg. She is grieving too. 'What will we do?' I ask her. 'Your companion and my partner is gone. She's never coming back.' All I can do is put my arms around her body, then I just lie down on the floor next to her. We comfort each other. After a few minutes, I get up. I look around the kitchen. I glance up to the mezzanine where Ann Louise would meditate. I smell the lavish display of flowers from friends and family. I shake my head and I think, *Just one foot in front of the other.* It becomes my motto, as the emptiness inside me deepens and hollows me out in the days ahead.

*

Towards the end of June I enter Leinster House through the overpass adjacent to the ministerial corridor. It's a 'back door' so to speak. The privacy suits me – no members of the public are allowed here. Though it's midsummer, the cold air hits my body. The glass overpass holds no insulation. Today the unsympathetic air permeates my spirit too. I head to the

Dáil chamber – not the main entrance, I just cannot bear it yet. Memories surface and I stop. I am back in St James's Hospital; it is the afternoon of the day we lost Ann Louise. My phone rings. It is Micheál Martin, leader of Fianna Fáil. 'I am so sorry, Katherine. Please, please, give yourself time. Do not return too soon. The work will wait.'

It has been almost two weeks since my neighbours lowered her, with exceptional respect and love, into the ground. My family had left, slowly, since that time. Not before, though, President Higgins had invited us to the Áras to present me with my ministerial seal of office, because I was in hospital the night he presented seals to the other ministers. That was the only bright day of those weeks, as we all sat together on the gorgeous furniture of his reception room, hoping and waiting for the splendid ambiance and remarkable company to offer some kind of balm. It did. The president's compassion soothed us all. I knew, though, that work would be a longer deliverance from the immeasurable grief and deep shock that was living in my body.

By sheer willpower I return to the present and wind my way through another narrow corridor that sits behind the chamber. It brings me to the main entrance. I pause. An usher greets my eyes with kindness and shakes my hand. Leinster House staff are not unlike family. (I loved every one of them, knew most by name.)

He opens the door for me. There's nothing else to do now except to go through it. Inside I am at the second tier, just above the seats in the chamber. I must answer some questions about my children and youth affairs portfolio. I look down and see many of the TDs still engaged in 'leader's questions'. Mary Lou McDonald, deputy leader of Sinn Féin, glances up and sees me. Again, eyes meet. She quietly arranges the papers in front of her, rises from her seat and climbs the steps. We embrace with no words, and both sob.

I pull myself together, descend the stairs, take up my seat and prepare to answer questions. But before any questions are asked, several TDs, from all sides of the house, stand up one by one to offer me sympathy. Gerry Adams remarks that he did not know Ann Louise very well, but remembers meeting her in a Leinster House corridor one morning. 'She was so gracious to me, asked me one or two political questions, and then moved on. I felt her warm-heartedness. I am so sorry, Minister Zappone.' Others acknowledge her great contribution to education and to the marriage equality movement. Brendan Howlin, leader of the Labour Party, concludes the sympathies: 'She was a gentle warrior. The nation owes her a great debt.'

I let the tears flow. I do not try to hold them back. Words remain in my throat. Eventually I stand, whisper 'thank you' and begin my speech, wrapped in parliamentarian care.

*

Does anything last? I wonder. If not, does it really matter what one does? I have to believe that it does. She did. I must keep some grip on living in the world without her.

At the end of June I go to my first public meeting. It has been scheduled for some time and I do not want to miss it. I do not want anyone to stand in for me. It is the first meeting I hold for former residents of the mother and baby and county homes. There are over 120 participants in the Westin Hotel's ballroom in Dublin. People have travelled across the country and from farther afield. I have appointed Jim Halley, past chairman of the Chartered Institute of Arbitration and an internationally respected mediator and facilitator, to lead a wide-ranging four-month consultation process to hear from the people who lived in these institutions. I want open and consistent engagement with them. I want to listen, learn and respond. For me, this represents an integral practice of transitional justice. The government, the state, *has* to listen.

I approach the podium to make an opening statement. I get out the first sentence, and then I stop. I struggle to speak through my tears. I know they know what I have been through. I thank them for being there. I tell them that I know they understand grief, in its most complex manner. Some of them have already expressed how deeply they appreciate that I would still come to speak to them while steeped in my own sorrow. Unexpectedly, I am comforted by those to whom I ought to provide comfort and justice. Just as I was at Ann Louise's funeral. A group of former residents from the Tuam mother and baby institution had taken an early train from Galway to come to Dublin to pay their respects. The last time I had met them, we'd walked the grounds of the Tuam institution together.

The Westin meeting represents the first of many meetings. I am determined to hear from a wide cross-section, and bring all these voices to the cabinet table. Consultation, collaboration with survivors and what to do at Tuam. This is my agenda. The world watches. Death is all around me. I have lost what is most important. With nothing left to lose, my resolve for tangible justice builds.

*

One other piece of work awaited. Paul Downes was scheduled to meet me about preventing children's hunger in schools. Ann Louise and I had talked about this often over the years. She had been in and out of countless primary schools throughout her career, and had observed first-hand the impact of poverty and hunger on children's learning and well-being. Paul had set up a national working group on the issue through Dublin City University's Educational Disadvantage Centre. They had a vision. They wanted a 'free hot meals' programme supported by the state in every DEIS school (a school operating in an area of designated socio-economic disadvantage). It meshed with my own vision, but ministerial responsibility for hunger prevention did not land with me. It was a matter for the minister for social protection. Nevertheless, I held the meeting with Paul and stayed in touch with him on this throughout the next eighteen months. My officials were in the process of developing a cross-departmental ten-year national strategy to support the well-being of the first five years of a child's life. Maybe this would be the vehicle to advance policy on children's hunger in schools? I would need to be patient and begin my inside advocacy after the summer.

Later that day I visited my constituency of Dublin South-West. Schools were preparing for the summer break, and I had one more visit planned for Scoil Cnoc Mhuire junior school located in Killinarden, Tallaght. I loved that school and its principals I had met over the years. The children faced some of the biggest barriers to learning because of high rates of poverty and unemployment in the area. The community spirit, however, spread a blanket of indefatigable love. As I entered one of the classrooms that day, it erupted with excitement and a natural inquisitiveness. The children had prepared questions for me. I relished these moments.

'How old are you?' a red-headed boy asked.

'Older than your parents,' I responded.

'How *old* are you?' he insisted.

'I don't do age,' I answered quietly.

He stared at me, perplexed, then eagerly enquired, 'Are you American?'

I knelt down and gently looked into his eyes. 'Yes, I am from America. But I am Irish too. What is your favourite subject?'

With no hesitation he replied, 'Geography!' and we were off in another direction.

When I got home that night, I went to a bedroom closet, opened it and started sifting through my summer clothes, trying to decide what to pack for my trip to Seattle. I was heading home to my siblings, where I would rest and be comforted. After my parents moved out of our family home into an apartment, my sister Suzanne's house in the North Beach area became the family hub where we all gathered for dinners, birthday parties and other occasions. Their backyard flowers with cherry blossoms, roses, Japanese maple trees, tulips, rhododendrons and all sorts of other varieties, in beds surrounding pristine lawns – cut by my brother-in-law Karl.

Their beagle, Frankie – picked out from the litter by Ann Louise the last time she visited Seattle – would race around the garden, and finally come into the den to flop and sleep. I spent much of my two weeks just lying quietly on the sofa, reading one book after another. We did go out for a boat trip one early evening and cruised through Lake Union into the Puget Sound. I remember having a photo taken on that trip, as I raised a bottle of Miller Lite, with the Space Needle in the background. I sent that photo to many Irish friends, trying to say, 'I will be okay.'

CHAPTER 9

Emptiness

I met emptiness everywhere after I returned to Dublin, especially in our home. The kitchen, the sitting room, my study, her study, the garden, the dining-room table. Our bedroom. Ann Louise was nowhere. All I could feel was her absence. Our dog August slumped on most of those September days. Even when I walked her through the Slievethoul forest, at the back of The Shanty, she moved her four legs slower than my two. Rabbits and deer did not stir her interest. She stayed close as we took the full circle of the woods and eventually stepped onto the road to our gate. The letterbox was painted in Ann Louise's handwriting, white script on royal blue. The flowerbeds contained roses from her mother's garden and tulip bulbs she had planted for me for a special birthday. (They are my favourite flower. She invited her entire family and each one brought a shovel and a sack of bulbs.)

She was gone, but there were literary traces of her. Ann Louise had verse going on in various notebooks or on scraps of paper. They turned up from time to time in different places throughout The Shanty. She was there, and not there. Here is one I found, a card from Ann Louise from 26 May 2016 after I had received the state seal of the minister for children and youth affairs:

'Whatever one loves is.' (Sappho)
I have loved you since the day I met you.
This is your time. I'll adore and
support you forever.
Annie

I smiled. She often said to me, 'This is your time.' What confidence that gave me. I believed it to be true. And there were weighty political challenges ahead of me that became more manageable because she had such faith in me. My second children's budget was one of them. With the boost of the huge investment for the first one behind me, I began to imagine a fully fledged model of childcare, one with capacity in every county and town for the provision of top-quality care and early learning. Together with my departmental officials and under the leadership of Assistant Secretary General Bernie McNally, we delivered the second year of free pre-school for all families. I established – for the first time – a legal entitlement for parents to the National Childcare Scheme (inclusive of state subsidies for fees) where the bulk and scale of the first-year investment went towards low-income families. Those who earned less, or did not earn at all, received the highest childcare subsidies. The lower-middle-income families did not receive much in the beginning, which my Fine Gael partners did not like. But cabinet accepted that those households on the lowest income were my priority as a progressive Independent. If they wanted – as I did – the lower-to-middle-income families to receive more financial support, then the minister for public expenditure would just have to give me a more generous budget. Sometimes he did, and sometimes he did not.

I was clear with my officials that I wanted to image, and begin to design, a public model of childcare – whereby the state establishes a system of early learning and after-school care – that is resourced and/or delivered by government (akin to our education system and practised in several European countries, such as Finland, which holds gender equality as a national policy priority). I had been arguing for a model like this since I was a senator. My officials and I held several internal meetings to examine the possibility and the kind of investment required. Ireland was so low on the totem pole of investment in this arena, compared to our European counterparts, that enormous sums of money would be required and this would take a lot of time. We agreed that our ten-year strategy would outline the initial critical steps.

Most political strategies like this tail off when governments change or the macroeconomics shift. So I asked the civil servants to design something that would be futureproof. That was my brief, and Magdalene Hayden, my parliamentary assistant, worked closely with them so that she could feed our earlier ideas, based on the Finnish model, into the work. Under my leadership, we completed the National Early Years Strategy named 'First Five'. All the recommendations were accepted by the government, and Leo Varadkar joined me to launch it in Dublin one fine day. A nascent sense of the centrality of care for a productive economy and inclusive society – in a way that ensured gender equity – was now a commitment. The implementation of 'First Five' will continue as the whole-of-government strategy for a ten-year period (until 2028), even though new political partners have been in charge. Integral to this strategy was the development of a new model of public funding for childcare, which is still being followed – a quantum leap of investment for children and families. Another government and Minister Roderic O'Gorman also deserves much credit for this. But we drew the map.

When I could work on something as significant as this, I felt less emptiness. But then I would return home in the evening and, as I stepped into The Shanty through the side door, I almost immediately would lose the sense of meaning and purpose generated by the work. I just had to keep going, though. How could I do that? What would take away even a little of the existential vacancy that I felt?

One night that feeling was more intense than others. I went into Ann Louise's study and rooted around her desk and bookcase, desperate to find another trace of her. And there it was – another small notebook, with her beautiful script on the second sheet:

Emptiness

*Even when your world is falling apart, if you have a strong
imagination, you'll believe your dreams will come true.*

This is what Ann Louise wrote as a blind person reaching
for sight and a healed brain. I just sank down on her study
chair. I closed my eyes. *She tried so hard*, I thought. I struggled desperately to let her spirit replenish mine. As I opened
my eyes, I found an A4 sheet printed in a large, bold-faced
font. She had been experimenting with definitions as part
of the writing of her book.

Resilience
*The ability of a substance or object to spring back into
shape.*

Elasticity
The capacity to recover quickly from difficulties, toughness.

Psychological resilience
*Defined as an individual's ability to successfully adapt to
life tasks in the face of social disadvantage or highly
adverse conditions.*

*Resilience is not a rare ability — it is found in the average
individual and it can be learned and developed by virtually
anyone. It should be considered a process rather than a
trait to be had.*

*People who demonstrate resilience are people with an
optimistic attitude and positive emotionality and are, by*

practice, able to effectively balance negative emotions with positive ones.

She is amazing. Somehow I will get through this, I thought. Someday the emptiness will recede. Maybe. The pain under my breastplate was so intense at times, though, I would stay later at work than necessary to try and ignore it. Finally I decided that maybe a couple of nights in a hotel during the middle of each week would bring me some kind of companionship. Even the company of strangers would be better than feeling alone in my home. In addition, my commute was getting longer and longer as Dublin traffic increased, sometimes taking up to two hours each way. It wore me down. My resilience – the kind Ann Louise wrote about – was low. Buswells Hotel, just across the street from Leinster House's main gate, became my haven. With reduced rates for TDs, including a sumptuous Irish breakfast and kind staff, I looked forward to Tuesday and Wednesday nights. It helped to break the intensity of wanting human contact while simultaneously feeling so solitary.

Meaningful work in a big job saved me too. In early September I asked the new taoiseach to hold a meeting with Ibrahim Halawa's father, sisters, myself and the minister for foreign affairs, Simon Coveney. While our Irish embassy officials were doing all they could in Egypt to secure Ibrahim's release, on the outside it felt as if things had stalled. Perhaps our new taoiseach would be willing to inject some of his own momentum and leadership. Leo agreed to meet the family. A room was secured in Government Buildings. I arrived first, then Ibrahim's father and sisters. Actually it was the first time I had been in the company of Hussein Halawa, Ibrahim's father. As the imam of the Islamic Cultural Centre of Ireland, he exuded a quiet spiritual leadership. The taoiseach and Simon Coveney listened intently to the pain and patience of the Halawas. When Leo spoke directly to Hussein, it felt like an engagement of leader to leader. The taoiseach promised he would do all he could to support Ibrahim's freedom.

*

I left for the Kennedy Summer School – a festival of Irish and American history, culture and politics, founded by Noel Whelan – soon after the meeting. Noel had invited me to be interviewed by him to kick off the school that September. I thought I could do it, with him at my side. The special Oireachtas committee considering the report of the citizens' assembly on the eighth amendment had started to meet, so it might be a good opportunity to say something that would influence those TD colleagues who were members, but opposed to repeal.

The sun is shining in New Ross, County Wexford. It feels so good. We drive towards St Michael's Theatre where the interview will take place. Eugene has to slow down. Protestors line the streets with placards of babies in wombs, saying 'Go Home Minister Zappone'. We pull to the side of the road at the entrance and Noel is there. He is a gorgeous man of immense stature. He is not going to let anyone touch me. Other colleagues, including Brian Murphy, huddle around and swiftly move me inside. I feel shaken, but safe in their embrace. The interview goes well. I am heard, though a pang of loneliness surfaces as I think about how much I wish I could phone Ann Louise afterwards.

When I return to Dublin at the end of the weekend, I contact the taoiseach's office to see if there is any news to report on Ibrahim's case. No information is forthcoming. To this day I am not privy to the exchanges made between Dublin and Cairo after my meeting with the taoiseach and Ibrahim's family. But on 18 September 2017, after four years of detention, Ibrahim is acquitted of all charges in an Egyptian court. Enda Kenny and Leo Varadkar, Ibrahim's Northern Irish and international legal team, our minsters for foreign affairs (Charlie Flanagan and Simon Coveney) and their diplomatic officials, Ireland's Amnesty International, members of the European Parliament, especially Sinn Féin MEP Lynn Boylan, and Ibrahim's extraordinary sisters all worked according to their different roles with immense compassion and competence to bring about this day.

*

Four weeks later, on 16 October, Hurricane Ophelia thumped Ireland, the worst storm to hit us in fifty years and also a major Atlantic hurricane. The day before, my next-door neighbours Ruth and Seán begged me to stay in town that night. We had seen the warnings, and they knew the potential impact of the winds better than anyone in our townland of Glenaraneen. Seán's family had lived there for over forty years and, as farmers, knew how weather behaves better than anyone. Ruth herself was a hurricane watcher, for a hobby!

She had travelled to the States for a few holidays just to watch them whip up. While Ann Louise and I had always minded our tall hardwood trees lining the property – with regular visits from the local tree surgeon to oversee their health and ensure their sturdiness in high winds – this was different. The winds that morning had already picked up and I was frightened. Not simply for my own safety, but for our precious home.

I took Seán and Ruth's advice. I stayed in Buswells. Their home was on higher ground than The Shanty but with more shelter. As the storm came through, branches and trees fell; there were power cuts everywhere. A huge tree from the neighbour's property on the other side of The Shanty crashed through the French windows and landed in the middle of my sitting room. Thank God I was not there. By the middle of the next afternoon, Seán had organised other neighbours to take out the tree, chainsaw it into moveable pieces, sweep up the shattered glass and board up the windows with sturdy cardboard. Ruth phoned a local glazier, and by the time I returned home, all was well again. That day Seán and Ruth became part of my family. While my most precious Ann Louise was gone, the void in my heart started to lessen.

On 20 October Ibrahim is released from prison. Three days later I receive a telephone call from Simon Coveney. 'Katherine, Ibrahim arrives from Egypt tomorrow morning early. Unfortunately, I am not able to be there. Are you free to go to welcome him home, on behalf of the Irish government?'

'Of course, Simon,' I say, with great relief and contentment.

In fact, it was the first time since Ann Louise's passing that

I felt any touch of happiness. When Ann Louise was well enough to conduct a conversation in hospital, we had often spoken about Ibrahim and what he must be going through.

On 24 October, Ibrahim Halawa touches down at Dublin airport. Officials have arranged for a private meeting room for Ibrahim to greet his family first. I have been invited to the room too. There are lots of Halawas, of all ages. We watch out. He comes through the doors with a huge smile, greets his father, mother, sisters, brothers and younger members of the family. I wait. He turns and I am introduced to him. Another big smile crosses his face: 'Minister Zappone!' I feel his strong, warm embrace. There will be many more times, as I continue to visit him in his family home in Firhouse, Tallaght. I am so proud that they are my constituents. I want to make sure that he receives all the medical and personal support the state has to offer, now that he is free. His family are some of the most inspiring people with whom I have ever campaigned, in particular his sisters Somaia, Fatima and Omaima. After he greets everyone and has a cup of tea, he approaches the doors. They open to the crowd that has assembled to welcome him home. He is jubilant, as is the crowd, as is his family. As I am. For this remarkable moment.

*

I return to work. As a former trained ethical theologian, frustration and dissatisfaction builds in me over the next critical months of the Repeal campaign. I reach for the energy to put out a comprehensive political-ethical argument in

234

favour of women's reproductive rights. Radio and television interviews, tweets and doorsteps do not offer any genuine opportunity for this. Furthermore, many civil society advocates want to stay a mile away from the 'religious' question. Their view is: we became mired in it thirty-four years ago when the eighth amendment cemented itself into our constitution. My view is: as Irish people, we need to be ethically liberated from Roman Catholicism to vote for reproductive justice.

My dilemma is solved when I receive an invitation from President Brian MacCraith of Dublin City University to give a public lecture on 7 December 2017. In two weeks' time the Oireachtas special committee will publish its report and recommendations to government on what to do about the eighth amendment. I accept the president's invitation and prepare at length for the talk, hoping to use the opportunity as a moment to educate. The evening arrives and, as I enter the lecture hall, I feel Ann Louise's presence. I begin with a story from her life, never shared publicly before.

I am so pleased to accept the invitation to deliver this lecture here . . . the academic home of my late beloved spouse, Dr Ann Louise Gilligan.

It was Ann Louise who first introduced me to the impact of the eighth amendment on young women's lives in Ireland. Not long after the amendment was inserted into the Irish constitution, Ann Louise listened to the story of one of her young students, a woman starting out on a career to become a primary school teacher in Catholic Ireland. She found herself pregnant because her contraceptive method had failed her. Her entire future was at stake.

Ann Louise listened with empathy and love, and supported this young woman to take the boat to England. If 'the authorities' had found out, the student would have lost her career and Ann Louise would have lost her job. Nothing about this circumstance was right. Not then, not now. Thankfully, no one did find out about the trespassing of Irish law. The woman graduated, and Ann Louise continued her radical way of teaching, practising the vision of freedom she offered to her students.

So, I offer these words in memory of Ann Louise.

I continue to lay out how we can build a Republic of justice, equality and empathy for women and pregnant people.

I conclude by arguing that true reproductive justice requires a politics of love. I quote the powerful words of the author bell hooks that 'love is the practice of freedom'. Deciding whether or not to have an abortion is about aspiring to freedom, it is not a debate or a contest of rights in a woman's life. If she feels she needs an abortion – having given her circumstances deep consideration – then she will break the law or even harm herself to find a way. This is what stories told to the citizens' assembly – in public or through written submissions – reveal. A politics of love demands that we legislate in order to free women from these non-choices. As citizens, we have the power to change our constitutional law so that women can make decisions in the open, with support, in their country and in their own home. Those gathered are quiet when I finish. There is no negative reaction. Then a couple of women tell their own stories about their struggles in deciding to have an abortion or indeed to have a child. We are all moved by their honesty and their desire for freedom.

*

The Oireachtas committee on the eighth amendment of the constitution finishes its deliberations and publishes its report on 20 December 2017. Under the exceptionally able chair-womanship of Senator Catherine Noone, the committee recommends to government that a referendum should be held and that unrestricted abortions should be allowed for up to twelve weeks.

Now it is over to the government to decide. Will we choose to hold a referendum, to put Repeal to the people? Will it be a simple 'Repeal' as the Oireachtas committee recommends, or will we put a referendum before the people that not only excises the eighth amendment, *but* replaces it with a new amendment that gives the Oireachtas the power to legislate for the termination of pregnancies? This second option requires us, as a government, to *own* the decision to put Repeal to the people, and to provide an outline of what a new law might look like if women are given the right to their reproductive healthcare. Or shall we do nothing? These are the options Taoiseach Varadkar puts before his ministerial colleagues in early January.

We speak at length about these issues over time and many share, with heartfelt honesty, how they have struggled with it, over much of their lives and particularly over the last year.

During one of our debates, Joe McHugh writes a note to me that: 'Men over fifty have been volunteering to me that they will be voting yes on the basis that it is "time to give women a say in their own health". I think the campaign should reach out to this group and make sure they vote.' I write a note back: 'I agree, Joe. Over to you. x.' The dimpled smile starts to come, followed by the Donegal chuckle.

I prepare for the cabinet meeting wherein we would decide what to do. I place the arguments in my well-worn Moleskine black notebook, writing out what I want to say. I often do, when I am nervous and want to make sure that I remember all my points. I want to use words carefully, with both respect and forthrightness. I keep my notes to three points:

> I acknowledge and appreciate the minister for health's [Simon Harris] willingness to outline how his listening to the views and experiences of women has shaped his thinking . . . and changed his mind. Bravo. Listening to women's experience provides, I think, a prime resource for ethical decision-making on an issue such as this. Of course, there is great diversity in that experience, but most women just wish to be the moral agents of their own choice, and that is what I am saying 'yes' to in Repeal.
>
> But, what about the 'unborn'? I believe that the foetus does have value. Yes. It is a form of early human life and as pregnancy progresses, that potential comes closer to realisation. We have a duty to recognise that value by providing and supporting healthy, voluntary pregnancy and appropriate medical care — by placing further limitations on access to abortion (after at least twelve weeks) as

pregnancy progresses. But foetal life is not the same as the life of a pregnant woman. (Thomas Aquinas says that the soul enters the foetus forty days after conception — for males — ninety days for females). The lives of the foetus and the pregnant woman <u>are not equal</u>.

Catholicism does <u>not</u> have an ethical tradition of an <u>absolute</u> approach to the taking of human life. Augustine, in the third century, put forward the 'just war theory'. There are, he argued, acceptable ways to justify the killing of another human being. And he laid out reasons or justifications whereby it is not unethical to go to war.

Should it not be the case, then, that there are reasons/ justifications whereby we can legislate to terminate a pregnancy? And that it is not wrong to do so?

While I am no longer Catholic, not for a long time, I respect those who are, and most of my colleagues would name themselves as such. I do not know how much of a difference my views make to them. What I do know is that we decide to put a referendum to the people. We agree to ask them to repeal the eighth amendment and to replace it with a simple amendment making clear that the Oireachtas could legislate the termination of pregnancy. This proposal we own and will campaign for it together.

On 22 March the Abortion Rights Campaign, the National Women's Council of Ireland, the Coalition to Repeal the Eighth Amendment, the Irish Family Planning Association, Amnesty International, the Irish Council for Civil Liberties, Termination for Medical Reasons, the Union of Students in Ireland and many more groups form 'Together for Yes'. Ailbhe Smyth (the

Coalition), Orla O'Connor (National Women's Council) and Gráinne Griffin (Abortion Rights Campaign) co-direct the campaign. (*Time* magazine would go on to list them among the 100 most influential people in the world in 2019.)

I had met Ailbhe in the early 1980s when I first came to Ireland. We ended up on the same platform one morning in the Berkeley Court Hotel. The Women's Political Association hosted the event. I was a theologian then; she was an academic. Though religion and feminism did not mix well in the minds of most Irish feminists at the time, Ailbhe's radical spirit opened her to anyone and any side that worked for freedom. I was grateful for that. Another grand feminist of the time had written to me, 'Women like you should be knee-capped'! I had to ask Ann Louise what knee-capped meant. All such a long time ago now. Ailbhe's fierceness held a soft centre and we became friends.

Soon after 'Together for Yes' forms, we decide to stay connected – out of the limelight. We want to open a line of communication, from the outside of civil society power to the inside of political power, not an unusual practice in politics when the stakes are high. So, every Sunday morning I find a quiet spot in our Shanty home, often the conservatory at the front of the house. Filled with Ann Louise's blossoming flowers, no matter what time of year, its sweet-smelling environment calms my body and mind.

'Hello, Ailbhe? . . . this is a good week . . . I can't tell you what we said at cabinet, but here's the tenor . . .'

'Hello, Katherine . . . we met with the leaders of all political parties . . . a genuine openness is coming . . . I can't tell you what our next public event will be yet, but it will feature . . .'

Emptiness

We honour our comrades, we keep confidences, and we each find better ways to negotiate.

*

On 25 May 2018, 66.4 per cent of the electorate voted in favour of repealing the eighth amendment of the constitution and replacing it with the words of the thirty-sixth amendment: 'Provision may be made by law for the regulation of the termination of pregnancy.' Our voice as Irish people, once again, echoed around the world.

Maybe Ann Louise heard it. It was her day too. She abhorred the extinguishing of women's moral agency and advocated for women's religious freedom in a patriarchal Catholic institution. She was punished for that, as I have described earlier. But Ann Louise was a woman who willingly and valiantly paid the price to champion liberty, time and again. She spent her entire life imaging the possible. Encouraging others to do the same was integral to her teaching, activism and philosophy.

On the back of another envelope I found after the Repeal victory, Ann Louise had written in her most distinctive penmanship (again, though blind):

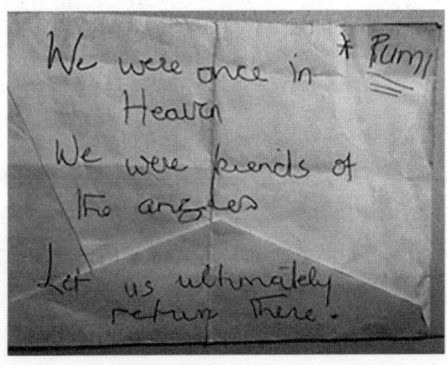

Why was our time so short after such amazing victories? Did she know it would be short? Where did she go?

*

I was looking forward to a slightly slower pace after the referendum victory. But that was not to be. At the beginning of the following week my secretary general informed me that extensive examination and cross-checking of records by Tusla had uncovered proof that a number of adopted children had been registered incorrectly. On 29 May I announced publicly that clear and robust evidence existed of 126 cases of illegally registered births. The survivors name these 'illegal adoptions'. This occurs when a child is placed with a couple or individual who are not the parents, but the birth is then registered as if the child had been born to them. My announcement came fourteen months after dealing with the shock and horror of children's remains being found at Tuam's mother and baby institution. Survivors, advocates and journalists declared that the evidence of illegal adoptions was just the tip of the iceberg.

What was I to do?

I took a cycle on a Wicklow road a few days later and pedalled down a laneway to Manor Kilbride Cemetery where Ann Louise is buried. She often said 'image the possible', especially during times when change seemed impossible. I had the phrase etched on her gravestone, and I sat beside it that afternoon and made a phone call to Mary Robinson, Ireland's former president. We talked about how Ireland, as a state and a society, has caused too much pain. We acknowledged that there has been an imbalance of power, that women and children have had no voice. And we discussed the possibility of a truth-telling process in Ireland, broader than anything done so far.

A few days later I drafted one page on a possible 'truth-telling' undertaking for Ireland. I asked my friend Fionnuala Ní Aoláin to review it, and then I organised a meeting with Leo Varadkar. When the taoiseach and I met, I described my intense feeling that it was time for Ireland to do something akin to a 'truth and reconciliation' commission, many of which have been established throughout the world – the South African one being the best-known example. There have been so many forms of the institutional abuse of women and children, and some men, across the various settings of industrial schools, Magdalene laundries, and mother and baby institutions. I sensed he was really listening. I talked about what it could be, why we needed it, why now, and what form it could take. He had said in public that the illegal adoptions opened up another 'dark chapter' in Ireland's history. I reminded him of those words and pleaded that we must face this as part of our national story. To listen and learn. To offer a collective apology. To hold a solemn moment. That the Decade of Centenaries offered us an opportunity to ensure that we recognise and memorialise the entire history of our state. He asked me to send a note to him in light of our conversation. I did. He responded shortly thereafter.

Katherine
Thanks for this. It follows up well on our discussion earlier.
I am a great believer in the cathartic power of

truth-telling and the power of narrative and am more
convinced about restorative justice than I was in the past.

I'd really appreciate if you could consult with other
relevant ministers and experts in the field with a view to
working up a proposal for government to consider. I
appreciate it's very much a cross-government matter so
obviously any costs, the need for a secretariat, etc. that
may arise would have to come from central resources rather
than your department. We can discuss that with Paschal at
a later date.

See you at the weekend
Leo

I was thrilled with such a genuine and helpful response. He understood what I was talking about, and he outlined the beginnings of its operationalisation. I set off. Working with Irish, UK and Spanish experts, we formulated proposals for 'A Forum on Truth, Gender and Transformation', using the guiding principle of transitional justice. Such an approach would encompass a coming to terms with varied forms of the abuse of women, girls and boys in different institutional settings during the greater part of the Republic's history. Those most affected – survivors and their families – would be central to the design and implementation of the next steps. Patricia Ryan, Jerry O'Connor – my political team – and I met with several ministers, and the attorney general Séamus Woulfe, to present the proposals. We incorporated their responses into an amended draft cabinet memorandum. Formulated and positive action was about to be taken when the ticking political clock called time on the government. But I was so close, and I had the taoiseach's support.

At least the vision had been articulated inside the corridors of political power. This might make it easier for something similar to happen in the future. My knowledge of that, from time to time, ameliorated some of the emptiness that surrounded those days. But that was my rational intellect operating, and it had only so much capacity to build emotions of acceptance and hope for the new. Just *one* conversation with Ann Louise about these momentous issues would have settled my spirit and helped me to see other ways to keep going. Just one conversation would have sparked my confidence to move quickly into other strategies. While I was getting used to the absence of her counsel, there was nothing that could ever replace it. Her wisdom, rooted so deeply in love, nailed it every time. But it was way too soon for her creative power to grow inside my heart. Way too soon.

CHAPTER 10

The Tide of Politics

The rhythmic rise and fall of the sea aptly represents my last eighteen months of Irish politics. The tide's flow reaches a full peak before ebbing. Given my grief, I certainly did not expect any peaks to be visiting me. I was wrong. August, usually a sleepy month for political activity, took on a very different pace and hue in 2018. The country was preparing for Pope Francis. I was pretty clear in my own head that my engagement would be minimal. I would be faithful to my ministerial obligations and attend his speech in Dublin Castle. All of us had been commanded to be there by the taoiseach. But I did not want anything further. I had not been a proper 'pope-watcher' for years. Though Francis from time to time did appear to break away from the weight and politics of Catholic tradition, little had changed for LGBTQ+

folks. And I was one of them. We were not welcome in his domain on our own terms.

I was at home in The Shanty when I received a phone call from Martin Fraser, secretary general of the taoiseach's department. Lisa Hughes had let me know that he wanted to speak with me. I had just got off the phone with Leo, who had rung to ask if I had any advice for him about what to say to the pope in his welcome address at Dublin Castle. But Martin wanted something different.

'Hi, minister, how are you today?'

I had recently celebrated the first anniversary of Ann Louise's passing, and the gaping sadness was like a daily companion. 'Okay,' I responded.

He continued: 'I have a request. It's about the pope's visit. Would you be willing to represent the government of Ireland when Pope Francis arrives at Áras an Uachtaráin to hold a meeting with our president?'

I was taken aback. I didn't want to be viewed as welcoming a man who stands over the church's treatment of LGBTQ+ people, and I told Martin that.

'But we think a photo of a lesbian minister greeting the pope would be a powerful symbol of the new Ireland,' he said.

I started to recognise an opportunity. I agreed, but only if I could have a word with the pope.

'We are asking you to shake his hand, minister, along with about fifteen others, to welcome him to Ireland. You might have thirty seconds.'

That's enough, I thought. What should I say to him? I had to get it right. What did Francis need to know? Whose voices did he need to hear? My deep-seated sadness made room for some excitement. I phoned Patricia and Jerry straight away: 'I will be meeting the pope and will have thirty seconds to deliver a message to him.'

'Tuam, minister. You must speak to him about Tuam,' said Patricia.

'Yes, that's what I thought. It can only be a few lines. And I want to speak to him in Italian! Let's get to work!'

The month before I had taken a short break in Siena. Ann Louise and I had once travelled there during an Italian holiday and I had always been fascinated with Catherine of Siena, and had studied all her writings during my theological days. This time, however, I needed a holiday to recuperate from the intensity of work and loss, and also to not have to be totally alone. I decided to try to learn some Italian. I hoped I had some affinity for it. After all, my father's people were from Gildone, a hill town in the province of Campobasso, in the Molise region of southern Italy.

Siena is known for its language schools so I signed up for one, Saena Iulia, housed in the historic residential Palace of the Magnificent, home to Siena's legendary sixteenth-century governor Pandolfo Petrucci. God, it was hot in July. However, my instructors became my companions, and when we headed to the cool mountains one night for some extraordinary al fresco opera and linguine, I felt stirrings of comfort and contentedness. At the end of my stay I had to admit – finally – to linguistic confoundment. Nevertheless, the sun restored my Italian body. I had no idea, however, how fortuitous this trip would become.

Patricia, Jerry and I worked assiduously on the lines that I wanted to deliver to the pope, on behalf of the victims and survivors of Tuam, and other mother and baby institutions throughout Ireland, and their families. Once we had the sentences that we thought best captured the message, I got in contact with Mauro, the manager of the Siena school. I explained to him that I would be meeting the pope, and why, and that I wished to speak with him in Italian. I asked if he and his team could provide me with the best translation of my few words. An audio recording would also be helpful, to ensure that my pronunciation was proper and could be heard as an authentic attempt to get the tongue right. Mauro's response was swift and generous: 'Of course, minister. It would be our greatest pleasure.' My memory says that they spent quite a bit of time not only getting the translation perfect, but also recording it, and that he asked Elettra, one of my instructors, to provide the recording in a woman's voice. I spent the next couple of days in the Brittas, County Dublin sunshine, walking around my home and Shanty garden, listening intently to the audio recording, and doing my very best to get the accent correct, and to memorise it all.

The next week I also decided to write to the country leader of the Sisters of Bon Secours Ireland. This religious order ran the Tuam mother and baby institution between 1925 and 1961. I believed that they shared some of the responsibility for the children's remains. I knew that, whatever option the government would choose to deal sensitively and respectfully with the human remains found at the site, it would be costly. I thought it reasonable to seek discussions with the order about sharing a proportion of these costs with the state.

Thus began an exchange of letters and phone calls between my department and the sisters. I perceived that there was some resistance on their part, but I was determined. As a trained theologian, I had knowledge of their religious world-view. I wanted to listen to their concerns and to understand genuinely how they viewed their ethical obligation for the past in the present.

Would they begin the reckoning from a place of love? If not in the past, why not now?

Equally, I believed that all relevant parties, including the state and the Sisters of Bon Secours, had, at a minimum, a shared moral responsibility to ensure that appropriate action was taken to compassionately respond to this tragic situation.

The sisters agreed to meet with me on 5 September.

*

It is 25 August. The day to greet the pope has arrived. Eugene drives me through Phoenix Park. We are too early, in fact, so he pulls over about a half a mile from the entrance to the Áras and turns on the radio. A former pilot, Eugene tunes it to air traffic control at Dublin airport. My immense set of nerves start to dissipate as we both listen to the exuberance in the Irish broadcaster's voice as he describes the landing of the pope's jet on Irish soil. 'Touchdown!'

'Okay, Eugene, let's go.'

Deep breaths. We arrive and I join the greeting line. The Irish navy's guard of honour is called to attention and the army band plays the papal anthem and the Irish national anthem as the pope steps out of the car.

Three dignitaries shake the pope's hand and then I walk up. I turn first to my right where our president and Mrs Higgins stand, and say '*Dia dhuit, a Uachtaráin*'. I had a week in Donegal trying to learn Irish that summer. While linguistic confoundment persisted, I did learn greetings.

I then turn to the pope and look up – he is so tall! I say, from memory,

Benevenuto Papa Francesco,

Io sono responsabile per la Tuam Mother and Baby Home.

In questo posto sono stati trovati resti di bambini nel sistema fognario.

Spero che la chiesa faccia ammenda per il suo ruolo in questo vergognoso capitolo.

È importante.

Le scriverò tutto in dettaglio.

Suddenly I am terrified that he will respond in Italian, and I won't know what he has said. Instead, he bends down slightly, looks straight into my eyes as he clasps my hands and says in English, 'Thank you for saying that.' I am stunned, and moved.

I walk on quickly, turn to my left where I see a bank of

journalists and photographers and hear them clamour, 'What did she say to the pope?' I am whisked away by a government official to bring me straight to Dublin Castle where Taoiseach Varadkar will give his speech of welcome to the pope and the pope will speak to the Irish people. I slip into a seat between the attorney general and the minister for health. The pope is halfway through his prepared script when he mentions the scandal of abuse of young people by members of the church and then he pauses and glances up to look at the audience over his reading glasses. He says, off the cuff, albeit decidedly, 'My heart . . . the words of the minister for children are still in my heart. Thank you for your words.'

I am blown away. Mary McAleese, sitting immediately in front of me, turns around to give a thumbs-up. Both men beside me whisper out loud, 'Katherine, what did you say to the pope?' I do not answer them. I leave quietly and quickly after the event. While a bus is waiting to take ministers away from Dublin Castle, I decide to ditch that trip. My political team and I have agreed that I will not discuss my message to the pope on that day. We don't want to take away the focus on President Higgins's discussions with him and his communication to the media about their exchange. Not that we had ever imagined the pope's public acknowledgement of my message. Later in the day, the pope is also quoted from a press conference on the jet back to Rome saying that I had been 'very balanced', and adding: '[S]he made me understand that the church has something to do with this. That lady had a dignity that touched my heart, and now I have the memo there that I will study when I get home.'

We are bombarded with media requests. I phone Jerry;

we decide to stick to our original plan and take up just one media request for the following morning. He contacts Miriam O'Callaghan's radio show team to organise the exchange. The next day Miriam begins with, 'Katherine, what did you say to the pope?!' I rehearse the Italian words on air and then offer the English translation:

Welcome Pope Francis.

I am responsible for the Tuam Mother and Baby Home.

Children's remains were found in what appears to be a sewage system there.

I hope the church will make reparation for its part in this shameful chapter.

It is important.

I will write to you with details.

The pope, as indicated to the media, began to study my letter to him on the way back to Rome. The first lines crystallised my view of the church's responsibility to make reparations for its part in a very shameful chapter of Irish history. The note gave Francis the background to the mother and baby institutions, including the establishment of a commission of investigation, and its confirmation of the presence of human remains on the site of the former Bon Secours mother and baby institution in Tuam. I told him that I had instructed an expert team to determine the options open to us to fulfil our duty to these children and that the team had done so. I concluded by saying that there had been little compassion shown to children and their mothers in this institution and, while we could not change what had happened to them, we could give the little ones dignity in death. Given the role of the church in this shameful chapter of recent Irish history, I said it was my belief that it should play a practical role in redressing the hurt and damage by contributing substantially to the cost of whatever option would be decided by the government – willingly, unconditionally and quickly. Nothing less would do to properly demonstrate remorse.

*

The Forensic Expert Group had delivered its report to me at the end of 2017, outlining five options for how the government could respond to Tuam – ranging from 'memorialisation' of the site, with no further investigative work, to full forensic excavation and recovery of all human remains and DNA testing for possible identification. We had placed the report with the stakeholders for consultation. We sought legal advice from the attorney general's office, which indicated that new legislation would be required for the full excavation option. I requested, from Dr Geoffrey Shannon – at the time the Government's Special Rapporteur on Child Protection – a human rights analysis of the government's obligation to respond. His report made it very clear that we had a duty to act. Notably, this aligned with the advice of the attorney general's office that, from a human rights perspective, the government had a duty to alleviate the suffering of relatives and survivors. In mid-July 2018, I established the Collaborative Forum – with Mr Gerry Kearney as its first chair and Dr Gráinne Healy as its second – a group of twenty representative members of those who spent time in the mother and baby institutions, or were closely associated with those who did. Their job was to identify, discuss and prioritise the issues of concern to them and provide reports and recommendations to the minister. At its inaugural meeting, I indicated that my own preference was for full excavation and identification, and asked them to consider these matters as part of their deliberations. They were in no doubt that full excavation, exhumation and dignified reinterment was the only option acceptable.

*

On Tuesday, 23 October 2018, the government accepted my recommendation for a full forensic excavation, and for the remains to be exhumed, identified where possible and reburied. We had estimated that the costs for such an operation could range between €6 million and €13 million. The decision was informed by detailed technical advice and, most importantly, by compassion and respect for the rights and dignity of the children interred on the site. I was relieved that my cabinet colleagues responded as they did. We had travelled quite a distance to get to that day. Many of the survivors and their advocates strongly welcomed the decision. Catherine Corless said she was 'shocked' that the government chose to pursue the exhumation. She did not expect that we would go that far. But she added, 'I see it as a huge statement for justice.'

At the press conference I offered my personal apologies to the victims and to those affected by the events at Tuam. (From a legal perspective, the state's apology could not be offered until the commission had completed its work. Taoiseach Martin would go on to acknowledge that mothers and children had been failed by the Republic, and to issue the government's formal regrets on 23 January 2021.) That same morning I announced that the Bon Secours Sisters had agreed to contribute €2.5 million towards the cost of this work. They made this decision before the commission of investigation established evidence in a final report. I was very grateful for the sisters' response. It was the right thing to do.

While the legal and technical challenges (including the government's decision to develop new legislation for forensic excavation) should not be underestimated, a comprehensive, compassionate and scientific approach provided us with the best opportunity to find answers to the many deeply personal questions of former residents and their families. Such a task had never been undertaken or contemplated previously.

Three weeks later, I received a letter from Pope Francis, in response to our meeting in Dublin and my subsequent letter to him.

Minister Zappone,
I wish to assure you of my prayerful solidarity and concern
for this sad situation, and I pray in particular that efforts

made by the government and by the local Churches and religious congregations will help face responsibly this tragic chapter in Ireland's history.

From the Vatican,
13 November 2018 Francis

Initially, I was unimpressed with his letter. Though solidarity is important, we needed money. I wondered whether his promise to pray was an abdication of his power or an expression of it. I will never know.

*

As we approached Christmas 2019 there were rumblings that a motion of no-confidence in the minister for health, Simon Harris, would be put to the Dáil immediately after the break. The rumour mill began to churn. Leo Varadkar was considering dissolving the Dáil. He did not want to lose the no-confidence vote. That's what we heard. And on 14 January 2020 that is what he did. He called an end to the government of which I was a part, of which Ann Louise had been so proud.

I was walking towards the lift just off the ministerial corridor when I heard the news. *How can I possibly run, without her?* was my first thought. I sighed. *I guess that is what I will do, though. There's still so much to be done. She would want me to try.*

My campaign team geared up once again, this time with Claire Murphy heading strategy and tactics, ably assisted by Ruth Frost, Shane McGough, Alan Edge and many faithful others. Campaigning could be brutal on some days through the winter weather. We were warmed by the fact, though, that the TeamZappone crew filled up with friends, family and members of the marriage equality clan. A couple of memories stand out. No matter what else was happening, the Hogan family squad was out. Mary and Dara Hogan – my cousins through marriage – lived in Rathfarnham and covered that part of the constituency for me. On several days they were accompanied by their pug, Clifford, who wore his own special KZ hi-vis vest! Nothing like a dog's presence to start a good conversation on the doorstep.

It was tough going at times, though. The government was not popular; the voters wanted change. One afternoon a constituent started to attack me verbally with violent threats. A shouting match began. I am not proud of that. Thank goodness Alan Edge came to rescue me, gently pulling me away from the angry quarrel and stepping in to continue the dialogue while trying to bring down the temperature. Perhaps most disturbing of all, though, is that this campaign was the first time we had experienced a heavy onslaught of vile messages against me through the social media channels. One day my team started to see printed leaflets denouncing me and my 'witch-like' activities. With further investigation, they found a full website, with my name on it alongside election 2020, that had been created by Enoch Burke – the teacher subsequently jailed for his refusal to stay away from Wilson's Hospital School, because his personal stance on gender transition did not align with the school's. The website he had designed about me outlined how I taught that witch-craft is a positive force, that Tusla is the new KGB and that my beliefs 'weaken parents'.

On 8 February 2020, after a valiant fight, I lost my Independent seat. I had the sixth greatest number of votes after first preferences and transfers, but there were only five seats. Now I would live with a double loss. Ann Louise and the seat for Dublin South-West both gone. The second loss could not nearly compare to the first. Perhaps that is why I did not feel devastated as I left the Citywest count centre that day. While I had grown to love the practice of politics as one of the greatest passions of my life, the impact of its loss felt mitigated by something much more existential. All I could think of was, *What will I do now?* My work as a minister had kept me going after Ann Louise's loss. How could I now maintain some desire to keep going without her? It felt like the tide of politics had started its inescapable ebb.

Not so fast. Returns from general election 2020 did not offer any political party enough seats to govern, and there were no obvious combinations of political parties or Independents to get a government up and running quickly. Negotiations had started but a further complicating factor hit Ireland, and the globe, which slowed down government formation considerably – Covid-19. We had to find ways to decelerate its devastating path, both within Ireland and throughout the world. This was the primary task for the government. Until another government was formed, it was statutory practice for former ministers – whether re-elected or not – to stay at their posts. Though unelected, I maintained my portfolio as minister for children and youth affairs for another four and a half months.

Because of Covid, cabinet meetings had to make swift decisions of the utmost importance. Initially many meetings were held 'virtually', transitioning to gathering in several rooms in Government Buildings to retain the requirements of social distancing, and finally moving to one of the very large meeting rooms in Dublin Castle. One of our first and most fundamental tasks was to negotiate answers to the question: how should we impose the heavy Covid safety restrictions on behaviour, businesses and institutional settings in a way that might also save the economy and society? The gravity of those early meetings produced enormous tension. As we closed schools, childcare facilities, many public services and businesses, the ministers for finance and for social protection knew that a plan to rescue employees' livelihoods and help businesses and public services to stay connected to their workers was urgently required.

Paschal Donohoe and Heather Humphreys, the two ministers, wanted to establish a temporary wage subsidy scheme for employers to keep their employees and, for those who did not qualify for that scheme, to set a pandemic unemployment payment at €350 per week. My departmental staff had raised objections to aspects of this proposal, but little attention was paid to them. Convinced that this approach would destabilise if not drastically reduce the childcare sector, I explained to the taoiseach that most childcare providers would not qualify for the wage subsidy scheme. They were making less than €350 per week, so they would automatically sign on for a better deal with an unemployment payment. I predicted that a huge exodus of childcare workers from their employers would begin.

Little attention was paid to my arguments. I had to do something to stop this train coming down the tracks, so I flatly refused to support the proposal as written. Subsequently, Martin Fraser, aware of my definitiveness, spoke with me and promised it would be settled, in a meeting with my officials. I agreed to this, and the taoiseach's department told my officials to 'sort it', which they did together in the next days. On that basis, I gave my approval to the proposal.

We later presented our plan to the childcare sector, at our first formal Zoom meeting with them. The centrepiece was a Temporary Wage Subsidy Childcare Scheme whereby childcare workers would receive €350 from their employer, funded directly by the exchequer through the Department of Children and Youth Affairs. In effect, the state was now paying the wages of childcare workers, and it was considered to be a fair wage. This had not been done before. The proposals were received with unanimous affirmation. I had never previously secured that from all quarters in the sector.

The next morning, though, I took a phone call from Paschal Donohoe to say that I had made his job 100 per cent more difficult with other cabinet members. Part of me found his comments devastating. I insisted, however, that it was the right thing to do. The call did not end well, though we both mustered politeness. Many thought I was taking a solo flight, for my own reputation. It was solo, I suppose, but not for myself. I had already lost my seat. In the midst of all the other grave decisions to be made, I had this unexpected shot to complete one more critical plank for childcare. A step-change in compensation for the childcare professionals, something that I had felt ardent about from the very beginning of my term of office. Eventually, it was perceived to be the sensible thing to do. It was later acknowledged as a government decision that was a prime factor in saving the childcare sector during the pandemic.

Fine Gael, Fianna Fáil and the Greens started to close an agreement on a unique type of coalition, a primary component being to share the role of taoiseach between the civil war political parties. Fine Gael and Fianna Fáil – age-old adversaries – began to lay down their swords to govern together for the first time. But not before one more historic moment. Back in September 2019, I had been appointed an Irish government special envoy for Ireland's candidature for election to the United Nations Security Council. I had already promoted a seat for Ireland during numerous bilateral and multilateral meetings in New York and in Africa, including Lesotho, Botswana, Kenya, Namibia and South Africa, and I had addressed the Security Council on a number of occasions. I loved this work. It was intellectually stimulating as I learned quickly the history and values of various UN member states and 'sold' Ireland to them as a country that would bring their concerns to the Security Council table. Interviews with foreign ministers, presidents and finance ministers – on their own turf – were exhilarating, especially when I asked, 'Will you vote for Ireland?' and they said, 'Yes!'

It was an intense, exceptionally creative and lengthy campaign, led by Leo Varadkar, Simon Coveney, minister for foreign affairs, Niall Burgess, the secretary general of the Department of Foreign Affairs, and Geraldine Byrne Nason, Ireland's UN ambassador in New York. I was one of twelve people who advocated diplomatically for the UN seat, and together we made the case for the strong and independent role Ireland would play on the Security Council. In spite of tremendous competition from Norway and Canada, we won the seat on 18 June 2020. It was a momentous achievement. Ireland's voice and values would contribute to international decisions about peace and security for the next two years.

Seven days later, the new government took up the reins as the global pandemic continued. What had begun with a phone call in a Carmelite church on Clarendon Street almost ten years earlier, and the extraordinary joy and hope I felt as I stepped into Irish politics with Ann Louise by my side, was over. It was such hard work, and I gave it all I had. I loved the highs – and negotiated the lows – of three successful referenda campaigns, sharing amazing fun and moments of terror with my political, campaign and civil service teams. How would we solve the next problem? What would we say to the media? How could we continue to give hope, even during the most troubling times? That big cabinet table, all those people sitting around it – almost every Tuesday morning – ready to fight their corner, but willing to support fellow ministers during the most difficult times. I felt respect for each one, regardless of differences in style, beliefs, values and manner. Every day I felt the heavy but privileged weight of collectively governing towards a better future for Ireland. I will never forget the long line of cabinet colleagues, former taoisigh and our president in the front row at Ann Louise's funeral and how their presence helped me to go on.

All I could do was look away from the Seanad, the Dáil, Government Buildings and my department. They were behind me. All I had was myself, though with everything that made my life so rich. All I could do was muster some hope for a future with a little of that joy and meaning again someday.

I gathered the few mementoes left in my departmental office, and Lisa and I – masked – walked out of the almost empty building to my car, with Eugene standing by to bring me to The Shanty for the last time.

CHAPTER 11

Finding Home

It did not take me long to decide to leave Ireland, once work as a TD and a minister had finished in July 2020. I had lost my political seat and the country was in the midst of the Covid-19 shutdown. A new government had been formed. I had no sense of home without Ann Louise. My grief did not lessen and, at times, it felt unbearable. Though my friends held me tight, loneliness crept under my skin as soon as I was not with them.

As part of my preparations for departure, I drove to the Little Sugar Loaf mountain one afternoon, as I had done countless times before over the past thirty-seven years. Ascending the narrow country road, passing sheep and wheat fields, I turned onto the gravel path to the home of Ann

Louise's sister, June, and her husband, Michael. Though these were pandemic times, it was a glorious day and so we could meet in their conservatory. It opened onto a full-bloomed garden, with a row of roses transplanted from Imelda's home (the mother of Ann Louise and June) not far from where I sat.

We had coffee and tea, Michael smoked his pipe, and we talked about my plans for the upcoming year. I told them I was going to America. No further professional opportunities – political or otherwise – beckoned in Ireland. New York was calling. I had loved my times in this big city as the Irish government's special envoy to advocate for a seat on the United Nations Security Council. Indeed, my mother was from the city. My father had received an MBA from Columbia University after his time in the army in the Second World War. He courted her there, proposed to her at the back of St Patrick's Cathedral, and in 1950 they were married in Riverdale, the northwestern portion of New York City's borough of the Bronx. It would be a bit like coming home, full circle.

How does all this sound? I wondered to myself as I examined June's grapevine, carefully. Let's face it. This was just part of the rationale. The other bit landed squarely on looking for new love. Would I be brave enough to say this to Ann Louise's sister? I did not know. I was tired of being brave. Tea, coffee, scones and jam finished, I started to sweat, but no words came.

June turned to me and said, 'Now, Katherine, we want you to know that we really hope you find someone else.'

Speechless, I just nodded, tears in my eyes. I now had the blessing of Ann Louise's family to look for another. It was a permission of sorts. I took it with gratitude.

My sister Suzanne concurred with June's view. She knew, along with Mark, that I ached for some intimacy and joy. In fact, she'd listened to me describe one or two of the women who had already turned my head. I wore a T-shirt I had bought for one of them. Having known her for a couple of months, I built up enough courage to say something – honestly, I can't even remember the words now. She was bending down to unlock her bicycle on Dawson Street. My awkward words drifted to a pause.

Her head swooped up and she said, 'You want a romantic relationship? I am not a lesbian!'

'Oh, okay! See you later!' I said, not feeling at all the nonchalance I pretended.

So how does one do this, later on in life? There were two others. They were straight as well. I left for America, and New York, filled with as much hope as I could muster. I was unaware of how deep the grief was. Probably just as well. It might have slowed me down.

*

My first stop was Seattle. My hometown never fails to lift my spirits. Philip, third in our family, phones as Suzanne and Mark drive me to Ballard where I will stay in Suzanne and Karl's spacious home with its soothing gardens. 'Hey, sis, come out to see us when you can. We're all wearing masks. Oh! Gotta go, here comes a guy I'm selling a car to. Love you. Bye.'

I'll get through this, I quietly muse. *I am home. I am in my hometown.*

*

I am from a proud Democratic household. That's how our parents raised us. I made a personal commitment four years before, at an election-night watch party in the Guinness Storehouse, Dublin, when I saw Donald Trump take power. In 2020, I promised myself that I would do more than use my vote. I would pump time, effort and energy into the campaign. Now it was time to honour that personal pledge.

I move to New York and join the Biden–Harris team there. I never envision that working on the campaign will be mostly either in front of a laptop or in a study. I am appointed a training leader to teach volunteers how to use the campaign apps as they make calls to the various states. Virtual town halls have us connecting and rallying supporters. The razzmatazz that characterises US politics has adapted itself to Twitter, Facebook and Instagram.

The presidential campaign keeps me company for my first three months in New York. I am very lucky to land a rent-controlled apartment in a big old Upper West Side building. It is a sublet from a friend of a friend of my brother's, who had fled the city during Covid. I love the doormen, the handymen and the superintendent. They are like family, always there for you. The dining-room windows open a vista onto birches, oak trees and Japanese zelkova, all co-existing happily with humans in the small park below.

*

The morning of the 2020 US presidential election, when all the world is held in the balance, I switch on the television to *Morning Joe* (MSNBC) and do not turn it off until days later, on Saturday, 7 November. We get an urgent email message from campaign headquarters to log online in thirty minutes. The entire country-wide Biden–Harris team gather to listen to Biden's unflappable campaign manager, Jennifer O'Malley Dillon, list the executive team's predictions for each state, one by one, to let us know that Biden *will* win. At midday, I just could not stay in the apartment any longer. I walk, almost run, towards the Hudson river, and turn up Riverside Drive to go north. At 110th Street I decide to head to Broadway, and then I hear the sounds – the banging of pots, just a couple, then more, and more and more, and people hanging out of their apartment windows, striking pans louder and louder. I shout, 'He's won!' and sprint to Broadway to join the people spilling out of their buildings to become crowds.

My video tweet, from the centre of Broadway, goes viral: '#Huge emotion as NYC celebrates.' A friend messages me from Ireland: 'You have literally saved the world.'

*

The pandemic did not lend itself well to falling in love. Grocery shopping, outdoor exercise and a weekly visit on a 'timed ticket' to the Metropolitan Museum of Art were the only times I found myself in the physical presence of other human beings. I compared notes with my smart niece Kaitlin who lives in Seattle. She was looking for a romantic partner too. We agreed that her apps would probably not suit me! What should I do? I felt quite protective as a former public person. I did not need or want the destructive unkindness of social media.

I longed for companionship coupled with physical intimacy. I knew that this would not be the same as my first big love. I did struggle, though, with fidelity to Ann Louise. We had promised each other 'till death us do part'. What did this mean now? She is dead, and I am not. Will I be forever married to her? Is it possible to have a second 'love of your life'? I do not have answers for these questions yet.

What I do know now, completely, is that Ann Louise would want me to be happy.

*

Early one morning at the end of January 2021 I received an email from my cherished English friend Michael Little. We had started working together at the beginning of 2000, in Ireland, when he came to provide expertise for the development of Atlantic Philanthropies' Children & Youth Programme. His email relayed sad news about a colleague of ours from the Atlantic days, Charles Roussel, who had lost his wife, Wyn, in October 2020. I sent my sympathies and let him know that I had moved back to the States. Charles responded quickly and our subsequent Zoom nourished us both. He had known and admired Ann Louise, and our partnership. We were both a bit in the same boat. In the course of the conversation I shared with him that I was open to looking for another love. He didn't say much. We agreed to talk again soon.

Two weeks after that, Charles sent me an e-introduction to one of his colleagues, Jennifer, who lived in New York. Charles had described her to me as a 'formidable femme' (!) and, 'by the way, a lesbian'. Oh my goodness. Was she partnered? I wondered. Jennifer and I exchanged emails. It sounded like she was awfully busy, but she responded quickly and positively to my suggestion to meet at the Morgan Library & Museum, originally the personal library of J.P. Morgan, now holding collections of manuscripts, rare books and works of art. She had received the first vaccine and so had I. It seemed safe enough with timed tickets as well. Jennifer said that a David Hockney exhibition was opening – one of her favourite artists – and offered to buy the tickets. I thanked her and then looked her up online. Wow. Gorgeous. The date was set: 6 March.

Towards the end of February I also received a phone call from Simon Coveney. We had worked together, with the Irish United Nations embassy staff, to earn Ireland's seat on the UN Security Council. I had been appointed special envoy in 2019 to bolster Ireland's profile in the final months of the campaign and had led twenty-five bilateral meetings at the UN in New York and in the African countries of Kenya, Lesotho, Botswana and Namibia. I had loved every minute of it and was overjoyed when Ireland's victory was announced.

Simon initiated the call by expressing his delight at the Biden–Harris win. He was aware of my involvement because I had been a regular contributor to the Irish media during the last months of the US presidential campaign. Our conversation then turned to the future. He had been thinking about the priorities for Ireland's two years on the Security Council and wondered if I had any ongoing interest in LGBTQ+, diversity and equity issues in the international arena. I said, 'Of course!' He indicated that there might be a role I could play, for Ireland, on these topics. I heard a lightness and ambition in his voice. We agreed to talk further within the next month.

Early in March Simon phoned me again. After the call ended, I looked out my apartment window at the wintry park outside and thought, *This feels like a new beginning.* I understood that he was offering me an opportunity to represent Ireland again. The details needed to be hammered out, and he would leave that to his officials. We would keep this in confidence until then and Simon suggested that June might be a good month to announce my role as special envoy for LGBTQ+ rights, as a way of celebrating Pride. My heart started to feel full again.

*

I push through the weighty glass doors of the entrance to the Morgan Library on Saturday afternoon, 6 March. I see a tall, masked, graceful woman looking at the door intently, and I think it must be her.

She walks towards me with quiet purpose. 'Katherine?'

I put my red-gloved hand out to greet her. 'Jennifer?'

Hmm . . . thoughtful and gentle, I think. Her eyes sensual, her spirit kind. I feel at ease in her presence, from the very beginning. We take the Hockney exhibit at our own pace, then join each other and walk together through Hockney's canvases. At one point, we both sit on a bench to view a portfolio of tender drawings of his mother. I savour Jennifer's presence and am comfortable next to her. We look more than talk.

After the viewings, neither of us wants to end the day. Jennifer had mentioned a drink. It is dinnertime, though, and things are going well! She agrees to take me through the streets to see if we can find a restaurant. We are saved from the icy winds and slightly post-apocalyptic mood of Park Avenue South by a Thai restaurant. It has everything one needs at this point – warmth, light, food, drink and an open front door. We talk and talk and talk. She is South African, has lived and worked in America for many years. Towards the end of the meal I learn that she is a Buddhist, indeed training to be a teacher of Buddhism. Wow, again. While I understand little about Buddhist traditions, her commitment to spirit work impresses me deeply. What a rare, intriguing combination of so many attributes. I can see her face now, too. No mask while eating. Her face is beautiful.

Over the course of the next number of months a bond deepened between us. We spent more and more time together, and moments of joy began to fill my body again. Her companionship stimulated my mind and heart. Jennifer had received a doctorate in politics from Oxford and had gone on to work in research, strategic communications and public affairs. Our common interests helped us to build a pathway towards partnership.

Jennifer's mother Betty, sister Linda and nephew Rhys live in the UK. She always visits them in the summer. While Covid protocols remained solidly in place, it was possible to travel and so we planned a trip: my first opportunity to meet her family. I was so keen to meet them, especially her eighty-nine-year-old mother. We also arranged for time in Dublin. I wanted her to meet my Irish family and to introduce her to my friends and colleagues. I wanted to say to them, *This is what you have given to me – the capacity to love again.* Their embrace, and that of my own family, kept me alive and on the footpath as I grieved the greatest loss of my life. Jennifer was excited to see me in my role of political leader and changemaker, and to witness me on home turf for the first time. I hoped that Dublin would be open enough from Covid restrictions to host a 'thank you' gathering at the Merrion Hotel for members of my family, my former department, political team and fellow activists. One year earlier I had left them in a locked-down country, with no opportunities to say thank you or goodbye. Their professional support and enormous kindness had enabled me to heal to the point of being able to love again.

I made contact with Dorothy MacCann at the Merrion Hotel to ascertain if it was possible to plan a July reception. Ann Louise and I thought the world of Dorothy. She had taken over as chair of An Cosán's board during a very rocky time for the organisation. Things had not been going well. We needed a whip-smart businesswoman and one who understood the ethos of empowering education for those who missed out on a first chance. Dorothy did her job: listening to all sides, managing conflict and negotiating the next phase of the organisation's development. An Cosán simply would not be where it is today without her quiet, effective and generous leadership.

Our exchange over the next couple of months about planning a reception included an ongoing caveat: we had to adhere to government Covid restrictions. Ireland was opening, cautiously, though we were aware that things could turn and we kept this uppermost in our minds as the planning progressed. I decided to send out invitations in early June – to give people time – knowing that I could always rescind if necessary. That's the way we planned it. I trusted the Merrion with its high professional standards. I knew that many of my expected guests, especially those working within the civil service or public arena, would also check to ensure that the night out would be Covid-compliant. And they did.

The evening finally arrived. Jennifer flew in from Canterbury in Kent to join me. Quarantine requirements had been lifted on 19 July. We were thrilled. The Merrion Hotel said we were good to go, and staff met me before other guests arrived to outline the Covid-specific protocols that would be in place. The reception would be held *outside*, guests were to be seated at tables to avoid mingling, and mask-wearing was recommended.

My remarks to the guests gathered outside in the lovely courtyard of the Merrion on the evening of the reception opened with:

Family, friends, colleagues. No woman is an island.
Certainly not in public life. So, I want to thank you. To
express my gratitude for your support during my ministry.
What an extraordinary country we live in. I am so proud
to be Irish. Of its – our – culture. Of its – our – people. It
always nourishes my soul to return home, as we continue
to live in one another's shelter.

I announced the posthumous publication of Ann Louise's
book that I had edited, *Reclaiming the Secret of Love* (2021).
I quoted her inspiring words, 'Our hope for a new future
lies in an imagination rooted in love.' I introduced the guests
to Jennifer; they welcomed her with open hearts. I thanked
the forty-eight guests by name, and concluded, 'What I
achieved, negotiated or simply bore witness to could not
have been done without you. I carry you in my heart, as I
return to my other homeland.'

The Tuesday after we arrived back in New York from
Dublin and Britain, the cabinet approved my appointment
as the Irish government's special envoy on freedom of opinion
and expression. The night before the Merrion, Simon
Coveney had phoned to say that he would be bringing my
appointment before cabinet at its next meeting in six days'
time. I was delighted, and Jennifer and I returned to the US
with great anticipation.

By the Wednesday, subsequent to a leak from cabinet
about the appointment, my whole world began to change.
I was accused of lobbying the minister, and Simon Coveney
was criticised for a lack of transparency and appropriate
procedures in the appointment process. Some public

representatives insisted that I had lobbied for the job in their exchange with Simon during a meeting of the Oireachtas Committee on Foreign Affairs and Defence. Newspaper articles carried headlines for several days to the effect that '*Coveney denies Zappone lobbied him*' while at least one newspaper asserted that I had '*personally lobbied Simon Coveney for the Special Envoy job*' (*Irish Examiner*, 28 July 2021). Simon publicly acknowledged that mistakes had been made in the appointment process, and that he bore the responsibility for these, yet he stood firm in committee meetings and Dáil debates that I *did not* lobby him. The taoiseach, Leo Varadkar, clarified that special envoys had been appointed for years, usually directly by the minister for foreign affairs or the taoiseach, and these positions had never been advertised in the past nor required cabinet approval. Nevertheless, the taoiseach accepted – as did the minister – that a review of appointment procedures and internal communications for special envoys would be necessary in the future.

As the political and media story intensified, I recognised that the credibility of the role itself had been damaged beyond repair. Simon and I talked by phone and I told him that I would not be accepting the appointment. Exhausted and dazed, Jennifer and I climbed a large rock on the northwestern side of Central Park later that morning and found a quiet place to sit. There, she helped me to write the statement in which I turned down the offer:

Statement from Dr Katherine Zappone re Special Envoy on Freedom of Opinion and Expression

While I am honoured to have been appointed by the Government to be the Special Envoy on Freedom of Opinion and Expression, it is clear that criticism of the appointment process has impacted the legitimacy of the role itself.

It is my conviction that a Special Envoy role can only be of real value to Ireland and to the global community if the appointment process is acceptable to all parties.

For this reason, I have decided not to accept this appointment, and I have recommended to the Minister for Foreign Affairs that the appointment process be revised and re-started.

It was not over. Later that same day another story broke – that my Merrion Hotel reception had not followed Covid regulations. I did not understand. Covid restrictions, according to government communications and regulations, had been followed strictly. I was shocked.

Overnight, I became a person in public Irish commentary whom I could not recognise. My character, values and political legacy were being ripped to pieces. I was attacked, almost every day, for two months. I was accused of holding a 'large exclusive gathering of politicians and others' just days before the Irish cabinet appointed me as a special envoy. A picture was painted of me as elitist, corrupt and dishonourable.

It felt so sore. I trembled with fear early each morning as I reached for my phone. Many days, a headline denouncing or questioning my integrity would land. My future opportunities to work for Ireland vanished before my eyes. This wounded me profoundly – personally and professionally – and the effects continue to this day. By August, a frenzy had erupted. There were calls to name names. The media wanted to know who had attended the Merrion event. Shame on them! Through some digging, they discovered that, in addition to Leo Varadkar, one other politician had attended, along with my former secretary general and my past political advisors. Several friends and colleagues were phoned, with demands to know if they had been there. A friend told me that one of the 'red tops' had offered €20,000 for the guest list. Another said she eventually had to record a voicemail to say that she was not in the country for the summer, and calls would not be returned. Paddy Cosgrave, founder of the Web Summit, tweeted an offer of €50,000 – paid in cryptocurrency – for the list. The intensity of this pursuit had the added impact of silencing some of those who might have spoken in my defence.

It turned out that, in terms of Covid restrictions, a significant lack of clarity existed between what was allowed and what was not allowed at the time of the event at the Merrion Hotel. This was due to a non-alignment between government regulations in public health measures (yes, it is allowed) and the industry guidelines of Fáilte Ireland (no, it is not allowed). This discrepancy was clarified on 4 August by the attorney general who ruled that the event *was* in compliance with Covid-19 regulations. The Government Press Office released the following statement:

The Government has been advised by the Attorney General that regulations provide for organised outdoor events and gatherings up to 200 people, including social, recreational, exercise, cultural, entertainment or community events. Further updates will be made to the guidelines to ensure that people have clarity about how organised outdoor events may operate into the future.

My reception effectively led to a clarification of pandemic rules around outdoor hospitality. Fáilte Ireland lifted its more restrictive guidelines two days after the attorney general's statement.

Technically, there was no wrongdoing, but it was too late. The gathering had taken on a life of its own – in social media, on the public airwaves, in the press and in the chambers of Leinster House. I was asked time and again to comment, and even to appear before the Oireachtas Committee on Foreign Affairs. It was a very difficult call, but I ultimately felt that any appearance or commentary would ignite the story again, and, with so much against me, there would be no space for a fair hearing.

What had happened?

Media reports and party-political attacks within the Dáil claimed that I had broken the Covid-19 regulations to hold my reception. Restaurants, cafés and pubs were not holding large outdoor gatherings because they were following the Fáilte Ireland guidelines. Furthermore, numbers allowed to attend funerals and weddings had been restricted significantly, just six wedding guests and ten funeral mourners in February 2021 and then fifty guests for both by July. Confirmations and communions were not being held during the period.

My reception at the Merrion came at a time when the public consciousness carried the weight of this loss, for families, communities and the country.

*

It is 24 September 2021, a couple of months after the controversy erupted, and things have not yet died down. I walk with heaviness into the utility room to drop my garbage in the communal bin. Each floor of this old apartment building has a room like this. I am so weary. In the previous three days, several Irish news reporters, in town for a United Nations event, have come repeatedly to the entrance of my apartment building, trying to get the doormen to call me downstairs. Jimmy, a staff member of the building, looks up at me from his work emptying recyclables and asks, 'Who are you? You're either a whistleblower, or you're gay.' Stunned, I answer, 'I am not a whistleblower.'

Just yesterday, Jimmy had been assigned by Carlos, the superintendent, to protect me as I fled by the fire escape to avoid the photographer staked out for hours across the street. They were not budging until their telephoto lens got a mug shot. The others who came would introduce themselves to the doormen as 'my friend' or ask 'Does Katherine Zappone live here? For how long? How big is her apartment?' I am angry and afraid. I feel invaded.

Because Jimmy wanted to know who I was, the next day I leave a copy of the memoir I authored with Ann Louise in 2008 at the front desk of the apartment building. I have no idea how it will be received – but it is all I could think of to let Jimmy and his colleagues know a little about who I was and am. A couple of days pass, and I meet Eric, another staff member, as I come out of the lift one morning. He tells me that one of his colleagues, Paul, has taken the book home. Then he asks, 'Do you have another copy? I want to give it to my wife.' Stunned again, yet this time relieved, I smile and say I will get him one.

*

Several months later Carlos and I had a longer conversation about what the staff referred to as the 'paparazzi time'. He told me a little more about what he and his fellow workers did to shield me and keep the photographers and journalists at bay. He was clear that '[o]ur job is to protect our tenants'. One of the days it got so intense, though, he did wonder, 'Are we helping a murderer? Is she wanted? Or is she in danger?'

I tried to explain as best I could what had gone on in Ireland, expecting that the cultural differences might make it difficult for him to understand. After a (perhaps too) lengthy explanation on my part, he looked up and asked, 'Is that all it was?' And then with a twinkle in his eye he declared, 'I am disappointed!'

*

Life in New York moved on, somewhat, and I started to seek professional opportunities in the autumn of 2021. It was difficult. With Covid restrictions still in place, and a World

Wide Web full of controversial headlines about my 2021 Irish summer, openings that I had imagined only months previously did not materialise. I was, however, invited to give once-off lectures on gender and progressive politics in New York University and Princeton University. I was appointed to a *Lancet* Covid-19 international commission taskforce and wrote some articles on humanitarian relief and social protection. During the same period Jennifer resigned her lecturing post at New York University's School of Professional Studies to explore new opportunities. She started a consultancy soon after and I received a one-year appointment as a visiting scholar at the Leitner Center for International Law and Justice at Fordham University law school.

Nevertheless we were both at a crossroads professionally. I sought long-term work that could make a difference and she wanted to do something that she could be truly passionate about. Our partnership was flourishing, though, and we talked often about where we wanted to make a home together. Jennifer felt a draw to the United Kingdom, especially to be closer to her family. We explored Oxford, and I was genuinely open to the possibility. America no longer held the same pull for me. I was surprised. Perhaps it was the polarised political climate, or the absence of social justice friends and colleagues. America had changed from a nation that once was the beacon of democracy to one that wrestled to sustain its egalitarian and self-governing character. I could not find a place to plant myself properly so that I might mine my political experience and re-envision what was needed now for the intersection of human rights and politics.

What about Ireland? I felt Irish in my soul upon my

arrival in the early 1980s. I had Irish in my blood – my great-grandmother Catherine Brady was from Virginia, County Cavan – but it was more than that. For me Ireland has a culture of kindness, a respect for spirituality and wide-open hospitality wrapped around a passion for justice and creativity. When I first arrived in the country, it felt like coming home. Would that be possible again? I really was not sure. Frankly, I was afraid to put my foot on Irish soil, thinking that I would be vilified and cast out as soon as I was recognised.

I needed to return for family reasons, however, and did so in early 2022. I slipped in quietly, kept to myself and my family (by marriage), and eventually travelled to Dublin airport for the return journey, relieved that no one had spotted me. Arriving at the departure gate, however, I heard 'Minister Zappone, is that you?' A woman with her three young children faced me. *Oh God*, I thought, *here it comes*.

'I wanted to just thank you for all you did for me and my children while you were a minister. It made our lives easier and much more manageable,' she said.

I was stunned and could not find any words.

She continued: 'They threw you under a bus, Minister Zappone. I am so sorry that you had to endure that. But many of us are grateful for all you did.'

I thanked her for her words, and she and her family left to board their flight.

That simple exchange pushed my heart open to Ireland again. Maybe I could come home. Maybe the decency of the Irish people would be shown towards me. I had missed Ireland so much. Most of my friends, colleagues and Irish family live here. And then one day Jennifer asked me, 'Katherine, why don't we move to Ireland? I think you would be happy there, more than any place else.'

We arrived at the end of June 2023. Once before, the Irish people had opened their hearts to me and allowed me to make a home-place among them. I hoped it would happen again. Ireland is where I became myself. It is a softer place to live in than New York City. As a politician, I had wanted to help shape a Republic of equality, empathy, justice and love. I still want to contribute to this mission. Jennifer was willing to come with me. It would bring her closer to her family and might allow her to find a new way to pursue her greatest passion – practising and teaching Buddhism. She found a good job quickly in Dublin and has become part of the Buddhist Sangha in the Kadampa tradition located in Templeogue. It all felt like it was meant to be, for both of us.

I had sold The Shanty a couple of years earlier, so we found a place to live in the city centre. Unexpectedly, I started to feel Ann Louise's presence again, and in a qualitatively different way. As I passed certain street corners or buildings, or walked through specific sections of St Stephen's Green, her spirit would fill me up in a new way. She was a Dub, through and through, and I could sometimes hear her sing a favourite song, 'In Dublin's fair city . . .', just like she used to. I feel accompanied by her again.

Being here, and completing this memoir in Dublin, also grants gifts unanticipated. With more time to reflect about the summer of 2021, in my home-place, I am learning important lessons. One comes from having time to read *Taking the Arrow Out of the Heart* (2018) by Alice Walker.

She says, 'No one escapes a time in life when the arrow of sorrow, of anger, of despair pierces the heart.' She asks how we can overcome our natural instinct to cherish our wounded self and to spend our life railing at the archer. Instead of this empty and exhausting crusade, she asks how we might take the arrow from our heart and turn towards the 'medicine of Life', to heal and flourish once more.

*

I sure felt like bringing down the archer! But that does no good, as Walker notes. I need to take an arrow out of my heart. I know now that the 'medicine of Life' means that I must reassess what I think and say about an acutely wounding time. While I have no more to say about the government appointment, bar the loss I feel, I do understand better now why so many felt so aggrieved with my Merrion Hotel reception. Whereas technically it may have been *allowed* by regulation, was it *appropriate* for the time, in light of all that so many others had suffered? No. I think not. And I do regret that. I am sorry.

*

I am also pursuing the 'medicine of life' in other ways. One such way is by attending classes on Buddhism with Jennifer. I am learning all sorts of new things about the power of the mind, and how we can make choices to interpret our experiences in ways that seed peace and happiness, no matter how painful they may feel initially. One evening we were completing our study of the text *The New Heart of Wisdom* (1988) by Geshe Kelsang Gyatso. This passage really struck a chord:

> In the practice of patience we should never allow ourself to become angry or discouraged, by temporarily accepting difficulties or harm from others. When we practise patience we are wearing the supreme inner armour that directly protects us from physical sufferings, mental pain and other problems . . . Anger destroys our merit, or good fortune, so that . . . it will be difficult to fulfil our wishes, especially our spiritual aims.

It is time to lay down my anger. To become myself once again. In the end, all we can hope for is to realise our capacity for love. To image the possible.

APPENDIX

Notes from Ann Louise

Ann Louise's words, in speaking personally or publicly or in her writing, were always inspiring, smart and often very funny. I'm including a selection of them here, writing notes that she was compiling as part of a book she was trying to write subsequent to her brain haemorrhages. While she was unable to complete the book, I think they are worthy of publication, as part of my testament to her in my memoir. And she gets the last word!

On the Discipline of Healing

Most of us are familiar with the exhortation that to live well requires discipline.

However, what is seldom expressed is that healing calls for a daily commitment to discipline –

or

that healing well calls for extraordinary discipline.

Lessons on the Fragility of Life

Permanence is not part of the prominence of the human condition – rather –

as the Buddhists teach, change and death are among the few certainties we all come to know.

On Love

When someone loves you it's like they shine a light on you and you become the best you can be.

I want to write a chapter on K – the extraordinary consolation of every time I would open my eyes – consolation that you were there – the glance of love. I would feel such solace.

On Visiting the Sick

Those who have never been seriously ill carry in that privileged comportment often a presumption that they know how to advise those who are ill.

Balancing on the Fulcrum of Healing

Holding in balance all the advice one receives on how to heal is a challenge in itself.

The warnings that one mustn't do too much give rise to fear every time one increases one's fitness programme – will a further ten minutes added to my daily walk be a step too far?

On the other hand, laziness, lethargy, and lack of engagement with life can stunt and delay a return to full health.

Writing Note 4

Sometimes the unfurling of *memories* can offer hope-filled images for coping with revelations of the present. Images that offer consolation.

While not a great advocate of the 'philosophy' of positive thinking, I do have an optimistic temperament and a strong imagination which tilts towards imaging the possible.

Writing Note 6

Lying in a bed-filled ward I was struck by the quiet, the stillness and the silence. This brought solace, as temperamentally I am allergic to chit-chat, piped music and the mindless menu of soaps.

In the stillness my mind drifted with no nudging to one of my most treasured memories.

Every Monday night of winter my mother would don her coat, take me by the hand and together we would head for the Merrion Road to the residential school for the blind, in time for evening devotions. Once inside we would assume our position at the back of the church. Then, hand-by-hand, quietly large numbers of women and children would file into multiple rows of heavy oak benches.

A bell would sound and out would come a tall man all dressed up in a big heavy gold frock with a white skirt underneath. The boy behind him was swinging a silver container with smoke ascending from it. I loved the smell which I learned later was called 'incense', made up of frankincense and myrrh. Then as the boy waved his smoke, the man, called a 'priest' I was told, put something round and white into the middle of a magnificent huge gold ornament, all embedded with jewels. He turned toward us, lifted it up and down, back and forth, and my mother bowed her head, as did all those sightless in the benches.

Within moments the organ would resonate and fill the space and then the choir assisted by my mother from her back seat bench would begin. The singing was in a different language. Again, I learned later that it was Latin, a language I loved throughout my life.

In the end after the final 'Ave Maria' was sung, the blind people filed out wearing dark glasses and some held white canes. As they went through their door I could hear their laughter, some of the voices were from children and others sounded like older women, but they sounded happy and full of fun. The nuns snuffed out the candles on the altar, and the pure wax aroma filled my nostrils. I too felt happy.

If I were to name my image of heaven, it would simply be the experience of these Monday nights. Every sense was engaged, which is probably why the memories have not faded with time but grown more intense. In this experience, the melding of earth and heaven put no strain on the belief of the existence of either. It enhanced my belief as a child of the existence of both. I think it was the silence.

These experiences allowed me to grow older reflecting:

If there is a heaven, then there must be earth in heaven because I have encountered heaven on earth.

Ann Louise's Retirement Speech from St Patrick's College, Drumcondra

The final abiding feeling that I have lived with as I pass over this threshold, is a sense of enormous freedom. One cannot anticipate what one will feel when you make a decision to resign your job – but truthfully this is the strongest emotion. As a feminist and as a lesbian woman, it has not always been easy to work for my entire career within institutions managed by the Catholic Church.

When one's very identity contests the presumptive normativity all around you, you always live somewhat as an outsider, gazing in toward the accepted centre. This is not necessarily a negative place from which to view the world but it does give a different angle. Here I wish to give testament to those colleagues who think and believe in a manner very different to myself, but who have always been gracious and accepting of my difference – an example perhaps of catholicity with a small 'c' at best.

In saying this I wish to thank each and every one of my colleagues and the wider college community for their gracious acceptance, kindness and support shown to Katherine, my beloved partner, who has always been made feel welcome here.

A well-known poet asks: 'What are you going to do with your wild and precious years?'

I suppose I'll continue to swim upstream and will also continue to dialogue with the centre that holds, but I will feel more free to have a different relationship to that centre.

Acknowledgements

There are so many people who have helped me to shape this work, and so many others I want to thank for being part of my story in ways that taught me hope time and again. My parents, Kathie and Bob Zappone, fit in both lists. So do my sister Suzanne Zappone Hoover, my brother Mark Zappone and my niece Hilda McEvoy. Suzanne, Mark and Hilda appear often in the memoir. Their care as I traversed sorrow and loss kept me alive and able to continue my political work.

I started to write a few lines not long after Ann Louise had passed away. Thanks to some of my women writer friends who kept me company, especially in the early days: Fiona de Londras, Emilie Pine, Ruth Rubio-Marín, Sara Cantillon, Linda Cullen, Una Mullally and Fionnuala Ní Aoláin.

Other members of my family celebrated often with Ann Louise and I, and grieved with me: Bob, Maggi and their children Zach, Lucy and Annie; Philip, Julie and their children

Joel, Brooke and Marie; Suzanne's husband Karl and their daughter Kaitlin; June and Michael Kelly and their children, partners and family; Sally and Bruce McKeever; Hilda and Dermot McEvoy; Shane Kelly and Muireann Howley; Colin and Trina Kelly; and Arthur and Margi Gilligan. Ruth Frost and Seán Healy, whose home is next door to The Shanty, became family to me as well as neighbours.

No woman is an island, and the circle of friends and colleagues – many of whom I shared with Ann Louise – stepped up for us during the years this memoir covers with prodigious love and singular political intelligence. Thanks to our friends Kay Conroy and Mary Paula Walsh, Gráinne Healy and Trish O'Connor, Denise Charlton and Paula Fagan, Peadar Kirby and Toni Ryan, Ailbhe Smyth, Orla Howard and Gráinne Courtney, Moninne Griffith and Clodagh Robinson, Andrew Hyland, Gerard Quinn and Anne Motherway, Niall Crowley, Michael Farrell, Paul Downes, Noeline Blackwell, Lia O'Hegarty and John MacMenamin, Suzanne Egan, Lydia Foy, Rosemary Haughton and Nancy Schwoyer, Daire and Katie Keogh, Dr Máire Slevin, Rachel Matthews-McKay, Michael Murphy and Terry O'Sullivan, Dorothy and Peter MacCann, Karen O'Connor, Darragh Genockey, Philippa and Helen Ryder, Sonia and Jeffrey Sachs.

I want to give a very special mention to the healing team – as we called them – who helped me to provide around the clock care for Ann Louise while she was in hospital for 87 days. The hospital staff in the Mercer's Institute for Successful Aging (MISA) at St James's welcomed them with open arms and all together we ensured that Ann Louise always had love around her. The healing team comprised some of her closest women friends: Hilda McEvoy, Toni Ryan, Anne Genockey, Mary McEvaddy, Gráinne Dowling, Noeleen Quigly and Anne O'Reilly. Claire Murphy met with us weekly to schedule the rota of care and help us to review Ann Louise's medical and spiritual needs, progress and relapses.

Ann Louise's medical and administrative teams – in both Beaumont Hospital and St James's MISA Centre – were some of the most compassionate and skilful scientific healers that I have ever met. And she loved them all. Special thanks to Professor Norman Delanty and his team, and the 'brain ward' folks in Beaumont, and to the MISA medics and nurses, led by Dr Joe Harbison, assisted by Dr Ruth McDonagh, Roisín Kelly, nurses, physiotherapists, neurologists on call, administrators, cleaners and cooks, and Professor Rose Ann Kenny. Thank you to Véronique Glénat of the Alliance Française Dublin for sharing her story.

Throughout the years, women and men who became part of the An Cosán family were a prime community for Ann Louise and myself. Their generosity, leadership and belief in a poverty-free Ireland inspired us every day. I say thank you to our first management team, our CEOs, our board chairs and members, our staff and volunteers, our funders and especially our learners. In 2026, the organisation will mark its fortieth anniversary as a community education and early years learning organisation. In March 2025, Trinity College Dublin published a research report on the health and wellbeing landscape of Tallaght, Dublin, providing a comprehensive analysis of progress and challenges over the years. The people of An Cosán should be very proud of its findings.

The *KAL* case, as we called it in the early years beginning in 2004, would never have got off the ground if it were not for the magnanimity of our legal team: Ivana Bacik, Phil O'Hehir, Kevin Brophy, Gerard Hogan, Michael Collins and those who assisted them. The many witnesses in our case *Zappone & Gilligan v. the Revenue Commissioners & Others* (2006, 2008) provided amazing evidence and lots of copy for the daily reports. Advocates and friends, those who formed the KAL Advocacy Initiative and established Marriage Equality, will for ever be in our hearts. Our legal case would not have made the impact that it did without them.

Thanks to my 'political' friends – those policy and legal enthusiasts – whom I met to understand the technical, legal and public policy issues I grappled with as senator or minister: Brian Murphy, Brian Hunt, Geoffrey Shannon, Fergus Ryan, Ursula Barry, Micheál Collins, Eilionór Flynn, Tanya Ní Mhuirthile, Broden Giambrone, David Dodd, David Kenny, Brian Sheehan, Colm O'Gorman, Liam Herrick, Caoilfhionn Gallagher, Katie O'Byrne, Darragh Mackin, Tom O'Donnell, Mary Murphy and Rory O'Donnell. To a person, they are brilliant, committed and compassionate lawyers or public policy maestros.

In my early years as a senator, I had the extraordinary opportunity to learn from men who became my closest colleagues to 'save the Seanad'. Their enthusiasm, astuteness and historical and constitutional knowledge taught me many things I would never have learned about politics otherwise. Thanks to Feargal Quinn, Michael McDowell, Joe O'Toole and especially Noel Whelan. Noel appears several times in this memoir, before his untimely passing in 2019. I am grateful to my friend Eamonn Mac Aodha for introducing us, and hope that my stories provide solace and some joy to his wife Sinéad McSweeney and his son Seamus.

There are other politicians I wish to mention by name. Former taoiseach Enda Kenny is a master politician, with kindness at his core. Though I am not of his political ideological persuasion, our mutual respect for each other is what I will remember most. I learned every day from former taoiseach Leo Varadkar's political intelligence and intuition, his sense of fun, appreciation of history and artful communication skills. We, too, held mutual respect. Eamon Gilmore and Joan Burton, tánaistes during my time in politics, inspired me in their commitment to the ideals of Labour. It was a great privilege to sit around the big cabinet table every week with ministerial colleagues and I appreciated the commitment and ambition of each one: Frances Fitzgerald, Michael Noonan, Richard Bruton, Simon Coveney, Charlie Flanagan, Paschal Donohoe, Heather Humphreys, Simon Harris, Josepha Madigan, Michael Creed, Denis Naughton, Shane Ross, Mary Mitchell O'Connor, Regina Doherty, Paul Kehoe, Finian McGrath, Eoghan Murphy, Joe McHugh and Michael Ring. I benefited many times from the advice and colleagueship of attorney generals Máire Whelan and Séamus Woulfe.

I have had a privileged friendship with two of Ireland's presidents and their partners: Mary and Martin McAleese and Michael D. and Sabina Higgins. I learn often from their moral authority and love of Ireland.

I hold deep affection and gratitude for members of my political and constituency teams, and for the civil servants who worked side by side with me to get things done. Every day the counsel of Jerry O'Connor, my communications advisor, and Patricia Ryan, my policy advisor, ensured that my words, actions and relationships would help me to be the best minister I could be. Advisors Dónall Geoghegan and Sinead Farrell brought expertise and care to each piece of our work together. Lisa Hughes, my private secretary, and Orla McGovern, my diary secretary, always tried to keep me on the straight and narrow, and we had so much fun together, as they enabled my efficiency as a minister. My drivers Eugene O'Sullivan and Paudie Sheehan were gentlemen to their fingertips and trusted professionals. Fergal Lynch, secretary general of the Department of Children and Youth Affairs, was a meticulous, kind and effective colleague. I could always count on his commitment, creativity and respect. He and I were ably assisted by the department's management team: Bernie McNally, Elizabeth Canavan, Dermot Ryan, Eimear Fisher, Michelle Shannon, Laura McGarrigle, Conor Rowley and Anne-Marie Brooks. Martin Fraser, Geraldine Byrne Nason and Robert Watt are accomplished and thoughtful colleagues, always supportive. And then there was my Dublin South-West constituency team – what a great group of committed professionals who were with me: Ruth Frost, Claire Murphy, Shane Gough and Alan Edge.

Thanks to others who offered important friendship during the writing process, including: Michael Little, Miriam O'Callaghan, Seán Boylan, Charles Roussel, Loretta Brennan Glucksman, Linda Hogan, Marcos Giannantonio, Maurizio Mastrangelo, Paschal Gannon and Jason Doyle. Thanks to the poets Anne Francis O'Reilly and Michael Murphy for sharing your poems. A special mention too for Ibrahim Halawa. Staff of the National Library of Ireland, especially Ciara Kerrigan, Avice-Clare McGovern and Maria O'Shea, were exceptionally helpful, assisting me to access the collection of my papers that I donated to the National Library. Directors and the team at the Tyrone Guthrie Centre provided the beautiful space, hospitality and support at the beginning and completion of this work. It is a remarkable place.

I spent almost six years drafting and re-drafting this memoir. My agent, Jonathan Williams, believed in the potential of the manuscript at its earliest stages. What a gentleman, meticulous professional and towering figure in the Irish publishing landscape. I love working with him. The early editorial assistance of Seán Farrell recast my approach to writing personal narrative. His precision and sensitivity, as well as refined talent, made a significant difference to the calibre of my memoir. I am honoured to be published by Hachette Books Ireland. Ciara Considine, publisher, conducts her craft with creativity, generosity and directness. I trusted her from the very beginning. Catherine Gough's careful read and editorial recommendations lifted the standard of the narrative. And I enjoyed working with other members of the Hachette Books Ireland team, including Stephen Riordan and Elaine Egan.

Jennifer Scott, my partner, is a remarkable woman. She read every word – several times – and taught me about the elegance and rigour of writing. Her generous heart meets mine every moment, and she blesses me with a new path.